MALCOLM GLADWELL

Talking to Strangers

What We Should Know about the People We Don't Know

PENGUIN BOOKS

PENGUIN BOOKS

UK | USA | Canada | Ireland | Australia
India | New Zealand | South Africa

Penguin Books is part of the Penguin Random House group of companies
whose addresses can be found at global.penguinrandomhouse.com.

First published in the United States of America by Little, Brown and Company 2019
First published in Great Britain by Allen Lane 2019
Published in Penguin Books 2020
002

Text copyright © Malcolm Gladwell, 2019

The moral right of the author has been asserted

Printed and bound in Great Britain by Clays Ltd, Elcograf S.p.A.

A CIP catalogue record for this book is available from the British Library

ISBN: 978–0–141–98849–8

www.greenpenguin.co.uk

For Graham Gladwell, 1934–2017

Contents

Author's Note

Many years ago, when my parents came down to visit me in New York City, I decided to put them up at the Mercer Hotel. It was a bit of mischief on my part. The Mercer is chic and exclusive, the kind of place where the famous and the fabulous stay. My parents—and particularly my father—were oblivious to that kind of thing. My father did not watch television, or go to the movies, or listen to popular music. He would have thought *People* magazine was an anthropology journal. His areas of expertise were specific: mathematics, gardening, and the Bible.

I came to pick up my parents for dinner, and asked my father how his day had been. "Wonderful!" he said. Apparently he had spent the afternoon in conversation with a man in the lobby. This was fairly typical behavior for my father. He liked to talk to strangers.

"What did you talk about?" I asked.

"Gardening!" my father said.

"What was his name?"

"Oh, I have no idea. But the whole time people were coming up to him to take pictures and have him sign little bits of paper."

If there is a Hollywood celebrity reading this who remembers chatting with a bearded Englishman long ago in the lobby of the Mercer Hotel, please contact me.

For everyone else, consider the lesson. Sometimes the best conversations between strangers allow the stranger to remain a stranger.

"Step out of the car!"

1.

In July 2015, a young African American woman named Sandra Bland drove from her hometown of Chicago to a little town an hour west of Houston, Texas. She was interviewing for a job at Prairie View A&M University, the school she'd graduated from a few years before. She was tall and striking, with a personality to match. She belonged to the Sigma Gamma Rho sorority in college, and played in the marching band. She volunteered with a seniors group. She regularly posted short, inspirational videos on YouTube, under the handle "Sandy Speaks," that often began, "Good morning, my beautiful Kings and Queens."

I am up today just praising God, thanking His name. Definitely thanking Him not just because it's my birthday, but thanking Him for growth, thanking Him for the different things that He has done in my life over this past year. Just looking back at the twenty-eight years I have been on this earth, and all that He has shown me. Even though I have made some mistakes, I have definitely messed up, He still loves me, and I want to let my Kings and Queens know out there to that He still loves you too.

Bland got the job at Prairie View. She was elated. Her plan was to get a master's degree in political science on the side. On the afternoon of July 10 she left the university to get groceries, and as she made a right turn onto the highway that rings the Prairie View campus, she was pulled over by a police officer. His name was Brian Encinia: white, short dark hair, thirty years old. He was courteous—at least at first. He told her that she had failed to signal a lane change. He asked her questions. She answered them. Then Bland lit a cigarette, and Encinia asked her to put it out.

Their subsequent interaction was recorded by the video camera on his dashboard, and has been viewed in one form or another several million times on YouTube.

Bland: I'm in my car, why do I have to put out my cigarette?
Encinia: Well, you can step on out now.
Bland: I don't have to step out of my car.
Encinia: Step out of the car.
Bland: Why am I...
Encinia: Step out of the car!

Bland: No, you don't have the right. No, you don't have the right.

Encinia: Step out of the car.

Bland: You do not have the right. You do not have the right to do this.

Encinia: I do have the right, now step out or I will remove you.

Bland: I refuse to talk to you other than to identify myself. [*crosstalk*] I am getting removed for a failure to signal?

Encinia: Step out or I will remove you. I'm giving you a lawful order. Get out of the car now or I'm going to remove you.

Bland: And I'm calling my lawyer.

Bland and Encinia continue on for an uncomfortably long time. Emotions escalate.

Encinia: I'm going to yank you out of here. [*Reaches inside the car.*]

Bland: OK, you're going to yank me out of my car? OK, all right.

Encinia: [*calling in backup*] 2547.

Bland: Let's do this.

Encinia: Yeah, we're going to. [*Grabs for Bland.*]

Bland: Don't touch me!

Encinia: Get out of the car!

Bland: Don't touch me. Don't touch me! I'm not under arrest—you don't have the right to take me out of the car.

Encinia: You are under arrest!

Bland: I'm under arrest? For what? For what? For what?

Encinia: [*To dispatch*] 2547 County FM 1098. [*inaudible*] Send me another unit. [*To Bland*] Get out of the car! Get out of the car now!

Bland: Why am I being apprehended? You're trying to give me a ticket for failure...

Encinia: I said get out of the car!

Bland: Why am I being apprehended? You just opened my—

Encinia: I'm giving you a lawful order. I'm going to drag you out of here.

Bland: So you're threatening to drag me out of my own car?

Encinia: Get out of the car!

Bland: And then you're going to [*crosstalk*] me?

Encinia: I will light you up! Get out! Now! [*Draws stun gun and points it at Bland.*]

Bland: Wow. Wow. [*Bland exits car.*]

Encinia: Get out. Now. Get out of the car!

Bland: For a failure to signal? You're doing all of this for a failure to signal?

Bland was arrested and jailed. Three days later, she committed suicide in her cell.

2.

The Sandra Bland case came in the middle of a strange interlude in American public life. The interlude began in

4

the late summer of 2014, when an eighteen-year-old black man named Michael Brown was shot to death by a police officer in Ferguson, Missouri. He had just, allegedly, shoplifted a pack of cigars from a convenience store. The next several years saw one high-profile case after another involving police violence against black people. There were riots and protests around the country. A civil rights movement, Black Lives Matter, was born. For a time, this was what Americans talked about. Perhaps you remember some of the names of those in the news. In Baltimore, a young black man named Freddie Gray was arrested for carrying a pocket knife and fell into a coma in the back of a police van. Outside Minneapolis, a young black man named Philando Castile was pulled over by a police officer and inexplicably shot seven times after handing over his proof of insurance. In New York City, a black man named Eric Garner was approached by a group of police officers on suspicion that he was illegally selling cigarettes, and was choked to death in the ensuing struggle. In North Charleston, South Carolina, a black man named Walter Scott was stopped for a nonfunctioning taillight, ran from his car, and was shot to death from behind by a white police officer. Scott was killed on April 4, 2015. Sandra Bland gave him his own episode of "Sandy Speaks."

Good morning, my beautiful Kings and Queens....I am not a racist. I grew up in Villa Park, Illinois. I was the only black girl on an all-white cheerleading squad....Black people, you will not be successful in this world until you learn how to work with white people. I want the white folks to really understand out there that black people are doing as much as we can...and we can't help but get pissed off when we see situations where it's clear that the black life didn't matter. For those of you who question why he was running away, well goddamn, in the news that we've seen of late, you can stand there and surrender to the cops and still be killed.

Three months later, she too was dead.

Talking to Strangers is an attempt to understand what really happened by the side of the highway that day in rural Texas.

Why write a book about a traffic stop gone awry? Because the debate spawned by that string of cases was deeply unsatisfying. One side made the discussion about racism—looking down at the case from ten thousand feet. The other side examined each detail of each case with a magnifying glass. What was the police officer *like*? What did he do, precisely? One side saw a forest, but no trees. The other side saw trees and no forest.

Each side was right, in its own way. Prejudice and incompetence go a long way toward explaining social dysfunction in the United States. But what do you do with either of those diagnoses aside from vowing, in full earnestness, to try harder next time? There are bad cops. There are biased cops. Conservatives prefer the former interpretation, liberals the latter. In the end the two sides canceled each other out. Police officers still kill people in this country, but those deaths no longer command the news. I suspect that you may have had to pause for a

6

moment to remember who Sandra Bland was. We put aside these controversies after a decent interval and moved on to other things.

I don't want to move on to other things.

3.

In the sixteenth century, there were close to seventy wars involving the nations and states of Europe. The Danes fought the Swedes. The Poles fought the Teutonic Knights. The Ottomans fought the Venetians. The Spanish fought the French—and on and on. If there was a pattern to the endless conflict, it was that battles overwhelmingly involved neighbors. You fought the person directly across the border, who had always been directly across your border. Or you fought someone inside your own borders: the Ottoman War of 1509 was between two brothers. Throughout the majority of human history, encounters—hostile or otherwise—were rarely between strangers. The people you met and fought often believed in the same God as you, built their buildings and organized their cities in the same way you did, fought their wars with the same weapons according to the same rules.

But the sixteenth century's bloodiest conflict fit none of those patterns. When the Spanish conquistador Hernán Cortés met the Aztec ruler Montezuma II, neither side knew anything about the other at all.

Cortés landed in Mexico in February of 1519 and slowly made his way inland, advancing on the Aztec capital of

Tenochtitlán. When Cortés and his army arrived, they were in awe. Tenochtitlán was an extraordinary sight—far larger and more impressive than any of the cities Cortés and his men would have known back in Spain. It was a city on an island, linked to the mainland with bridges and crossed by canals. It had grand boulevards, elaborate aqueducts, thriving marketplaces, temples built in brilliant white stucco, public gardens, and even a zoo. It was spotlessly clean—which, to someone raised in the filth of medieval European cities, would have seemed almost miraculous.

"When we saw so many cities and villages built in the water and other great towns on dry land, we were amazed and said that it was like the enchantments," one of Cortés's officers, Bernal Díaz del Castillo, recalled. "And some of our soldiers even asked whether the things that we saw were not a dream?…I do not know how to describe it, seeing things as we did that had never been heard of or seen before, not even dreamed about."

The Spanish were greeted at the gates of Tenochtitlán by an assembly of Aztec chiefs, then taken to Montezuma. He was a figure of almost surreal grandeur, carried on a litter embroidered with gold and silver and festooned with flowers and precious stones. One of his courtiers advanced before the procession, sweeping the ground. Cortés dismounted from his horse. Montezuma was lowered from his litter. Cortés, like the Spaniard he was, moved to embrace the Aztec leader—only to be restrained by Montezuma's attendants. No one *embraced* Montezuma. Instead, the two men bowed to each other.

"Art thou not he? Art thou Montezuma?"

Montezuma answered: "Yes, I am he."

No European had ever set foot in Mexico. No Aztec had ever met a European. Cortés knew nothing about the Aztecs, except to be in awe of their wealth and the extraordinary city they had built. Montezuma knew nothing of Cortés, except that he had approached the Aztec kingdom with great audacity, armed with strange weapons and large, mysterious animals—horses—that the Aztecs had never seen before.

Is it any wonder why the meeting between Cortés and Montezuma has fascinated historians for so many centuries? That moment—500 years ago—when explorers began traveling across oceans and undertaking bold expeditions in previously unknown territory, an entirely new kind of encounter emerged. Cortés and Montezuma wanted to have a conversation, even though they knew nothing about the other. When Cortés asked Montezuma, "Art thou he?," he didn't say those words directly. Cortés spoke only Spanish. He had to bring two translators with him. One was an Indian woman named Malinche, who had been captured by the Spanish some months before. She knew the Aztec language Nahuatl and Mayan, the language of the Mexican territory where Cortés had begun his journey. Cortés also had with him a Spanish priest named Gerónimo del Aguilar, who had been shipwrecked in the Yucatán and learned Mayan during his sojourn there. So Cortés spoke to Aguilar in Spanish. Aguilar translated into Mayan for Malinche. And Malinche translated the Mayan into Nahuatl for Montezuma—and when Montezuma replied, "Yes, I am," the long translation chain ran in reverse. The kind of easy face-to-face interaction that each had

9

lived with his entire life had suddenly become hopelessly complicated.*

Cortés was taken to one of Montezuma's palaces—a place that Aguilar described later as having "innumerable rooms inside, antechambers, splendid halls, mattresses of large cloaks, pillows of leather and tree fibre, good eider-downs, and admirable white fur robes." After dinner, Montezuma rejoined Cortés and his men and gave a speech. Immediately, the confusion began. The way the Spanish interpreted Montezuma's remarks, the Aztec king was making an astonishing concession: he believed Cortés to be a god, the fulfillment of an ancient prophecy that said an exiled deity would one day return from the east. And he was, as a result, surrendering to Cortés. You can imagine Cortés's reaction: this magnificent city was now effectively his.

But is that really what Montezuma meant? Nahuatl, the language of the Aztecs, had a reverential mode. A royal figure such as Montezuma would speak in a kind of code, according to a cultural tradition in which the powerful projected their status through an elaborate false humility. The word in Nahuatl for a *noble,* the historian Matthew

---

* The idea that Montezuma considered Cortés a god has been soundly debunked by the historian Camilla Townsend, among others. Townsend argues that it was probably just a misunderstanding, following from the fact that the Nahua used the word *teotl* to refer to Cortés and his men, which the Spanish translated as *god.* But Townsend argues that they used that word only because they "had to call the Spaniards something, and it was not at all clear what that something should be....In the Nahua universe as it had existed up until this point, a person was always labeled as being from a particular village or city-state, or, more specifically, as one who filled a given social role (a tribute collector, prince, servant). These new people fit nowhere."

Restall points out, is all but identical to the word for *child*. When a ruler such as Montezuma spoke of himself as small and weak, in other words, he was actually subtly drawing attention to the fact that he was esteemed and powerful.

"The impossibility of adequately translating such language is obvious," Restall writes:

> The speaker was often obliged to say the opposite of what was really meant. True meaning was embedded in the use of reverential language. Stripped of these nuances in translation, and distorted through the use of multiple interpreters…not only was it unlikely that a speech such as Montezuma's would be accurately understood, but it was probable that its meaning would be turned upside down. In that case, Montezuma's speech was not his surrender; it was his acceptance of a Spanish surrender.

You probably remember from high-school history how the encounter between Cortés and Montezuma ended. Montezuma was taken hostage by Cortés, then murdered. The two sides went to war. As many as twenty million Aztecs perished, either directly at the hands of the Spanish or indirectly from the diseases they had brought with them. Tenochtitlán was destroyed. Cortés's foray into Mexico ushered in the era of catastrophic colonial expansion. And it also introduced a new and distinctly modern pattern of social interaction. Today we are now thrown into contact all the time with people whose assumptions, perspectives, and backgrounds are different from our own. The modern world is not two brothers feuding for control of the

Ottoman Empire. It is Cortés and Montezuma struggling to understand each other through multiple layers of translators. *Talking to Strangers* is about why we are so bad at that act of translation.

Each of the chapters that follows is devoted to understanding a different aspect of the stranger problem. You will have heard of many of the examples—they are taken from the news. At Stanford University in northern California, a first-year student named Brock Turner meets a woman at a party, and by the end of the evening he is in police custody. At Pennsylvania State University, the former assistant coach of the school's football team, Jerry Sandusky, is found guilty of pedophilia, and the president of the school and two of his top aides are found to be complicit in his crimes. You will read about a spy who spent years undetected at the highest levels of the Pentagon, about the man who brought down hedge-fund manager Bernie Madoff, about the false conviction of the American exchange student Amanda Knox, and about the suicide of the poet Sylvia Plath.

In all of these cases, the parties involved relied on a set of strategies to translate one another's words and intentions. And in each case, something went very wrong. In *Talking to Strangers,* I want to understand those strategies— analyze them, critique them, figure out where they came from, find out how to fix them. At the end of the book I will come back to Sandra Bland, because there is something about the encounter by the side of the road that ought to haunt us. Think about how *hard* it was. Sandra Bland was not someone Brian Encinia knew from the neighborhood or down the street. That would have been easy: *Sandy!*

How are you? Be a little more careful next time. Instead you have Bland from Chicago and Encinia from Texas, one a man and the other a woman, one white and one black, one a police officer and one a civilian, one armed and the other unarmed. They were strangers to each other. If we were more thoughtful as a society—if we were willing to engage in some soul-searching about how we approach and make sense of strangers—she would not have ended up dead in a Texas jail cell.

But to start, I have two questions—two puzzles about strangers—beginning with a story told by a man named Florentino Aspillaga years ago in a German debriefing room.

Part One

Spies and Diplomats:
Two Puzzles

CHAPTER ONE

Fidel Castro's Revenge

1.

Florentino Aspillaga's final posting was in Bratislava, in what was then Czechoslovakia. It was 1987, two years before the Iron Curtain fell. Aspillaga ran a consulting company called Cuba Tecnica, which was supposed to have something to do with trade. It did not. It was a front. Aspillaga was a high-ranking officer in Cuba's General Directorate of Intelligence.

Aspillaga had been named intelligence officer of the year in the Cuban spy service in 1985. He had been given a handwritten letter of commendation from Fidel Castro himself. He had served his country with distinction in Moscow, Angola, and Nicaragua. He was a star. In Bratislava, he ran Cuba's network of agents in the region.

But at some point during his steady ascent through

the Cuban intelligence service, he grew disenchanted. He watched Castro give a speech in Angola, celebrating the Communist revolution there, and had been appalled by the Cuban leader's arrogance and narcissism. By the time of his posting to Bratislava, in 1986, those doubts had hardened.

He planned his defection for June 6, 1987. It was an elaborate inside joke. June 6 was the anniversary of the founding of the Cuban Ministry of the Interior— the all-powerful body that administered the country's spy services. If you worked for the General Directorate of Intelligence, you would ordinarily celebrate on June 6. There would be speeches, receptions, ceremonies in honor of Cuba's espionage apparatus. Aspillaga wanted his betrayal to *sting*.

He met up with his girlfriend Marta in a park in downtown Bratislava. It was Saturday afternoon. She was Cuban as well, one of thousands of Cubans who were guest workers in Czech factories. Like all Cubans in her position, her passport was held at the Cuban government offices in Prague. Aspillaga would have to smuggle her across the border. He had a government-issued Mazda. He removed the spare tire from the trunk, drilled an air hole in the floor, and told her to climb inside.

Eastern Europe, at that point, was still walled off from the rest of the continent. Travel between East and West was heavily restricted. But Bratislava was only a short drive from Vienna, and Aspillaga had made the trip before. He was well known at the border and carried a diplomatic passport. The guards waved him through.

In Vienna, he and Marta abandoned the Mazda, hailed

a taxi, and presented themselves at the gates to the United States Embassy. It was Saturday evening. The senior staff was all at home. But Aspillaga did not need to do much to get the guard's attention: "I am a case officer from Cuban Intelligence. I am an intelligence *comandante.*"

In the spy trade, Aspillaga's appearance at the Vienna embassy is known as a *walk-in.* An official from the intelligence service of one country shows up, unexpectedly, on the doorstep of the intelligence service of another country. And Florentino "Tiny" Aspillaga was one of the great walk-ins of the Cold War. What he knew of Cuba—and its close ally, the Soviet Union—was so sensitive that twice after his defection his former employers at the Cuban spy service tracked him down and tried to assassinate him. Twice, he slipped away. Only once since has Aspillaga been spotted. It was by Brian Latell, who ran the CIA's Latin American office for many years.

Latell got a tip from an undercover agent who was acting as Aspillaga's go-between. He met the go-between at a restaurant in Coral Gables, just outside Miami. There he was given instructions to meet in another location, closer to where Aspillaga was living under his new identity. Latell rented a suite in a hotel, somewhere anonymous, and waited for Tiny to arrive.

"He's younger than me. I'm seventy-five. He's by now probably in his upper sixties," Latell said, remembering the meeting. "But he's had terrible health problems. I mean, being a defector, living with a new identity, it's tough."

Even in his diminished state, though, it was obvious what Aspillaga must have been like as a younger man, Latell says: charismatic, slender, with a certain theatricality about him—a taste for risks and grand emotional gestures. When he came into the hotel suite, Aspillaga was carrying a box. He put it down on the table and turned to Latell.

"This is a memoir that I wrote soon after I defected," he said. "I want you to have this."

Inside the box, in the pages of Aspillaga's memoir, was a story that made no sense.

2.

After his dramatic appearance at the American embassy in Vienna, Aspillaga was flown to a debriefing center at a U.S. Army base in Germany. In those years, American intelligence operated out of the United States Interests Section in Havana, under the Swiss flag. (The Cuban delegation had a similar arrangement in the United States.) Before his debriefing began, Aspillaga said, he had one request: he wanted the CIA to fly in one of the former Havana station chiefs, a man known to Cuban intelligence as "el Alpinista," the Mountain Climber.

The Mountain Climber had served the agency all over the world. After the Berlin Wall fell, files retrieved from the KGB and the East German secret police revealed that they had taught a course on the Mountain Climber to their agents. His tradecraft was impeccable. Once, Soviet intelligence officers tried to recruit him: they literally placed bags of money in front of him. He waved them off, mocked them. The Mountain Climber was incorruptible. He spoke Spanish like a Cuban. He was Aspillaga's role model. Aspillaga wanted to meet him face-to-face.

"I was on an assignment in another country when I got a message to rush to Frankfurt," the Mountain Climber remembers. (Though long retired from the CIA, he still prefers to be identified only by his nickname.) "Frankfurt is where we had our defector processing center. They told me a fellow had walked into an embassy in Vienna. He had driven out of Czechoslovakia with his girlfriend in the trunk of his car, walked in, and insisted on speaking to me. I thought it was kind of crazy."

El Alpinista went straight to the debriefing center. "I found four case officers sitting in the living room," he remembers. "They told me Aspillaga was back in the bedroom making love with his girlfriend, as he had constantly since he arrived at the safe house. Then I went in and spoke to him. He was lanky, poorly dressed, as Eastern Europeans and Cubans tended to be back then. A little sloppy. But it was immediately evident that he was a very smart guy."

When he walked in, the Mountain Climber didn't tell Aspillaga who he was. He was trying to be cagey; Aspillaga was an unknown quantity. But it was only a matter of minutes before Aspillaga figured it out. There was a moment of shock, laughter. The two men hugged, Cuban style.

"We talked for five minutes before we started into the details. Whenever you are debriefing one of those guys, you need someone that proves their bona fides," the Mountain Climber said. "So I just basically asked him what he could tell me about the [Cuban intelligence] operation."

It was then that Aspillaga revealed his bombshell, the news that had brought him from behind the Iron Curtain to the gates of the Vienna embassy. The CIA had a network of spies inside Cuba, whose dutiful reports to their case officers helped shape America's understanding of its adversary. Aspillaga named one of them and said, "He's a double agent. He works for us." The room was stunned. They had no idea. But Aspillaga kept going. He named another spy. "He's a double too." Then another, and another. He had names, details, chapter and verse. *That guy you recruited on the ship in Antwerp. The little fat guy with the mustache? He's a double. That other guy, with a limp, who works in the defense ministry? He's a double.* He continued on like that until he had listed dozens of names—practically the entire U.S. roster of secret agents inside Cuba. They were all working for Havana, spoon-feeding the CIA information cooked up by the Cubans themselves.

"I sat there and took notes," the Mountain Climber said. "I tried not to betray any emotion. That's what we're taught. But my heart was racing."

Aspillaga was talking about the Mountain Climber's people, the spies he'd worked with when he had been posted to Cuba as a young and ambitious intelligence officer. When he'd first arrived in Havana, the Mountain Climber had made a point of working his sources aggressively, mining them for information. "The thing is, if you have an agent who is in the office of the president of whatever country, but you can't communicate with him, that agent is worthless," the Mountain Climber said. "My feeling was, let's communicate and get some value, rather than waiting six months or a year until he puts up someplace else." But now the whole exercise turned out to have been a sham. "I must admit that I disliked Cuba so much that I derived much pleasure from pulling the wool over their eyes," he said, ruefully. "But it turns out that I wasn't the one pulling the wool over their eyes. That was a bit of a blow."

The Mountain Climber got on a military plane and flew with Aspillaga directly to Andrews Air Force Base outside Washington, DC, where they were met by "bigwigs" from the Latin American division. "In the Cuban section, the reaction was absolute shock and horror," he remembers. "They simply could not believe that they had been had so badly, for so many years. It sent shock waves."

It got worse. When Fidel Castro heard that Aspillaga had informed the CIA of their humiliation, he decided to rub salt in the wound. First he rounded up the entire cast of pretend CIA agents and paraded them across Cuba on a triumphant tour. Then he released on Cuban television an astonishing eleven-part documentary entitled *La Guerra de la CIA contra Cuba—The CIA's War against Cuba*. Cuban intelligence, it turned out, had filmed and recorded *everything* the CIA had been doing in their country for at least ten years—as if they were creating a reality show. *Survivor: Havana Edition*. The video was surprisingly high quality. There were close-up shots and shots from cinematic angles. The audio was crystal clear: the Cubans must have had advance word of every secret meeting place, and sent their technicians over to wire the rooms for sound.

On the screen, identified by name, were CIA officers supposedly under deep cover. There was video of every advanced CIA gadget: transmitters hidden in picnic baskets and briefcases. There were detailed explanations of which park bench CIA officers used to communicate with their sources and how the CIA used different-colored shirts to secretly signal their contacts. A long tracking shot showed a CIA officer stuffing cash and instructions inside a large, plastic "rock"; another caught a CIA officer stashing secret documents for his agents inside a wrecked car in a junkyard in Pinar del Rio; in a third, a CIA officer looked for a package in long grass by the side of the road while his wife fumed impatiently in the car. The Mountain Climber made a brief cameo in the documentary. His successor fared far worse. "When they showed that TV series," the Mountain Climber said, "it looked as though they had a guy with a camera over his shoulder everywhere he went."

When the head of the FBI's office in Miami heard about the documentary, he called up a Cuban official and asked for a copy. A set of videotapes was sent over promptly, thoughtfully dubbed in English. The most sophisticated intelligence service in the world had been played for a fool.

3.

This is what makes no sense about Florentino Aspillaga's story. It would be one thing if Cuba had deceived a group of elderly shut-ins, the way scam artists do. But the Cubans fooled the CIA, an organization that takes the problem of understanding strangers very seriously.

There were extensive files on every one of those double agents. The Mountain Climber says he checked them carefully. There were no obvious red flags. Like all intelligence agencies, the CIA has a division—counterintelligence—

whose job it is to monitor its own operations for signs of betrayal. What had they found? Nothing.*

Looking back on the episode years later, all Latell could do was shrug and say that the Cubans must have been really good. "They did it exquisitely," he said.

I mean, Fidel Castro selected the doubles that he dangled. He selected them with real brilliance...Some of them were trained in theatrical deception. One of

---

* The CIA makes a regular practice of giving its agents lie-detector tests—to guard against just the kind of treachery that Aspillaga was describing. Whenever one of the agency's Cuban spies left the island, the CIA would meet them secretly in a hotel room and have them sit for a polygraph. Sometimes the Cubans would pass; the head of the polygraph division personally gave a clean bill of health to six Cuban agents who ended up being doubles. Other times, the Cubans would fail. But what happened when they did? The people running the Cuban section dismissed it. One of the CIA's former polygraphers, John Sullivan, remembers being summoned to a meeting after his group gave the thumbs-down on a few too many Cuban assets. "They ambushed us," Sullivan said. "We were berated unmercifully....All these case officers were saying, 'You guys just don't know what you're doing,' et cetera, et cetera. 'Mother Teresa couldn't pass you.' I mean, they were really very, very nasty about it."

But can you blame them? The case officers chose to replace one method of making sense of strangers (strapping them to a polygraph machine) with another: their own judgment. And that is perfectly logical.

Polygraphy is, to say the least, an inexact art. The case officer would have had years of experience with the agent: met them, talked to them, analyzed the quality of the reports they filed. The assessment of a trained professional, made over the course of many years, ought to be more accurate than the results of a hurried meeting in a hotel room, right? Except that it wasn't.

"Many of our case officers think, 'I'm such a good case officer, they can't fool me,'" Sullivan said. "This one guy I'm thinking of in particular—and he was a very, very good case officer—they thought he was one of the best case officers in the agency." He was clearly talking about the Mountain Climber. "They took him to the cleaners. They actually got him on film servicing a dead drop. It was crazy."

them posed as a naïf, you know...He was really a very cunning, trained intelligence officer...You know, he's so goofy. How can he be a double? Fidel orchestrated all of this. I mean, Fidel is the greatest actor of them all.

The Mountain Climber, for his part, argues that the tradecraft of the CIA's Cuban section was just sloppy. He had previously worked in Eastern Europe, up against the East Germans, and there, he said, the CIA had been much more meticulous.

But what was the CIA's record in East Germany? *Just as bad as the CIA's record in Cuba.* After the Berlin Wall fell, East German spy chief Markus Wolf wrote in his memoirs that by the late 1980s

we were in the enviable position of knowing that not a single CIA agent had worked in East Germany without having been turned into a double agent or working for us from the start. On our orders they were all delivering carefully selected information and disinformation to the Americans.

The supposedly meticulous Eastern Europe division, in fact, suffered one of the worst breaches of the entire Cold War. Aldrich Ames, one of the agency's most senior officers responsible for Soviet counterintelligence, turned out to be working for the Soviet Union. His betrayals led to the capture—and execution—of countless American spies in Russia. El Alpinista knew him. Everyone who was high up at the agency did. "I did not have a high opinion of him," the Mountain Climber said, "because I knew him to be a lazy drunkard." But he and his colleagues never suspected that Ames was a traitor. "It was unthinkable to the old hands that one of our own could ever be beguiled by the other side the way Ames was," he said. "We were all just taken aback that one of our own could betray us that way."

The Mountain Climber was one of the most talented people at one of the most sophisticated institutions in the world. Yet he'd been witness three times to humiliating betrayal—first by Fidel Castro, then by the East Germans, and then, at CIA headquarters itself, by a lazy drunk. And if the CIA's best can be misled so completely, so many times, then what of the rest of us?

Puzzle Number One: Why can't we tell when the stranger in front of us is lying to our face?

CHAPTER TWO

Getting to Know der Führer

1.

On the evening of August 28, 1938, Neville Chamberlain called his closest advisor to 10 Downing Street for a late-night strategy session. Chamberlain had been the British prime minister a little over a year. He was a former businessman, a practical and plainspoken man, whose interests and experience lay with domestic affairs. But now he faced his first foreign-policy crisis. It involved Adolf Hitler, who had been making increasingly bellicose statements about invading the Sudetenland, the German-speaking portion of Czechoslovakia.

If Germany invaded Czechoslovakia, it would almost certainly mean a world war, which Chamberlain wanted desperately to avoid. But Hitler had been particularly reclusive in recent months, and Germany's intentions were so opaque that the rest of Europe was growing nervous. Chamberlain was determined to resolve the impasse. He dubbed his idea, which he put to his advisors that night, Plan Z. It was top secret. Chamberlain would later write that the idea was "so unconventional and daring that it rather took [Foreign Secretary Lord] Halifax's breath away." Chamberlain wanted to fly to Germany and demand to meet Hitler face-to-face.

One of the odd things about the desperate hours of the late 1930s, as Hitler dragged the world toward war, was how few of the world's leaders really knew the German leader.* Hitler was a mystery. Franklin Roosevelt, the American president throughout Hitler's rise, never met him. Nor did Joseph Stalin, the Soviet leader. Winston Churchill, Chamberlain's successor, came close while researching a book in Munich in 1932. He and Hitler twice made plans to meet for tea, but on both occasions Hitler stood him up.

The only people in England who spent any real amount of time with Hitler before the war were British aristocrats friendly to the Nazi cause, who would sometimes cross the Channel to pay their respects or join the Führer at parties. ("In certain moods he could be very funny," the fascist socialite Diana Mitford wrote in her memoirs. She dined with him frequently in Munich. "He did imitations of marvelous drollery.") But those were social calls. Chamberlain was trying to avert world war, and it seemed to him

---

* The one exception was Canadian prime minister William Lyon Mackenzie King. He met Hitler in 1937. He *loved* him. He compared him to Joan of Arc.

that he would benefit from taking the measure of Hitler for himself. Was Hitler someone who could be reasoned with? Trusted? Chamberlain wanted to find out.

On the morning of September 14, the British ambassador to Germany sent a telegram to Hitler's foreign minister, Joachim von Ribbentrop. Would Hitler like to meet? Von Ribbentrop replied the same day: yes. Chamberlain was a masterly politician with a gift for showmanship, and he artfully let the news slip. He was going to Germany to see if he could avert war. Across Britain, there was a shout of celebration. Polls showed that 70 percent of the country thought his trip was a "good thing for peace." The newspapers backed him. In Berlin, one foreign correspondent reported that he had been eating in a restaurant when the news broke, and the room had risen, as one, to toast Chamberlain's health.

Chamberlain left London on the morning of September 15. He'd never flown before, but he remained calm even as the plane flew into heavy weather near Munich. Thousands had gathered at the airport to greet him. He was driven to the train station in a cavalcade of fourteen Mercedes, then had lunch in Hitler's own dining car as the train made its way into the mountains, toward Hitler's retreat at Berchtesgaden. He arrived at five in the evening. Hitler came and shook his hand. Chamberlain would later report every detail of his first impressions in a letter to his sister Ida:

Halfway down the steps stood the Führer bareheaded and dressed in a khaki-coloured coat of broadcloth with a red armlet and a swastika on it and the military cross on his breast. He wore black trousers such as we wear in the evening and black patent leather lace-up shoes. His hair is brown, not black, his eyes blue, his expression rather disagreeable, especially in repose and altogether he looks entirely undistinguished. You would never notice him in a crowd and would take him for the house painter he was.

Hitler ushered Chamberlain upstairs to his study, with just an interpreter in tow. They talked, sometimes heatedly. "I am ready to face a world war!" Hitler exclaimed to Chamberlain at one point. Hitler made it plain that he was going to seize the Sudetenland, regardless of what the world thought. Chamberlain wanted to know whether that was *all* Hitler wanted. Hitler said it was. Chamberlain looked at Hitler long and hard and decided he believed him. In the same letter to his sister, Chamberlain wrote that he had heard back from people close to Hitler that the German leader felt he had had a conversation "with a man." Chamberlain went on:

"In short I had established a certain confidence which was my aim, and on my side in spite of the hardness and ruthlessness I thought I saw in his face I got the impression that here was a man who could be relied upon when he had given his word."

Chamberlain flew back to England the next morning. At Heston Airport, he gave a quick speech on the tarmac. "Yesterday afternoon I had a long talk with Herr Hitler," he said. "I feel satisfied now that each of us fully understands what is in the mind of the other." The two of them would meet again, he promised, only this time closer to England. "That is to spare an old man such another long journey," Chamberlain said, to what those present remembered as "laughter and cheers."

2.

Chamberlain's negotiations with Hitler are widely regarded as one of the great follies of the Second World War. Chamberlain fell under Hitler's spell. He was outmaneuvered at the bargaining table. He misread Hitler's intentions, and failed to warn Hitler that if he reneged on his promises there would be serious consequences. History has not been kind to Neville Chamberlain.

But underneath those criticisms is a puzzle. Chamberlain flew back to Germany two more times. He sat with Hitler for hours. The two men talked, argued, ate together, walked around together. Chamberlain was the only Allied leader of that period to spend any significant time with Hitler. He made careful note of the man's behavior. "Hitler's appearance and manner when I saw him appeared to show that the storm signals were up," Chamberlain told his sister Hilda after another of his visits to Germany. But then "he gave me the double handshake that he reserves for specially friendly demonstrations." Back in London, he told his cabinet that he had seen in the Führer "no signs of insanity but many of excitement." Hitler wasn't crazy. He was rational, determined: "He had thought out what he wanted and he meant to get it and he would not brook opposition beyond a certain point."

Chamberlain was acting on the same assumption that we all follow in our efforts to make sense of strangers. We believe that the information gathered from a personal interaction is uniquely valuable. You would never hire a babysitter for your children without meeting that person first. Companies don't hire employees blind. They call them in and interview them closely, sometimes for hours at a stretch, on more than one occasion. They do what Chamberlain did: they look people in the eye, observe their demeanor and behavior, and draw conclusions. *He gave me the double handshake.* Yet all that extra information Chamberlain gathered from his personal interactions with Hitler didn't help him see Hitler more clearly. It did the opposite.

Is this because Chamberlain was naive? Perhaps. His experience in foreign affairs was minimal. One of his critics would later compare him to a priest entering a pub for the first time, blind to the difference "between a social gathering and a rough house."

But this pattern isn't confined to Chamberlain. It also afflicted Lord Halifax, who would go on to become Chamberlain's foreign secretary. Halifax was an aristocrat, a superb student at Eton and Oxford. He served as Viceroy of India between the wars, where he negotiated brilliantly with Mahatma Gandhi. He was everything Chamberlain was not: worldly, seasoned, deeply charming, an intellectual — a man of such resolute religiosity that Churchill dubbed him the "Holy Fox."

Halifax went to Berlin in the fall of 1937 and met with the German leader at Berchtesgaden: he was the only other member of England's ruling circle to have spent time with the Führer. Their meeting wasn't some meaningless diplomatic reception. It began with Halifax mistaking Hitler for a footman and almost handing him his coat. And then Hitler was Hitler for five hours: sulking, shouting, digressing, denouncing. He talked about how much he hated the press. He talked about the evils of communism. Halifax listened to the performance with what another British diplomat at the time called a "mixture of astonishment, repugnance, and compassion."

Halifax spent five days in Germany. He met with two of Hitler's top ministers—Hermann Göring and Joseph Goebbels. He attended a dinner at the British Embassy, where he met a host of senior German politicians and businessmen. When he returned home, Halifax said that it was "all to the good making contact" with the German leadership, which is hard to dispute. That's what a diplomat is supposed to do. He had gained valuable insights from their face-to-face encounter about Hitler's bullying and volatility. But what was Halifax's ultimate conclusion? That Hitler didn't want to go to war, and was open to negotiating a peace. No one ever thought Halifax was naive, yet he was as deluded after meeting with Hitler as Chamberlain was.

The British diplomat who spent the most time with Hitler was the ambassador to Germany, Nevile Henderson. He met Hitler repeatedly, went to his rallies. Hitler even had a nickname for Henderson, "The man with the carnation," because of the flower the dapper Henderson always wore in his lapel. After attending the infamous Nuremberg Rally in early September 1938, Henderson wrote in his dispatch to London that Hitler seemed so abnormal that "he may have crossed the borderline into insanity." Henderson wasn't in Hitler's thrall. But did he think Hitler had dishonorable intentions toward Czechoslovakia? No. Hitler, he believed, "hates war as much as anyone." Henderson, too, read Hitler all wrong.*

The blindness of Chamberlain and Halifax and Henderson is not at all like Puzzle Number One, from the previous chapter. That was about the inability of otherwise intelligent and dedicated people to understand when they are being deceived. This is a situation where *some* people were deceived by Hitler and others were not. And the puzzle is that the group who were deceived are the ones you'd expect *not* to be, while those who saw the truth are the ones you'd think *would* be deceived.

Winston Churchill, for example, never believed for a

---

* The Nazi official Henderson knew even better was Göring, Hitler's deputy. Henderson would go stag hunting with Göring. They had long conversations. Henderson was convinced that Göring wanted peace as well, and that underneath his Nazi bluster was a decent man. In a memoir of his time in Berlin, written just as war broke out, Henderson said that Göring "loved animals and children; and, before ever he had one of his own, the top floor at Karinhall contained a vast playroom fitted up with every mechanical toy dear to the heart of a modern child. Nothing used to give him greater pleasure than to go and play there with them. The toys might, it is true, include models of airplanes dropping heavy bombs which exploded on defenseless towns or villages; but, as he observed when I reproached him on the subject, it was not part of the Nazi conception of life to be excessively civilized or to teach squeamishness to the young." (In case you were wondering, that's what Nazism was really about: tough-minded child-rearing.)

moment that Hitler was anything more than a duplicitous thug. Churchill called Chamberlain's visit "the stupidest thing that has ever been done." But Hitler was someone he'd only ever read about. Duff Cooper, one of Chamberlain's cabinet ministers, was equally clear-eyed. He listened with horror to Chamberlain's account of his meeting with Hitler. Later, he would resign from Chamberlain's government in protest. Did Cooper know Hitler? No. Only one person in the upper reaches of the British diplomatic service—Anthony Eden, who preceded Halifax as foreign secretary—had both met Hitler and saw the truth of him. But for everyone else? The people who were right about Hitler were those who knew the least about him personally. The people who were wrong about Hitler were the ones who had talked with him for hours.

This could all be a coincidence, of course. Perhaps Chamberlain and his cohort, for whatever private reason, were determined to see the Hitler they wanted to see, regardless of the evidence of their eyes and ears. Except that the same puzzling pattern crops up everywhere.

3.

The judge was middle-aged, tall, white-haired, with an accent that put his roots squarely in the borough of Brooklyn. Let's call him Solomon. He had served on the bench in New York State for over a decade. He wasn't imperious or intimidating. He was thoughtful, with a surprisingly gentle manner.

This was a Thursday, which in his courtroom was typically a busy day for arraignments. The defendants were all people who had been arrested in the past twenty-four hours on suspicion of some kind of crime. They'd just spent a sleepless night in a holding cell and now they were being brought into the courtroom in handcuffs, one by one. They sat on a low bench behind a partition, just to Solomon's left. When each case was called, the clerk would hand Solomon a file containing the defendant's rap sheet, and he would start flipping through, bringing himself up to speed. The defendant would stand directly in front of Solomon, with his lawyer on one side and the district attorney on the other. The two lawyers would talk. Solomon would listen. Then he would decide if the defendant would be required to post bail, and if so, how much the bail should be. *Does this perfect stranger deserve his freedom?*

The hardest cases, he said later, involved kids. A sixteen-year-old would come in charged with some horrible crime. And he would know that if he set bail high enough, the child would end up in a "cage" in the city's notorious Rikers Island facility, where—he put it as delicately as he could—there's basically "a riot waiting to happen at every turn."* Those cases got even harder when he looked up into the courtroom and saw the kid's mom sitting in the gallery. "I have a case like this every day," he said. He had taken up meditation. He found that made things easier.

---

* The law has since been changed. A defendant must be eighteen years old or above to be sent to Rikers.

Solomon was faced day in, day out with a version of the same problem that had faced Neville Chamberlain and the British diplomatic service in the fall of 1938: he was asked to assess the character of a stranger. And the criminal justice system assumes, as Chamberlain did, that those kinds of difficult decisions are better made when the judge and the judged meet each other first.

Later that afternoon, for example, Solomon was confronted with an older man with thinning, close-cropped hair. He was wearing blue jeans and a guayabera shirt and spoke only Spanish. He'd been arrested because of an "incident" involving the six-year-old grandson of his girl-friend. The boy told his father right away. The district attorney asked for $100,000 bail. There was no way the man had the resources to raise that amount. If Solomon agreed with the DA, the man in the guayabera would go straight to jail.

On the other hand, the man denied everything. He had two previous criminal offenses—but they were misdemeanors, from many years ago. He had a job as a mechanic, which he would lose if he went to jail, and he had an ex-wife and a fifteen-year-old son whom he was supporting with that income. So Solomon had to think about that fifteen-year-old, relying on his father's paycheck. He also surely knew that six-year-olds are not the most reliable of witnesses. So there was no way for Solomon to be sure whether this would all turn out to be a massive misunderstanding or part of some sinister pattern. In other words, the decision about whether to let the man in the guayabera go free—or to hold him in jail until trial—was impossibly difficult. And to help him make the right call, Solomon did what all of us would

38

do in that situation: he looked the man right in the eyes and tried to get a sense of who he really was. So did that help? Or are judges subject to the same puzzle as Neville Chamberlain?

4.

The best answer we have to that question comes from a study conducted by a Harvard economist, three elite computer scientists, and a bail expert from the University of Chicago. The group—and for simplicity's sake, I'll refer to it by the economist's name, Sendhil Mullainathan—decided to use New York City as their testing ground. They gathered up the records of 554,689 defendants brought before arraignment hearings in New York from 2008 to 2013—554,689 defendants in all. Of those, they found that the human judges of New York released just over 400,000.

Mullainathan then built an artificial intelligence system, fed it the same information the prosecutors had given judges in those arraignment cases (the defendant's age and criminal record), and told the computer to go through those 554,689 cases and make its own list of 400,000 people to release. It was a bake-off: man versus machine. Who made the best decisions? Whose list committed the fewest crimes while out on bail and was most likely to show up for their trial date? The results weren't even close. The people on the computer's list were 25 percent less likely to commit a crime while awaiting trial than the 400,000 people released by the judges of

New York City. 25 percent! In the bake-off, machine *destroyed* man.*

To give you just one sense of the mastery of Mullainathan's machine, it flagged 1 percent of all the defendants as "high risk." These are the people the computer thought should never be released prior to trial. According to the machine's calculations, well over half of the people in that high-risk group would commit another crime if let out on bail. When the human judges looked at that same group of bad apples, though, they didn't identify them as dangerous at all. They released 48.5 percent of them! "Many of the defendants flagged by the algorithm as high

---

* Two technical points about the dueling lists of 400,000 defendants: When Mullainathan says that the computer's list committed 25 percent fewer crimes than the judge's list, he's counting failure to appear for a trial date as a crime. Second, I'm sure you are wondering how Mullainathan could calculate, with such certainty, who would or wouldn't end up committing a crime while out on pretrial release. It's not because he has a crystal ball. It's an estimate made on the basis of a highly sophisticated statistical analysis. Here's the short version. Judges in New York City take turns doing bail hearings. Defendants are, essentially, randomly assigned to them for consideration. Judges in New York (as in all jurisdictions) vary dramatically in how likely they are to release someone, or how prohibitively high they set bail. Some judges are very permissive. Others are strict. So imagine that one set of strict judges sees 1,000 defendants and releases 25 percent of them. Another set of permissive judges sees 1,000 defendants, who are in every way equivalent to the other 1,000, and releases 75 percent of them. By comparing the crime rates of the released defendants in each group, you can get a sense of how many harmless people the strict judges jailed, and how many dangerous people the permissive judges set free. That estimate, in turn, can be applied to the machine's predictions. When it passes judgment on its own 1,000 defendants, how much better is it than the strict judges on the one hand, and the permissive judges on the other? This sounds highly complicated, and it is. But it's a well-established methodology. For a more complete explanation, I encourage you to read Mullainathan's paper.

risk are treated by the judge as if they were low risk," Team Mullainathan concluded in a particularly devastating passage. "Performing this exercise suggests that judges are not simply setting a high threshold for detention but are mis-ranking defendants.... The marginal defendants they select to detain are drawn from throughout the entire predicted risk distribution." Translation: the bail decisions of judges are all over the place.

I think you'll agree that this is baffling. When judges make their bail decisions, they have access to three sources of information. They have the defendant's record—his age, previous offenses, what happened the last time he was granted bail, where he lives, where he works. They have the testimony of the district attorney and the defendant's lawyer: whatever information is communicated in the courtroom. And they have the evidence of their own eyes. What is my *feeling* about this man before me?

Mullainathan's computer, on the other hand, couldn't see the defendant and it couldn't hear anything that was said in the courtroom. All it had was the defendant's age and rap sheet. It had a fraction of the information available to the judge—*and it did a much better job at making bail decisions.*

In my second book, *Blink,* I told the story of how orchestras made much smarter recruiting decisions once they had prospective hires audition behind a screen. Taking information away from the hiring committee made for better judgments. But that was because the information gleaned from watching someone play is largely irrelevant. If you're judging whether someone is a good violin player, knowing whether that person is big or small, handsome or homely, white or black isn't going to help. In fact, it will probably only introduce biases that will make your job even harder.

But when it comes to a bail decision, the extra information the judge has sounds like it should be really useful. In an earlier case in Solomon's courtroom, a young man in basketball shorts and a gray T-shirt was charged with getting into a fight with someone, then buying a car with the man's stolen credit card. In asking for bail, the district attorney pointed out that he had failed to appear for his court date after two previous arrests. That's a serious red flag. But not all "FTAs" are identical. What if the defendant was given the wrong date? What if he would lose his job if he took off work that day, and decided it wasn't worth it? What if his child was in the hospital? That's what the defendant's lawyer told the judge: Her client had a good excuse. The computer didn't know that, but the judge did. How could that not help?

In a similar vein, Solomon said the thing he's most alert to in bail cases is "mental illness with an allegation of violence." Those kinds of cases are a judge's worst nightmare. They let someone out on bail, then that person stops taking their medication and goes on to commit some horrible crime. "It's shoot a cop," Solomon said.

> It's drive a car into a minivan, killing a pregnant woman and her husband. It's hurt a child. [It's] shoving somebody in front of a subway train and killing them. It's an awful situation at every possible angle.... No judge would ever want to be the one having made the release decision on that case.

Some of the clues to that kind of situation are in the defendant's file: medical records, previous hospitalizations, some mention of the defendant's being found not competent. But other clues are found only in the moment.

"You also will hear terms thrown around in the courtroom of 'EDP'—emotionally disturbed person," Solomon said.

That will come from either the police department who's brought them in and handed you an envelope that's from a doctor at a hospital where he's been screened at a psychiatric ER prior to arraignment.... Other times, that information will get into the DA's folder and the DA will ask questions.... That's a fact for me to think about.

He'll look at the defendant, in those cases—closely, carefully, searching for, as he put it,

sort of a glassy-eyed look, not being able to make eye contact. And not the adolescent unable to make eye contact because the frontal lobe hasn't developed. I'm talking about the adult off their meds....

Mullainathan's machine can't overhear the prosecutor talking about an EDP, and it can't see that telltale glassy-eyed look. That fact should translate into a big advantage for Solomon and his fellow judges. But for some reason it doesn't.

Puzzle Number Two: How is it that meeting a stranger can sometimes make us worse at making sense of that person than *not* meeting them?

5.

Neville Chamberlain made his third and final visit to Germany at the end of September 1938, two weeks after his first visit. The meeting was in Munich at the Nazi Party's offices—the Führerbau. Italian leader Benito Mussolini and French prime minister Édouard Daladier were also invited. The four of them met, with their aides, in Hitler's private study. On the morning of the second day, Chamberlain asked Hitler if the two of them could meet alone. By this point, Chamberlain felt he had the measure of his adversary.

When Hitler had said his ambitions were limited to Czechoslovakia, Chamberlain believed that "Herr Hitler was telling the truth." It was now just a matter of getting that commitment in writing.

Hitler took him to his apartment on Prinzregentenplatz. Chamberlain pulled out a piece of paper on which he had written a simple agreement and asked Hitler whether he would sign it. As the interpreter translated the words into German, "Hitler frequently ejaculated, *'Ja! Ja!'* And at the end he said, 'Yes I will certainly sign it,'" Chamberlain later wrote to one of his sisters. "'When shall we do it?' I said, 'now,' & we went at once to the writing table & put our signatures to the two copies which I had brought with me."

That afternoon, Chamberlain flew home to a hero's welcome. A crowd of journalists surged toward him. He took the letter from his breast pocket and waved it to the crowd. "This morning I had another talk with the German Chancellor Herr Hitler, and here is a paper which bears his name upon it as well as mine."

Then it was back to the prime minister's residence at 10 Downing Street.

"My good friends, this is the second time in our history that there has come back from Germany to Downing Street peace with honor. I believe it is peace for our time. We thank you from the bottom of our hearts."

The crowd cheered.

"Now I recommend you go home, and sleep quietly in your beds."

In March 1939, Hitler invaded the rest of Czechoslovakia. It had taken him less than six months to break his agreement with Chamberlain. On September 1, 1939, Hitler invaded Poland, and the world was at war.

We have, in other words, CIA officers who cannot make sense of their spies, judges who cannot make sense of their defendants, and prime ministers who cannot make sense of their adversaries. We have people struggling with their first impressions of a stranger. We have people struggling when they have months to understand a stranger. We have people struggling when they meet with someone only once, and people struggling when they return to the stranger again and again. They struggle with assessing a stranger's honesty. They struggle with a stranger's character. They struggle with a stranger's intent.

It's a mess.

6.

One last thing:

Take a look at the following word, and fill in the two blank letters. Do it quickly, without thinking.

G L _ _

This is called a word-completion task. Psychologists commonly use it to test things such as memory.

I completed G L _ _ as GLUM. Remember that. The next word is:

_ _TER

I completed that as HATER. Remember that too. Here are the rest of the words:

S_ _RE	STR_ _ _	B_ _T
P_ _N	GO_ _	PO _ _ _
TOU_ _	CHE_ _	BA_ _
ATT_ _ _	_ _OR	_RA_
BO_ _	SL_ _ _	_ _ _EAT
FL_ _T	SC_ _ _	
SL_T	_ _NNER	

I started out with GLUM and HATER and ended up with SCARE, ATTACK, BORE, FLOUT, SLIT, CHEAT, TRAP, and DEFEAT. That's a pretty morbid and melancholy list. But I don't think that says anything about the darkness of my soul. I'm not melancholy. I'm an optimist. I think that the first word, GLUM, popped into my head, and then I just continued in that vein.

A few years ago, a team of psychologists led by Emily Pronin gave a group of people that same exercise. Pronin had them fill in the blank spaces. Then she asked them the same question: What do you think your choices *say* about you? For instance, if you completed TOU_ _ as TOUCH, does that suggest that you are a different kind of person than if you completed it as TOUGH? The respondents took the same position I did. *They're just words.*

"I don't agree with these word-stem completions as a measure of my personality," one of Pronin's subjects wrote. And the others in the group agreed:

"These word completions don't seem to reveal much about me at all.... Random completions."

"Some of the words I wrote seem to be the antithesis of how I view the world. For instance, I hope that I am not always concerned about being STRONG, the BEST, or a WINNER."

"I don't really think that my word completions reveal that much about me.... Occurred as a result of happenstance."

"Not a whole lot.... They reveal vocabulary."

"I really don't think there was any relationship.... The words are just random."

"The words PAIN, ATTACK, and THREAT seem similar, but I don't know that they say anything about me."

But then things got interesting. Pronin gave the group other people's words. These were perfect strangers. She asked the same question. What do you think this stranger's choices reveal? And this time Pronin's panel completely changed their minds.

"He doesn't seem to read too much, since the natural (to me) completion of B_ _K would be BOOK. BEAK seems rather random, and might indicate deliberate unfocus of mind."

"I get the feeling that whoever did this is pretty vain, but basically a nice guy."

Keep in mind that these are the exact same people who just moments before had denied that the exercise had any meaning at all.

"The person seems goal-oriented and thinks about competitive settings."

"I have a feeling that the individual in question may be tired very often in his or her life. In addition, I think that he or she might be interested in having close personal interactions with someone of the opposite sex. The person may also enjoy playing games."

The same person who said, "These word completions don't seem to reveal much about me at all" turned around and said, of a perfect stranger:

"I think this girl is on her period.... I also think that she either feels she or someone else is in a dishonest

sexual relationship, according to the words WHORE,
SLOT (similar to slut), CHEAT."

The answers go on and on like this. And no one
seemed even remotely aware that they had been trapped in
a contradiction.

"I guess there is some relationship....He talks a lot
about money and the BANK. A lot more correlation
here."

"He seems to focus on competition and winning.
This person could be an athlete or someone who is
very competitive."

"It seems this individual has a generally positive
outlook toward the things he endeavors. Most words,
such as WINNER, SCORE, GOAL, indicate some
sort of competitiveness, which combined with the
jargon, indicate that he has some athletic competitive
nature."

If the panel had seen my GLUM, HATER, SCARE,
ATTACK, BORE, FLOUT, SLIT, CHEAT, TRAP, and
DEFEAT, they would have worried for my soul.

Pronin calls this phenomenon the "illusion of asymmetric insight." She writes:

The conviction that we know others better than they
know us—and that we may have insights about them
they lack (but not vice versa)—leads us to talk when
we would do well to listen and to be less patient than
we ought to be when others express the conviction

that they are the ones who are being misunderstood or judged unfairly.

This is the problem at the heart of those first two puzzles. The officers on the Cuba desk of the CIA were sure they could evaluate the loyalty of their spies. Judges don't throw up their hands at the prospect of assessing the character of defendants. They give themselves a minute or two, then authoritatively pass judgment. Neville Chamberlain never questioned the wisdom of his bold plan to avert war. If Hitler's intentions were unclear, it was his job, as prime minister, to go to Germany and figure them out.

We think we can easily see into the hearts of others based on the flimsiest of clues. We jump at the chance to judge strangers. We would never do that to ourselves, of course. We are nuanced and complex and enigmatic. But the stranger is easy.

If I can convince you of one thing in this book, let it be this: Strangers are not easy.

Part Two

Default to Truth

CHAPTER THREE

The Queen of Cuba

1.

Let's take a look at another Cuban spy story.

In the early 1990s, thousands of Cubans began to flee the regime of Fidel Castro. They cobbled together crude boats—made of inner tubes and metal drums and wooden doors and any number of other stray parts—and set out on a desperate voyage across the ninety miles of the Florida Straits to the United States. By one estimate, as many as 24,000 people died attempting the journey. It was a human-rights disaster. In response, a group of Cuban emigrés in Miami founded Hermanos al Rescate— Brothers to the Rescue. They put together a makeshift air force of single-engine Cessna Skymasters and took to the skies over the Florida Straits, searching for refugees from the air and radioing their coordinates to the Coast

Guard. Hermanos al Rescate saved thousands of lives. They became heroes.

As time passed, the emigrés grew more ambitious. They began flying into Cuban airspace, dropping leaflets on Havana urging the Cuban people to rise up against Castro's regime. The Cuban government, already embarrassed by the flight of refugees, was outraged. Tensions rose, coming to a head on February 24, 1996. That afternoon three Hermanos al Rescate planes took off for the Florida Straits. As they neared the Cuban coastline, two Cuban Air Force MiG fighter jets shot two of the planes out of the sky, killing all four people aboard.

The response to the attack was immediate. The United Nations Security Council passed a resolution denouncing the Cuban government. A grave President Clinton held a press conference. The Cuban emigré population in Miami was furious. The two planes had been shot down in international airspace, making the incident tantamount to an act of war. The radio chatter among the Cuban pilots was released to the press:

> "We hit him, *cojones,* we hit him."
> "We retired them, *cojones.*"
> "We hit them."
> "Fuckers."
> "Mark the place where we retired them."
> "This one won't fuck with us anymore."

And then, after one of the MiGs zeroed in on the second Cessna:

"Homeland or death, you bastards."

But in the midst of the controversy, the story suddenly shifted. A retired U.S. rear admiral named Eugene Carroll gave an interview to CNN. Carroll was an influential figure inside Washington. He had formerly served as the director of all U.S. armed forces in Europe, with 7,000 weapons at his disposal. Just before the Hermanos al Rescate shoot-down, Carroll said, he and a small group of military analysts had met with top Cuban officials.

> **CNN:** Admiral, can you tell me what happened on your trip to Cuba, who you spoke with and what you were told?
>
> **Carroll:** We were hosted by the Ministry of Defense. General Rosales del Toro.... We traveled around, inspected Cuban bases, Cuban schools, their partially completed nuclear power plant, and so on. In long discussions with General Rosales del Toro and his staff the question came up about these overflights from U.S. aircraft—not government aircraft, but private airplanes operating out of Miami. They asked us, "What would happen if we shot one of these down? We can, you know."

Carroll interpreted that question from his Cuban hosts as a thinly veiled warning. The interview continued:

> **CNN:** So when you returned, who did you relay this information to?
>
> **Carroll:** As soon as we could make appointments, we discussed the situation...with members of the State

Department and members of the Defense Intelligence Agency.

The Defense Intelligence Agency—the DIA—is the third arm of the foreign intelligence triumvirate in the U.S. government, along with the CIA and the National Security Agency. If Carroll had met with the State Department and the DIA, he had delivered the Cuban warning about as high up in the American government as you could go. And did the State Department and DIA take those warnings to heart? Did they step in and stop Hermanos al Rescate from continuing their reckless forays into Cuban airspace? Obviously not.[*]

Carroll's comments ricocheted around Washington, DC, policy circles. This was an embarrassing revelation. The Cuban shoot-down happened on February 24. Carroll's warnings to the State Department and DIA were delivered on February 23. A prominent Washington insider met with U.S. officials *the day before* the crisis, explicitly warned them that the Cubans had lost patience with Hermanos al Rescate, and his warning was ignored. What began as a Cuban atrocity was now transformed into a story about American diplomatic incompetence.

---

[*] The State Department had informed Hermanos al Rescate, through official channels, that any flight plan with Cuba as a destination was unacceptable. But clearly those warnings weren't working.

CNN: Admiral, the State Department had issued other warnings to Brothers to the Rescue about this, haven't they?

Carroll: Not effective ones.... They know that [Brothers] have been filing flight plans that were false and then going to Cuba, and this was part of the Cuban resentment, was that the government wasn't enforcing its own regulations.

CNN: But what about the position that these were unarmed civilian planes?

Carroll repeated what he had been told in Havana.

Carroll: That is a very sensitive question. Where were they? What were they doing? I'll give you an analogy. Suppose we had the planes flying over San Diego from Mexico, dropping leaflets and inciting against [California] Governor Wilson. How long would we tolerate these overflights after we had warned them against it?

Fidel Castro wasn't being invited onto CNN to defend himself. But he didn't need to be. He had a rear admiral making his case.

2.

The next three chapters of *Talking to Strangers* are devoted to the ideas of a psychologist named Tim Levine, who has thought as much about the problem of why we are deceived by strangers as anyone in social science. The second chapter looks at Levine's theories through the story of Bernie Madoff, the investor who ran the largest Ponzi scheme in history. The third examines the strange case of Jerry Sandusky, the Pennsylvania State University football coach convicted of sexual abuse. And this, the first, is about the fallout from that moment of crisis between the United States and Cuba in 1996.

Does anything about Admiral Carroll and the Cuban shoot-downs strike you as odd? There are an awful lot of coincidences here.

1. The Cubans plan a deliberate murderous attack on U.S. citizens flying in international airspace.
2. It just so happens that the day before the attack, a prominent military insider delivers a stern warning to U.S. officials about the possibility of exactly that action.
3. And, fortuitously, that warning puts that same official, the day *after* the attack, in a position to make the Cuban case on one of the world's most respected news networks.

The timing of those three events is a little too perfect, isn't it? If you were a public relations firm, trying to mute the fallout from a very controversial action, that's exactly how you'd script it. Have a seemingly neutral expert available—right away—to say, "I warned them!"

This is what a military counterintelligence analyst named Reg Brown thought in the days after the incident. Brown worked on the Latin American desk of the Defense Intelligence Agency. His job was to understand the ways in which the Cuban intelligence services were trying to influence American military operations. His business, in other words, was to be alert to the kinds of nuances, subtleties, and unexplained coincidences that the rest of us ignore, and Brown couldn't shake the feeling that somehow the Cubans had orchestrated the whole crisis.

It turned out, for example, that the Cubans had a source

inside Hermanos al Rescate—a pilot named Juan Pablo Roque. On the day before the attack, he had disappeared and resurfaced at Castro's side in Havana. Clearly Roque told his bosses back home that Hermanos al Rescate had something planned for the 24th. That made it difficult for Brown to imagine that the date of the Carroll briefing had been chosen by chance. For maximum public relations impact, the Cubans would want their warning delivered the day before, wouldn't they? That way the State Department and the DIA couldn't wiggle out of the problem by saying that the warning was vague, or long ago. Carroll's words were right in front of them on the day the pilots took off from Miami.

So who arranged that meeting? Brown wondered. *Who picked February 23?* He did some digging, and the name he came up with startled him. It was a colleague of his at the DIA, a Cuban expert named Ana Belen Montes. Ana Montes was a star. She had been selected, repeatedly, for promotions and special career opportunities, showered with accolades and bonuses. Her reviews were glowing. She had come to the DIA from the Department of Justice, and in his recommendation, one of her former supervisors described her as the best employee he had ever had. She once got a medal from George Tenet, the director of the CIA. Her nickname inside the intelligence community was the "Queen of Cuba."

Weeks passed. Brown agonized. To accuse a colleague of treachery on the basis of such semi-paranoid speculation was an awfully big step, especially when the colleague was someone of Montes's stature. Finally Brown made up his mind, taking his suspicions to a DIA counterintelligence officer named Scott Carmichael.

"He came over and we walked in the neighborhood for a while during lunch hour," Carmichael remembers of his first meeting with Reg Brown. "And he hardly even got to Montes. I mean most of it was listening to him saying, 'Oh God.' He was wringing his hands, saying, 'I don't want to do the wrong thing.'"

Slowly, Carmichael drew him out. Everyone who worked on Cuba remembered the bombshell dropped by Florentino Aspillaga. The Cubans were *good*. And Brown had evidence of his own. He'd written a report in the late 1980s detailing the involvement of senior Cuban officials in international drug smuggling. "He identified specific senior Cuban officers who were directly involved," Carmichael said, "and then provided the specifics. I mean, flights, the dates, times, the places, who did what to whom, the whole enchilada." Then a few days before Brown's report was released, the Cubans rounded up everyone he'd mentioned in his investigation, executed a number of them, and issued a public denial. "And Reg went, 'What the fuck?' There was a leak."

It made Brown paranoid. In 1994, two Cuban intelligence officers had defected and told a similar story: The Cubans had someone high inside American intelligence. So what was he to think? Brown said to Carmichael. Didn't he have reason to be suspicious?

Then he told Carmichael the other thing that had happened during the Hermanos al Rescate crisis. Montes worked at the DIA's office on Bolling Air Force Base, in the Anacostia section of Washington, DC. When the planes were shot down, she was called in to the Pentagon: if you were one of the government's leading Cuba experts, you were needed at the scene. The shoot-down happened on a Saturday. The following evening Brown happened to telephone, asking for Montes.

"He said some woman answered the phone and told him that Ana had left," Carmichael says. Earlier in the day, Montes had gotten a phone call—and afterward she'd been agitated. Then she'd told everyone in the situation room that she was tired, that there was nothing going on, that she was going home.

> Reg was just absolutely incredulous. This was just so counter to our culture that he couldn't even believe it. Everybody understands that when a crisis occurs, you're called in because you have some expertise that can add to the decision-making processes. And at the Pentagon, you were available until you were dismissed. It's just understood. If somebody at that level calls you in, because all of a sudden those North Koreans have launched a missile at San Francisco, you don't just decide to leave when you get tired and hungry. Everybody understands that. And yet she did that. And Reg was just, "What the hell?"

In Brown's thinking, if she really worked for the Cubans, they would have been desperate to hear from her: they would want to know what was happening in the situation room. Did she have a meeting that night with her handler? It was all a bit far-fetched, which is why Brown was so conflicted. But there *were* Cuban spies. He knew that. And here was this woman, taking a personal phone call and heading out the door in the middle of what was—

for a Cuban specialist—just about the biggest crisis in a generation. And on top of that, she's the one who had arranged the awfully convenient Admiral Carroll briefing?

Brown told Carmichael that the Cubans had wanted to shoot down one of the Hermanos al Rescate planes for years. But they hadn't, because they knew what a provocation that would be. It might serve as the excuse the United States needed to depose Fidel Castro or launch an invasion. To the Cubans it wasn't worth it—unless, that is, they could figure out some way to turn public opinion in their favor.

> And so he finds out that Ana was not just one of the people in the room with Admiral Carroll, but she's the one who organized it. He looked at that and went, "Holy shit, I'm looking at a Cuban counterintelligence influence operation to spin a story, and Ana is the one who led the effort to meet with Admiral Carroll. What the hell is that all about?"

Months passed. Brown persisted. Finally, Carmichael pulled Montes's file. She had passed her most recent polygraph with flying colors. She didn't have a secret drinking problem, or unexplained sums in her bank account. She had no red flags. "After I had reviewed the security files and the personnel files on her, I thought, *Reg is way off base here*," Carmichael said. "This woman is gonna be the next Director of Intelligence for DIA. She's just fabulous." He knew that in order to justify an investigation on the basis of speculation, he had to be meticulous. Reg Brown, he said, was "coming apart." He had to satisfy Brown's suspicions, one way or another—as he put it, to "document the living shit out of everything" because if word got out that Montes was under suspicion, "I knew I was gonna be facing a shit storm."

Carmichael called Montes in. They met in a conference room at Bolling. She was attractive, intelligent, slender, with short hair and sharp, almost severe features. Carmichael thought to himself, *This woman is impressive.* "When she sat down, she was sitting almost next to me, about that far away"—he held his hands three feet apart—"same side of the table. She crossed her legs. I don't think that she did it on purpose, I think she was just getting comfortable. I happen to be a leg man—she couldn't have known that, but I like legs and I know that I glanced down."

He asked her about the Admiral Carroll meeting. She had an answer. It wasn't her idea at all. The son of someone she knew at DIA had accompanied Carroll to Cuba, and she'd gotten a call afterward.

She said, "I know his dad, his dad called me, and he said, 'Hey, if you want the latest scoop on Cuba, you should go see Admiral Carroll,' and so I just called up Admiral Carroll and we looked at our schedules and decided the 23rd of February was the most convenient date that works for both of us, and that was it."

As it turned out, Carmichael knew the DIA employee she was talking about. He told her that he was going to call him up and corroborate her story. And she said, "Please do."

So what happened with the phone call in the situation

room, he asked her? She said she didn't remember getting a phone call, and to Carmichael it seemed as though she was being honest. It had been a crazy, hectic day, nine months before. What about leaving early?

> She said, "Well, yeah, I did leave." Right away, she's admitting to that. She's not denying stuff, which might be a little suspicious. She said, "Yeah, I did leave early that day." She says, "You know, it was on a Sunday, the cafeterias were closed. I'm a very picky eater, I have allergies, so I don't eat stuff out of vending machines. I got there around six o'clock in the morning, it was about…eight o'clock at night. I'm starving to death, nothing was going on, they didn't really need me, so I just decided I was going to get out of there. Go home and eat something."[*] That rang true to me. It did.

After the interview, Carmichael set out to double-check her answers. The date of the briefing really *did* seem like a coincidence. Her friend's son *had* gone to Cuba with Carroll.

> I learned that yeah, she does have allergies, she doesn't eat out of vending machines, she's very particular

---

[*] This was in fact true. Montes strictly controlled her diet, at one point limiting herself to "eating only unseasoned boiled potatoes." CIA-led psychologists later concluded she had borderline OCD. She also took very long showers with different types of soap and wore gloves when she drove her car. Under the circumstances, it's not surprising that people would explain away their suspicions about her often-strange behavior.

about what she eats. I thought, she's there in the Pentagon on a Sunday. I've been there, the cafeteria's not open. She went all day long without eating, she went home. I said, "Well, it kind of made sense."

What'd I have? I didn't have anything. Oh well.

Carmichael told Reg Brown not to worry. He turned his attention to other matters. Ana Montes went back to her office. All was forgotten and forgiven until one day in 2001, five years later, when it was discovered that every night Montes had gone home, typed up from memory all of the facts and insights she had learned that day at work, and sent it to her handlers in Havana.

From the day she'd joined the DIA, Montes had been a Cuban spy.

3.

In the classic spy novel, the secret agent is slippery and devious. We're hoodwinked by the brilliance of the enemy. That was the way many CIA insiders explained away Florentino Aspillaga's revelations: *Castro is a genius. The agents were brilliant actors.* In truth, however, the most dangerous spies are rarely diabolical. Aldrich Ames, maybe the most damaging traitor in American history, had mediocre performance reviews, a drinking problem, and didn't even try to hide all the money he was getting from the Soviet Union for his spying.

Ana Montes was scarcely any better. Right before she was arrested, the DIA found the codes she used to send her dispatches to Havana...in her purse. And in her apartment, she had a shortwave radio in a shoebox in her closet.

Brian Latell, the CIA Cuba specialist who witnessed the Aspillaga disaster, knew Montes well.

"She used to sit across the table from me at meetings that I convened, when I was [National Intelligence Officer]," Latell remembers. She wasn't polished or smooth. He knew that she had a big reputation within the DIA, but to him, she always seemed a bit odd.

> I would try to engage her, and she would always give me these strange reactions.... When I would try to pin her down at some of these meetings that I convened, on—"What do you think Fidel's motives are about this?"—she would fumble, in retrospect, the deer with the headlights in his eyes. She balked. Even physically she would show some kind of reaction that caused me to think, "Oh, she's nervous because she's just such a terrible analyst. She doesn't know what to say."

One year, he says, Montes was accepted into the CIA's Distinguished Analyst Program, a research sabbatical available to intelligence officers from across the government. Where did she ask to go? Cuba, of course.

"She went to Cuba funded by this program. Can you imagine?" Latell said. If you were a Cuban spy, trying to conceal your intentions, would you request a paid sabbatical in Havana? Latell was speaking almost twenty years after it had happened, but the brazenness of her behavior still astounded him.

She went to Cuba as a CIA distinguished intelligence analyst. Of course, they were delighted to have her, especially on our nickel, and I'm sure that they gave her all kinds of clandestine tradecraft training while she was there. I suspect—I can't prove it, but I'm pretty sure—she met with Fidel. Fidel loved to meet with his principal agents, to encourage them, to congratulate them, to revel in the success they were having together against the CIA.

When Montes came back to the Pentagon, she wrote a paper in which she didn't even bother to hide her biases.

There should have been all kinds of red flags raised and guns that went off when her paper was read by her supervisors, because she said things about the Cuban military that make absolutely no sense, except from [the Cubans'] point of view.

But did anyone raise those red flags? Latell says he never once suspected she was a spy. "There were CIA officers of my rank, or close to my rank, who thought she was the best Cuban analyst there was," he said. So he rationalized away his uneasiness. "I never trusted her, but for the wrong reasons, and that's one of my great regrets. I was convinced that she was a terrible analyst on Cuba. Well, she was. Because she wasn't working for us. She was working for Fidel. But I never connected the dots."

Nor did anyone else. Montes had a younger brother named Tito, who was an FBI agent. He had no idea. Her sister was also an FBI agent, who in fact played a key role in exposing a ring of Cuban spies in Miami. She had no idea. Montes's boyfriend worked for the Pentagon as well. His specialty, believe it or not, was Latin American intelligence. His job was to go up against spies *like his girlfriend.* He had no idea. When Montes was finally arrested, the chief of her section called her coworkers together and told them the news. People started crying in disbelief. The DIA had psychologists lined up to provide on-site counseling services. Her supervisor was devastated. None of them had any idea. In her cubicle, she had a quotation from Shakespeare's *Henry V* taped to her wall at eye level—for all the world to see.

The king hath note
of all that they intend,
By interception
Which they dream not of.

Or, to put it a bit more plainly: The Queen of Cuba takes note of all that the U.S. intends, by means that all around her do not dream of.

The issue with spies is not that there is something brilliant about *them.* It is that there is something wrong with *us.*

4.

Over the course of his career, the psychologist Tim Levine has conducted hundreds of versions of the same simple experiment. He invites students to his laboratory and gives them a trivia test. What is the highest mountain in Asia?

That kind of thing. If they answer the questions correctly, they win a cash prize.

To help them out, they are given a partner. Someone they've never met before, who is, unknown to them, working for Levine. There's an instructor in the room named Rachel. Midway through the test, Rachel suddenly gets called away. She leaves and goes upstairs. Then the carefully scripted performance begins. The partner says, "I don't know about you, but I could use the money. I think the answers were left right there." He points to an envelope lying in plain sight on the desk. "It's up to them whether they cheat or not," Levine explains. In about 30 percent of cases, they do. "Then," Levine goes on, "we interview them, asking, 'Did you cheat?'"

The number of scholars around the world who study human deception is vast. There are more theories about why we lie, and how to detect those lies, than there are about the Kennedy assassination. In that crowded field, Levine stands out. He has carefully constructed a unified theory about deception.* And at the core of that theory are the insights he gained from that first trivia-quiz study.

I watched videotapes of a dozen or so of those post-experiment interviews with Levine in his office at the University of Alabama at Birmingham. Here's a typical one, featuring a slightly spaced-out young man. Let's call him Philip.

---

* Levine's theories are laid out in his book, *Duped: Truth-Default Theory and the Social Science of Lying and Deception* (Tuscaloosa, AL: University of Alabama Press, 2019). If you want to understand how deception works, there is no better place to start.

Interviewer: All right, so...have you played Trivial Pursuit games...before?

Philip: Not very much, but I think I have.

Interviewer: In the current game did you find the questions difficult?

Philip: Yes, some were. I was like, "Well, what is that?"

Interviewer: If you would scale them one to ten, if one was easy and ten was difficult, where do you think you would put them?

Philip: I would put them [at] an eight.

Interviewer: An eight. Yeah, they're pretty tricky.

Philip is then told that he and his partner did very well on the test. The interviewer asks him why.

Philip: Teamwork.

Interviewer: Teamwork?

Philip: Yeah.

Interviewer: OK, all right. Now, I called Rachel out of the room briefly. When she was gone, did you cheat?

Philip: I guess. No.

Philip slightly mumbles his answer. Then looks away.

Interviewer: Are you telling the truth?

Philip: Yes.

Interviewer: Okay. When I interview your partner and I ask her, what is she going to say?

At this point in the tape, there's an uncomfortable silence, as if the student is trying to get his story straight.

"He's obviously thinking very hard," Levine said.

Philip: No.
Interviewer: No?
Philip: Yeah.
Interviewer: OK, all right. Well, that's all I need from you.

Is Philip telling the truth? Levine has shown the Philip videotape to hundreds of people and nearly every viewer correctly pegs Philip as a cheater. As the "partner" confirmed to Levine, Philip looked inside the answer-filled envelope the minute Rachel left the room. In his exit interview, he lied. And it's obvious. "He has no conviction," Levine said.

I felt the same thing. In fact, when Philip is asked, "Did you cheat?" and answers, "I guess. No," I couldn't contain myself, and I cried out, "Oh, he's terrible." Philip was looking away. He was nervous. He couldn't keep a straight face. When the interviewer followed up with, "Are you telling the truth?" Philip actually paused, as if he had to think about it first.

He was easy. But the more tapes we looked at, the harder it got. Here is a second case. Let's call him Lucas. He was handsome, articulate, confident.

Interviewer: I have to ask, when Rachel left the room, did any cheating occur?
Lucas: No.
Interviewer: No? You telling me the truth?
Lucas: Yes, I am.
Interviewer: When I interview your partner and I ask

her the same question, what do you think she's
going to say?

Lucas: Same thing.

"Everybody believes him," Levine said. *I* believed him.
Lucas was lying.

Levine and I spent the better part of a morning watching
his trivia-quiz videotapes. By the end, I was ready to throw
up my hands. I had no idea what to make of anyone.

The point of Levine's research was to try to answer one
of the biggest puzzles in human psychology: why are we so
bad at detecting lies? You'd think we'd be good at it. Logic
says that it would be very useful for human beings to know
when they are being deceived. Evolution, over many millions of years, *should* have favored people with the ability to
pick up the subtle signs of deception. But it hasn't.

In one iteration of his experiment, Levine divided
his tapes in half: twenty-two liars and twenty-two truth-
tellers. On average, the people he had watch all forty-four
videos correctly identified the liars 56 percent of the time.
Other psychologists have tried similar versions of the
same experiment. The average for all of them? 54 percent.
Just about everyone is terrible: police officers, judges,
therapists—even CIA officers running big spy networks
overseas. *Everyone.* Why?[*]

Tim Levine's answer is called the "Truth-Default Theory," or TDT.

---

[*] In my book *Blink,* I wrote of Paul Ekman's claim that a small number
of people are capable of successfully detecting liars. For more on the
Ekman-Levine debate, see the extended commentary in the Notes.

Levine's argument started with an insight that came from one of his graduate students, Hee Sun Park. It was right at the beginning of Levine's research, when he was as baffled as the rest of his profession about why we are all so bad at something that, by rights, we should be good at.

"Her big insight, the first one, was that the 54-percent deception-accuracy figure was averaging *across* truths and lies," Levine said. "You come to a very different understanding if you break out...how much people are right on truths, and how much people are right on lies."

What he meant was this. If I tell you that your accuracy rate on Levine's videos is right around 50 percent, the natural assumption is to think that you are just randomly guessing—that you have no idea what you are doing. But Park's observation was that that's not true. We're much *better* than chance at correctly identifying the students who are telling the truth. But we're much *worse* than chance at correctly identifying the students who are lying. We go through all those videos, and we guess—"true, true, true"—which means we get most of the truthful interviews right, and most of the liars wrong. We have a *default to truth:* our operating assumption is that the people we are dealing with are honest.

Levine says his own experiment is an almost perfect illustration of this phenomenon. He invites people to play a trivia game for money. Suddenly the instructor is called out of the room. *And she just happens to leave the answers to the test in plain view on her desk?* Levine says that, logically, the subjects should roll their eyes at this point. These are college students. They're not stupid. They've signed up for a psychological experiment. They're given a "partner," whom they've never met, who is egging them on to cheat. You would think that they might be even a little suspicious that things are not as they seem. But no!

"Sometimes, they catch that the instructor leaving the room might be a setup," Levine says. "The thing they almost never catch is that their partners are fake....So they think that there might be hidden agendas. They think it might be a setup because experiments are setups, right? But this nice person they are talking and chatting to? Oh no." They never question it.

To snap out of truth-default mode requires what Levine calls a "trigger." A trigger is not the same as a suspicion, or the first sliver of doubt. We fall out of truth-default mode only when the case against our initial assumption becomes definitive. We do not behave, in other words, like sober-minded scientists, slowly gathering evidence of the truth or falsity of something before reaching a conclusion. We do the opposite. We start by believing. And we *stop* believing only when our doubts and misgivings rise to the point where we can no longer explain them away.

This proposition sounds at first like the kind of hair-splitting that social scientists love to engage in. It is not. It's a profound point that explains a lot of otherwise puzzling behavior.

Consider, for example, one of the most famous findings in all of psychology: Stanley Milgram's obedience experiment. In 1961, Milgram recruited volunteers from New Haven to take part in what he said was a memory experiment. Each was met by a somber, imposing young man named John Williams, who explained that they were going to play the role of "teacher" in the experiment.

Williams introduced them to another volunteer, a pleasant, middle-aged man named Mr. Wallace. Mr. Wallace, they were told, was to be the "learner." He would sit in an adjoining room, wired to a complicated apparatus capable of delivering electrical shocks up to 450 volts. (If you're curious about what 450 volts feels like, it's just shy of the amount of electrical shock that leaves tissue damage.)

The teacher-volunteer was instructed to give the learner a series of memory tasks, and each time the learner failed, the volunteer was to punish him with an ever-greater electrical shock, in order to see whether the threat of punishment affected someone's ability to perform memory tasks. As the shocks escalated, Wallace would cry out in pain, and ultimately he started hammering on the walls. But if the "teacher" wavered, the imposing instructor would urge them on:

"Please continue."

"The experiment requires that you continue."

"It is absolutely essential that you continue."

"You have no other choice, you must go on."

The reason the experiment is so famous is that virtually all of the volunteers complied. Sixty-five percent ended up administering the maximum dose to the hapless learner. In the wake of the Second World War—and the revelations about what German guards had been ordered to do in Nazi concentration camps—Milgram's findings caused a sensation.

But to Levine, there's a second lesson to the experiment. The volunteer shows up and meets the imposing young John Williams. He was actually a local high-school biology teacher, chosen, in Milgram's words, because he was "technical-looking and dry, the type you would later see on television in connection with the space program." Everything Williams said during the experiment had been memorized from a script written by Milgram himself.

"Mr. Wallace" was in fact a man named Jim McDonough. He worked for the railroad. Milgram liked him for the part of victim because he was "mild and submissive." His cries of agony were taped and played over a loudspeaker. The experiment was a little amateur theatrical production. And the word *amateur* here is crucial. The Milgram experiment was not produced for a Broadway stage. Mr. Wallace, by Milgram's own description, was a terrible actor. And everything about the experiment was, to put it mildly, more than a little far-fetched. The electric-shock machine didn't actually give shocks. More than one participant saw the loudspeaker in the corner and wondered why Wallace's cries were coming from there, not from behind the door to the room where Wallace was strapped in. And if the purpose of the experiment was to measure learning, why on earth did Williams spend the entire time with the teacher and not behind the door with the learner? Didn't that make it obvious that what he really wanted to do was observe the person inflicting the pain, not the person receiving the pain? As hoaxes go, the Milgram experiment was pretty transparent. And just as with Levine's trivia test, people fell for it. They defaulted to truth.

"I actually checked the death notices in the *New Haven Register* for at least two weeks after the experiment to see if I had been involved and a contributing factor in the death of the so-called learner—I was very relieved that his name did not appear," one subject wrote to Milgram in a follow-up questionnaire. Another wrote, "Believe me, when no response came from Mr. Wallace with the stronger voltage I really believed the man was probably dead." These are adults—not callow undergraduates—who were apparently convinced that a prestigious institution of higher learning would run a possibly lethal torture operation in one of its basements. "The experiment left such an effect on me," another wrote, "that I spent the night in a cold sweat and nightmares because of the fear that I might have killed that man in the chair."

But here's the crucial detail. Milgram's subjects weren't hopelessly gullible. They had doubts—lots of doubts! In her fascinating history of the obedience experiments, *Behind the Shock Machine*, Gina Perry interviews a retired toolmaker named Joe Dimow, who was one of Milgram's original subjects. "I thought, 'This is bizarre,'" Dimow told Perry. Dimow became convinced that Wallace was faking it.

> I said I didn't know exactly what was going on, but I had my suspicions about it. I thought, "If I'm right in my suspicions, then he [the learner] is in collusion with them; he must be. And I'm not delivering shocks at all. He's just hollering out every once in a while."

But then Mr. Wallace came out of the locked room at the end of the experiment and put on a little act. He looked, Dimow remembers, "haggard" and emotional. "He came in with a handkerchief in his hand, wiping his face. He came up to me and he offered his hand to shake hands with me and he said, 'I want to thank you for stopping it'....When he came in, I thought, 'Wow. Maybe it really was true.'" Dimow was pretty sure that he was being lied to. But all it took was for one of the liars to extend the pretense a little longer—look a little upset and mop his brow with a handkerchief—and Dimow folded his cards.

Just look at the full statistics from the Milgram experiment:

I fully believed the learner was getting painful shocks.	56.1 percent
Although I had some doubts, I believed the learner was probably getting the shocks.	24 percent
I just wasn't sure whether the learner was getting the shocks or not.	6.1 percent
Although I had some doubts, I thought the learner was probably not getting the shocks.	11.4 percent
I was certain the learner was not getting the shocks.	2.4 percent

Over 40 percent of the volunteers picked up on something odd—something that suggested the experiment was not what it seemed. But those doubts just weren't enough to trigger them out of truth-default. That is Levine's point. You believe someone not because you have no doubts about them. Belief is not the absence of doubt. You believe someone because you don't have enough doubts about them.

I'm going to come back to the distinction between *some* doubts and *enough* doubts, because I think it's crucial. Just think about how many times you have criticized someone else, in hindsight, for their failure to spot a liar. *You should have known. There were all kinds of red flags. You had doubts.* Levine would say that's the wrong way to think about the problem. The right question is: were there enough red flags to push you over the threshold of belief? If there weren't, then by defaulting to truth you were only being human.

5.

Ana Belen Montes grew up in the affluent suburbs of Baltimore. Her father was a psychiatrist. She attended the University of Virginia, then received a master's degree in foreign affairs from Johns Hopkins University. She was a passionate supporter of the Marxist Sandinista government in Nicaragua, which the U.S. government was then working to overthrow, and her activism attracted the attention of a recruiter for Cuban intelligence. In 1985 she made a secret visit to Havana. "Her handlers, with her unwitting assistance, assessed her vulnerabilities and exploited her psychological needs, ideology, and personal pathology to recruit her and keep her motivated to work for Havana," the CIA concluded in a postmortem to her career. Her new compatriots encouraged her to apply for work in the U.S. intelligence community. That same year, she joined the DIA—and from there her ascent was swift.

Montes arrived at her office first thing in the morning, ate lunch at her desk, and kept to herself. She lived alone in a two-bedroom condo in the Cleveland Park neighborhood of Washington. She never married. In the course of his investigation, Scott Carmichael—the DIA counterintelligence officer—collected every adjective used by Montes's coworkers to describe her. It is an impressive list: *shy, quiet, aloof, cool, independent, self-reliant, stand-offish, intelligent, serious, dedicated, focused, hardworking, sharp, quick, manipulative, venomous, unsociable, ambitious, charming, confident, businesslike, no-nonsense, assertive, deliberate, calm, mature, unflappable, capable,* and *competent.*

Ana Montes assumed that the reason for her meeting with Carmichael was that he was performing a routine security check. All intelligence officers are periodically vetted so that they can continue to hold a security clearance. She was brusque.

"When she first came in she tried to blow me off by telling me—and it was true—she had just been named as the Acting Division Chief," Carmichael remembered. "She had a ton of responsibilities, meetings and things to do, and she just didn't have a lot of time." Carmichael is a disarmingly boyish man, with fair hair and a substantial stomach. He looks, by his own estimation, like the late comedian and actor Chris Farley. She must have thought she could bully him. "I dealt with it the way you normally do," he remembers:

> The first time you just acknowledge it. You say, "Oh, I understand. Yeah, I heard that, congratulations, great. I understand you've got a limited amount of time." And then you just kind of ignore it, because if it takes you twelve days, it takes twelve days. You don't let them go. But then she hit me with it again....She really made a point of it. I hadn't even settled in yet and she said, "Oh, but seriously, I've gotta leave by

two," or something like that, "because I've got all these things to do."

I'm like, "What the fuck?" That's what I'm thinking....I didn't lose my temper, but I lost my patience. "Look, Ana. I have reason to suspect that you might be involved in a counterintelligence influence operation. We need to sit down and talk about this." Bam! Right between the eyes.

Montes had been, by that point, a Cuban spy for nearly her entire government career. She had met with her handlers at least 300 times, handing over so many secrets that she ranks as one of the most damaging spies in U.S. history. She had secretly visited Cuba on several occasions. After her arrest, it was discovered that Fidel Castro had personally given her a medal. Through all of that, there hadn't been even a whiff of suspicion. And suddenly, at the start of what she thought was a routine background check, a funny-looking Chris Farley character was pointing the finger at her. She sat there in shock.

"She was just looking at me like a deer looking at the headlights, waiting for me to say another word, just waiting."

When Carmichael looked back on that meeting years later, he realized that was the first clue he had missed: her reaction made no sense.

I just didn't pick up on the fact that she never said, "What are you talking about?" Nothing like that. She didn't say a freaking word. She just sat there and was listening. If I'd been astute, I'd have picked up on that. No denial, no confusion, no anger. Anybody who has been told they're suspected of murder or something....If they're completely innocent it's like, "What do you mean?" They're going to say, "Wait a minute, you just accused me of some...I want to know what the fuck this is all about." Eventually, they'll get in your face, they'll really get in your face. Ana didn't do a freaking thing except sit there.

Carmichael had doubts, right from the beginning. But doubts trigger disbelief only when you can't explain them away. And he could easily explain them away. She was the Queen of Cuba, for goodness' sake. How could the Queen of Cuba be a spy? He had said that line to her—"I have reason to suspect that you might be involved in a counter-intelligence influence operation"—only because he wanted her to take the meeting seriously. "I was anxious to get into it and get to the next step. Like I said, I'm just patting myself on the back: 'That worked, that shut her up. I'm not going to hear any more of that crap anymore. Now, let's get to this, get this done.' That's why I missed it."

They talked about the Admiral Carroll briefing. She had a good answer. They talked about why she abruptly left the Pentagon that day. She had an answer. She was being flirty, a little playful. He began to relax. He looked down at her legs again.

Ana started doing this thing. She's got her legs crossed and she's bouncing her toe, like that. I don't know if it was conscious...but what I do know is, that catches your eye....We got more comfortable with one another, and she became just a little bit more flirty. Flirty? I don't know, but cute sometimes in some of her responses to questions.

They talked about the phone call. She said she never got a phone call, or at least she didn't remember getting one. It should have been another red flag: the people who were with her that day in the situation room distinctly remembered her getting a phone call. But then again, it had been a long and stressful day. They had all been in the middle of an international crisis. Maybe they had confused her with someone else.

There was one other thing—another moment when Carmichael saw something in her reaction that made him wonder. Near the end of the interview, he asked Montes a series of questions about what happened after she left the Pentagon that day. It was a standard investigative procedure. He just wanted as complete a picture as possible of her movements that evening.

He asked her what she did after work. She said she drove home. He asked her where she parked. She said in the lot across the street. He asked her if she saw anyone else as she was parking. Did she say hello to anyone? She said no.

I said, "OK, well, so what'd you do? You parked your car and you walked across the street"—and while I'm doing this is when the change of demeanor occurred. Keep in mind, I'd been talking to her for almost two hours and by that time, Ana and I were almost like buddies, not that close, but we have a great rapport going. She's actually joking about stuff and making funny remarks every once in a while about stuff—it's that casual and that warm, if you will.

Then all of a sudden, this huge change came over her. You could see it, one minute she's just almost flirting and stuff, having a good time....All of a sudden she changed. It's like a little kid who has been caught with his hand in the cookie jar, and he's got it behind his back, and Mom says, "What do you have?" She was looking at me and denying, but...with that look like, "What do you know? How do you know? Are you going to catch me? I don't want to get caught."

After her arrest, investigators discovered what had really happened that night. The Cubans had an arrangement with her: if she ever spotted one of her old handlers on the street, it meant that her spymasters urgently needed to talk to her in person. She should keep walking and meet them the following morning at a prearranged site. That night, when she got home from the Pentagon, she saw one of her old handlers standing by her apartment building. So when Carmichael asked her, pointedly, "Who did you see? Did you see anyone as you came home?" she must have thought that he knew about the arrangement—that he was on to her.

She was scared to fucking death. She thought I knew it and I didn't. I had no idea, I didn't know what I had. I knew I had something, I knew there was something. After the interview, I would look back on it...and what did I do? I did the same thing every human being does....I rationalized it away.

I thought, *Well, maybe she's been seeing a married guy…and she didn't want to tell me. Or maybe she's a lesbian or something and she was hooking up with a girlfriend that she doesn't want us to know [about], and she's worried about that.* I started thinking about all these other possibilities and I sort of accepted it, just enough so that I wouldn't keep going crazy. I accepted it.

Ana Montes wasn't a master spy. She didn't need to be. In a world where our lie detector is set to the "off" position, a spy is always going to have an easy time of it. And was Scott Carmichael somehow negligent? Not at all. He did what Truth-Default Theory would predict any of us would do: he operated from the assumption that Ana Montes was telling the truth, and—almost without realizing it—worked to square everything she said with that assumption. We need a trigger to snap out of the default to truth, but the threshold for triggers is high. Carmichael was nowhere near that point.

The simple truth, Levine argues, is that lie detection does not—*cannot*—work the way we expect it to work. In the movies, the brilliant detective confronts the subject and catches him, right then and there, in a lie. But in real life, accumulating the amount of evidence necessary to overwhelm our doubts takes time. You ask your husband if he is having an affair, and he says no, and you believe him. Your default is that he is telling the truth. And whatever little inconsistencies you spot in his story, you explain away. But three months later you happen to notice an unusual hotel charge on his credit-card bill, and the combination of that and the weeks of unexplained absences and mysterious phone calls pushes you over the top. That's how lies are detected.

This is the explanation for the first of the puzzles, why the Cubans were able to pull the wool over the CIA's eyes for so long. That story is not an indictment of the agency's competence. It just reflects the fact that CIA officers are—like the rest of us—human, equipped with the same set of biases to truth as everyone else.

Carmichael went back to Reg Brown and tried to explain.

> I said, "Reg, I realize what it looks like to you, I understand your reasoning that you think that this is a deliberate influence operation. Looks like it. But if it was, I can't point a finger [to] it to say she was part of a deliberate effort. It just doesn't make any sense....At the end of the day, I just had to close out the case."

6.

Four years after Scott Carmichael's interview with Ana Montes, one of his colleagues at the DIA met an analyst for the National Security Agency at an interagency meeting. The NSA is the third arm of the U.S. intelligence network, along with the CIA and the DIA. They are the code-breakers, and the analyst said that her agency had had some success with the codes that the Cubans were using to communicate with their agents.

The codes were long rows of numbers, broadcast at

regular intervals over shortwave radio, and the NSA had managed to decode a few snippets. They had given the list of tidbits to the FBI two and a half years before, but had heard nothing back. Out of frustration, the NSA analyst decided to share a few details with her DIA counterpart. The Cubans had a highly placed spy in Washington whom they called "Agent S," she said. Agent S had an interest in something called a "safe" system. And Agent S had apparently visited the American base at Guantánamo Bay in the two-week time frame from July 4 to July 18, 1996.

The man from the DIA was alarmed. "SAFE"* was the name of the DIA's internal computer-messaging archive. That strongly suggested that Agent S was at the DIA, or at least closely affiliated with the DIA. He came back and told his supervisors. They told Carmichael. He was angry. The FBI had been working on a spy case potentially involving a DIA employee for two and a half years, and they hadn't told him? He was the DIA's counterintelligence investigator!

He knew exactly what he had to do—a search of the DIA computer system. Any Department of Defense employee who travels to Guantánamo Bay needs to get approval. They need to send two messages through the Pentagon system, asking first for permission to travel and then for permission to talk to whomever they wish to interview at the base.

"Okay, so two messages," Carmichael said.

---

* SAFE stands for *Security Analyst File Environment.* I love it when people start with the acronym and work backward to create the full name.

He guessed that the earliest anyone traveling to Guantánamo Bay in July would apply for their clearances was April. So he had his search parameters: travel-authority and security-clearance requests from DIA employees regarding Guantánamo Bay made between April 1 and July 18, 1996. He told his coworker, "Gator" Johnson, to run the same search simultaneously. Two heads would be better than one.

> What [the computer system] did back in those days, it would set up a hit file. It would electronically stack up all your messages and tell you, "You've got X number of hits." I can hear Gator over there…I can hear him tapping away and I knew he hadn't even finished his query yet and I already had my hit file to go through, so I thought, I'm going through them real quickly, just to see if any [name] pops out at me, and that's when I'm pretty sure it was the twentieth one hit me. It was Ana B. Montes. The game was fucking over, and I mean it was over in a heartbeat.…I was really stunned—speechless stunned. I could have fallen out of my chair. I literally backed up—I was on wheels—I was literally distancing myself from this bad news.…I literally backed up all the way to the end of my cubicle and Gator is still going *dink-pink-tink-tink.*
>
> I said, "Oh shit."

CHAPTER FOUR

The Holy Fool

1.

In November 2003, Nat Simons, a portfolio manager for the Long Island–based hedge fund Renaissance Technologies, wrote a worried email to several of his colleagues. Through a complicated set of financial arrangements, Renaissance found itself with a stake in a fund run by an investor in New York named Bernard Madoff, and Madoff made Simons uneasy.

If you worked in the financial world in New York in the 1990s and early 2000s, chances are you'd heard of Bernard Madoff. He worked out of an elegant office tower in Midtown Manhattan called the Lipstick Building. He served on the boards of a number of important financial-industry associations. He moved between the monied circles of the Hamptons and Palm Beach. He had an imperious manner and a flowing mane of white hair. He was reclusive, secretive. And that last fact was what made Simons uneasy. He'd heard rumors. Someone he trusted, he wrote in the group email, "told us in confidence that he believes that Madoff will have a serious problem within a year."

He went on: "Throw in that his brother-in-law is his auditor and his son is also high up in the organization, and you have the risk of some nasty allegations, the freezing of accounts, etc."

The next day Henry Laufer, one of the firm's senior executives, wrote back. He agreed. Renaissance, he added, had "independent evidence" that something was amiss with Madoff. Then Renaissance's risk manager, Paul Broder—the person responsible for making sure the fund didn't put its money anywhere dangerous—weighed in with a long, detailed analysis of the trading strategy that Madoff claimed to be using. "None of it seems to add up," he concluded. The three of them decided to conduct their own in-house investigation. Their suspicions deepened. "I came to the conclusion that we didn't understand what he was doing," Broder would say later. "We had no idea how he was making his money. The volume numbers that he suggested he was doing [were] not supported by any evidence we could find." Renaissance had doubts.

So did Renaissance sell off its stake in Madoff? Not quite. They cut their stake in half. They hedged their bets. Five years later, after Madoff had been exposed as a fraud—the mastermind of the biggest Ponzi scheme in history—federal investigators sat down with Nat Simons and asked him to explain why. "I never, as the manager, entertained the thought that it was truly fraudulent,"

Simons said. He was willing to admit that he didn't understand what Madoff was up to, and that Madoff smelled a little funny. But he wasn't willing to believe that he was an out-and-out liar. Simons had doubts, but not enough doubts. He defaulted to truth.

The emails written between Simons and Laufer were discovered during a routine audit by the Securities and Exchange Commission (SEC), the agency responsible for monitoring the hedge-fund industry. It wasn't the first time the SEC had run across doubts about Madoff's operations. Madoff claimed to follow an investment strategy linked to the stock market, which meant that like any other market-based strategy, his returns ought to go up and down as the market went up and down. But Madoff's returns were rock steady—which defied all logic. An SEC investigator named Peter Lamore once went to see Madoff to get an explanation. Madoff's answer was that, essentially, he could see around corners; he had an infallible "gut feel" for when to get out of the market just before a downswing, and back into the market just before an upswing. "I asked him repeatedly," Lamore recalled later:

> I thought his gut feel was, you know, strange, suspicious. You know, I kept trying to press him. I thought there was something else…I thought, you know, he was getting some sort of insight into the overall broad market that other people weren't getting. So I repeatedly sort of pressed him on that. I asked Bernie repeatedly over and over again, and at some point, I mean, I'm not sure what else to do.

Lamore took his doubts to his boss, Robert Sollazzo, who had doubts too. But not *enough* doubts. As the SEC postmortem on the Madoff case concluded, "Sollazzo did not find that Madoff's claim to be trading on 'gut feel' was 'necessarily…ridiculous.'" The SEC defaulted to truth, and the fraud continued. Across Wall Street, in fact, countless people who had had dealings with Madoff thought that something didn't quite add up about him. Several investment banks steered clear of him. Even the real-estate broker who rented him his office space thought he was a bit off. But no one did anything about it, or jumped to the conclusion that he was history's greatest con man. In the Madoff case, *everyone* defaulted to truth—everyone, that is, except one person.

In early February 2009—just over a month after Madoff turned himself in to authorities—a man named Harry Markopolos testified at a nationally televised hearing before Congress. He was an independent fraud investigator. He wore an ill-fitting green suit. He spoke nervously and tentatively, with an upstate New York accent. No one had ever heard of him.

"My team and I tried our best to get the SEC to investigate and shut down the Madoff Ponzi scheme with repeated and credible warnings to the SEC that started in May 2000," Markopolos testified to a rapt audience. Markopolos said that he and a few colleagues put together charts and graphs, ran computer models, and poked around in Europe, where Madoff was raising the bulk of his money: "We knew then that we had provided enough red flags and mathematical proofs to the SEC for them where they should have been able to shut him down right then and there at under $7 billion." When the SEC did nothing, Markopolos came back in October 2001. Then again in 2005, 2007, and 2008. Each time he got nowhere. Reading slowly from his notes, Markopolos described years of frustration.

> I gift-wrapped and delivered the largest Ponzi scheme in history to them, and somehow they couldn't be bothered to conduct a thorough and proper investigation because they were too busy on matters of higher priority. If a $50 billion Ponzi scheme doesn't make the SEC's priority list, then I want to know who sets their priorities.

Harry Markopolos, alone among the people who had doubts about Bernie Madoff, did not default to truth. He saw a stranger for who that stranger really was. Midway through the hearing, one of the congressmen asked Markopolos if he would come to Washington and run the SEC. In the aftermath of one of the worst financial scandals in history, the feeling was that Harry Markopolos was someone we could all learn from. Defaulting to truth is a problem. It lets spies and con artists roam free.

Or is it? Here we come to the second, crucial component of Tim Levine's ideas about deception and truth-default.

2.

Harry Markopolos is wiry and energetic. He's well into middle age, but looks much younger. He's compelling and likable, a talker—although he tells awkward jokes that sometimes stop conversation. He describes himself as obsessive: the sort to wipe down his keyboard with disinfectant after he opens his computer. He is what's known on Wall Street as a *quant*, a numbers guy. "For me, math is truth," he says. When he analyzes an investment opportunity or a company, he prefers not to meet any of the principals personally; he doesn't want to make the Neville Chamberlain error.

> I want to hear and see what they're saying remotely through their public appearances, through their financial statements, and then I want to analyze that information mathematically using these simple techniques....I want to find the truth. I don't want to have a favorable opinion of somebody who glad-hands me, because that could only negatively affect my case.

Markopolos grew up in Erie, Pennsylvania, the child of Greek immigrants. His family ran a chain of Arthur Treacher's Fish & Chips outlets. "My uncles, they would chase after the people that did the dine and dash. They would go out there and catch them, make them pay," he remembers.

> I saw my dad get in fights with customers, chasing customers down. I saw people stealing silverware. Not even silverware—tableware....I remember one guy, he's huge, and he is eating off of other people's plates that have left the counter, and my uncle says, "You can't do that." And the guy says, "Yes I can, they didn't eat the food." So my uncle goes to the other

side of the counter, picks this guy up by his beard and lifts him up and he keeps lifting him up....And I'm thinking, my uncle's dead. This guy was like six foot six. My uncle's going to be killed. Fortunately, other customers in the restaurant stood up. Otherwise I think my uncle would've been a dead man.

The standard immigrant-entrepreneur story is about the redemptive power of grit and ingenuity. To hear Markopolos tell it, his early experiences in the family business taught him instead how dark and dangerous the world was:

I saw a lot of theft in the Arthur Treacher's. And so I became fraud-aware at a formative age, in my teens and early twenties. And I saw what people are capable of doing, because when you run a business, five to six percent of your revenues are going to be lost to theft. That's the Association of Certified Fraud Examiners' statistics. I didn't know the statistics when I was a young 'un. That organization didn't exist. But I saw it. I saw our chicken and shrimp sprout legs and walk out the back door on a regular basis. They would throw cases of that stuff in the back of their cars. That was the *employees*.

When Harry Markopolos was in business school, one of his professors gave him an A. But Markopolos double-checked the formula the professor used to calculate grades and realized that there had been a mistake. He had actually earned an A-minus. He went to the professor and complained. In his first job out of business school, he worked for a brokerage selling over-the-counter stocks, and one of the rules of that marketplace is that the broker must report any trade within ninety seconds. Markopolos discovered that his new employer was waiting longer than ninety seconds. He reported his own bosses to the regulators. *Nobody likes a tattletale,* we learn as children, understanding that sometimes pursuing what seems fair and moral comes with an unacceptable social cost. If Markopolos was ever told that as a child, he certainly didn't listen.

Markopolos first heard about Madoff in the late 1980s. The hedge fund he worked for had noticed Madoff's spectacular returns, and they wanted Markopolos to copy Madoff's strategy. Markopolos tried. But he couldn't figure out what Madoff's strategy was. Madoff claimed to be making his money based on heavy trading of a financial instrument known as a derivative. But there was simply no trace of Madoff in those markets.

"I was trading huge amounts of derivatives every year, and so I had relationships with the largest investment banks that traded derivatives," Markopolos remembers.

So I called the people that I knew on the trading desks: "Are you trading with Madoff?" They all said no. Well, if you are trading derivatives, you pretty much have to go to the largest five banks to trade the size that he was trading. If the largest five banks don't know your trades and are not seeing your business, then you have to be a Ponzi scheme. It's that easy. It was not a hard case. All I had to do was pick up the phone, really.

At that point, Markopolos was precisely where the people at Renaissance would be several years later. He had done the math, and he had doubts. Madoff's business didn't make sense.

The difference between Markopolos and Renaissance, however, is that Renaissance trusted the system. Madoff was part of one of the most heavily regulated sectors in the entire financial market. If he was really just making things up, wouldn't one of the many government watchdogs have caught him already? As Nat Simons, the Renaissance executive, said later, "You just assume that someone was paying attention."

Renaissance Technologies, it should be pointed out, was founded in the 1980s by a group of mathematicians and code-breakers. Over its history, it has probably made more money than any other hedge fund in history. Laufer, the Renaissance executive to whom Simons turned for advice, has a PhD in mathematics from Princeton University and has written books and articles with titles such as *Normal Two-Dimensional Singularities* and "On Minimally Elliptic Singularities." The people at Renaissance are brilliant. Yet in one crucial respect, they were exactly like the students in Levine's experiment who watched the instructor leave, spotted the envelope with the answers lying conspicuously on the desk, but couldn't quite make the leap to believe that it was all a setup.

But not Markopolos. He was armed with all the same facts but none of the faith in the system. To him, dishonesty and stupidity are everywhere. "People have too much faith in large organizations," he said. "They trust the accounting firms, which you should never trust because they're incompetent. On a best day they're incompetent, on a bad day they're crooked, and aiding and abetting the fraud, looking the other way."

He went on. "I think the insurance industry is totally corrupt. They've had no oversight forever, and they're dealing with trillions in assets and liabilities." He thought between 20 and 25 percent of public companies were cheating on their financial statements. "You want to talk of another fraud?" he said at one point, out of the blue. He had just published a memoir and was now in the habit of scrutinizing his royalty statements. He called them "Chinese batshit." The crooks he investigates, he said, have financial statements "more believable than my publisher's."

He said the one fact he keeps in mind whenever he goes to the doctor's office is that forty cents of every health-care dollar goes to either fraud or waste.

Whoever is treating me, I make sure I tell them that I'm a white-collar-criminal investigator, and I let them know that there's a lot of fraud in medicine. I tell them that statistic. I do that so they don't mess with me or my family.

There is no high threshold in Markopolos's mind before doubts turn into disbelief. He has no threshold at all.

3.

In Russian folklore there is an archetype called *yurodivy*, or the "Holy Fool." The Holy Fool is a social misfit—

eccentric, off-putting, sometimes even crazy—who none-theless has access to the truth. *Nonetheless* is actually the wrong word. The Holy Fool is a truth-teller *because* he is an outcast. Those who are not part of existing social hierarchies are free to blurt out inconvenient truths or question things the rest of us take for granted. In one Russian fable, a Holy Fool looks at a famous icon of the Virgin Mary and declares it the work of the devil. It's an outrageous, heretical claim. But then someone throws a stone at the image and the facade cracks, revealing the face of Satan.

Every culture has its version of the Holy Fool. In Hans Christian Andersen's famous children's tale "The Emperor's New Clothes," the king walks down the street in what he has been told is a magical outfit. No one says a word except a small boy, who cries out, "Look at the king! He's not wearing anything at all!" The little boy is a Holy Fool. The tailors who sold the king his clothes told him they would be invisible to anyone unfit for their job. The adults said nothing, for fear of being labeled incompetent. The little boy didn't care. The closest we have to Holy Fools in modern life are whistleblowers. They are willing to sacrifice loyalty to their institution—and, in many cases, the support of their peers—in the service of exposing fraud and deceit.

What sets the Holy Fool apart is a different sense of the possibility of deception. In real life, Tim Levine reminds us, lies are rare. And those lies that are told are told by a very small subset of people. That's why it doesn't matter so much that we are terrible at detecting lies in real life. Under the circumstances, in fact, defaulting to truth makes logical sense. If the person behind the counter at the coffee shop says your total with tax is $6.74, you can do the math yourself to double-check their calculations, holding up the line and wasting thirty seconds of your time. Or you can simply assume the salesperson is telling you the truth, because on balance most people do tell the truth.

That's what Scott Carmichael did. He was faced with two alternatives. Reg Brown said that Ana Montes was behaving suspiciously. Ana Montes, by contrast, had a perfectly innocent explanation for her actions. On one hand was the exceedingly rare possibility that one of the most respected figures at the DIA was a spy. On the other hand was the far more likely scenario that Brown was just being paranoid. Carmichael went with the odds: that's what we do when we default to truth. Nat Simons went with the odds as well. Madoff *could* have been the master-mind of the greatest financial fraud in history, but what were the chances of that?

The Holy Fool is someone who doesn't think this way. The statistics say that the liar and the con man are rare. But to the Holy Fool, they are everywhere.

We need Holy Fools in our society, from time to time. They perform a valuable role. That's why we romanticize them. Harry Markopolos was the hero of the Madoff saga. Whistleblowers have movies made about them. But the second, crucial part of Levine's argument is that we can't all be Holy Fools. That would be a disaster.

Levine argues that over the course of evolution, human beings never developed sophisticated and accurate skills to detect deception as it was happening because there is no advantage to spending your time scrutinizing the words and behaviors of those around you. The advantage to human beings lies in assuming that strangers are truthful. As he puts it, the trade-off between truth-default and the risk of deception is

> a great deal for us. What we get in exchange for being vulnerable to an occasional lie is efficient communication and social coordination. The benefits are huge and the costs are trivial in comparison. Sure, we get deceived once in a while. That is just the cost of doing business.

That sounds callous, because it's easy to see all the damage done by people like Ana Montes and Bernie Madoff. Because we trust implicitly, spies go undetected, criminals roam free, and lives are damaged. But Levine's point is that the price of giving up on that strategy is much higher. If everyone on Wall Street behaved like Harry Markopolos, there would be no fraud on Wall Street—but the air would be so thick with suspicion and paranoia that there would also *be* no Wall Street.*

---

* But wait. Don't we want counterintelligence officers to be Holy Fools? Isn't this just the profession where having someone who suspects everyone makes sense? Not at all. One of Scott Carmichael's notorious predecessors was James Angleton, who ran the counterintelligence operations of the CIA during the last decades of the Cold War. Angleton became convinced there was a Soviet mole high inside the agency. He launched an investigation that eventually covered 120 CIA officials. He couldn't find the spy. In frustration, Angleton ordered many in the Soviet division to pack their bags. Hundreds of people—Russian specialists with enormous knowledge and experience of America's chief adversary—were shipped elsewhere. Morale plummeted. Case officers stopped recruiting new agents.

4.

In the summer of 2002, Harry Markopolos traveled to Europe. He and a colleague were looking for investors for a new fund they were starting. He met with asset managers in Paris and Geneva and all the centers of capital across Western Europe, and what he learned stunned him. Everyone had invested with Madoff. If you stayed in New York and talked to people on Wall Street, it was easy to think that Madoff was a local phenomenon, one of many money managers who served the wealthy of the East Coast. But Madoff, Markopolos realized, was international. The size of his fraudulent empire was much, much larger than Markopolos had previously imagined.

It was then that Markopolos came to believe his life was in danger. Countless powerful and wealthy people out there had a deep-seated interest in keeping Madoff afloat. Was that why his repeated entreaties to regulators went nowhere? Markopolos's name was known to prominent people at the SEC. Until the Ponzi scheme was publicly exposed, he could not be safe.

He decided that the next logical step was to approach

Ultimately, one of Angleton's senior staffers looked at the crippling costs of more than a decade of paranoia and jumped to the final, paranoid conclusion: if you were the Soviet Union and you wanted to cripple the CIA, the most efficient way to do that would be to have your mole lead a lengthy, damaging, exhaustive hunt for a mole. *Which meant the mole must be Angleton.*

The final casualty of James Angleton's witch hunt? James Angleton. He was pushed out of the CIA in 1974, after thirty-one years. Had Scott Carmichael behaved like James Angleton and suspected everyone of being a spy, the DIA would have collapsed in a cloud of paranoia and mistrust like the CIA's Soviet division.

New York's attorney general, Eliot Spitzer, who had shown himself to be one of the few elected officials interested in investigating Wall Street. But he needed to be careful. Spitzer came from a wealthy New York City family. Was it possible that he, too, had invested with Madoff? Markopolos learned that Spitzer was going to be in Boston giving a speech at the John F. Kennedy Library. He printed out his documents on clean sheets of paper, removing all references to himself, and put them in a plain brown 9x12 envelope. Then, to be safe, he put that envelope inside a larger plain brown envelope. He wore a pair of gloves, so he left no fingerprints on the documents. He put on extra-heavy clothing, and over that the biggest coat he owned. He did not want to be recognized. He made his way to the JFK Library and sat unobtrusively to one side. Then, at the end of the speech, he went up to try to give the documents to Spitzer personally. But he couldn't get close enough—so instead he handed them to a woman in Spitzer's party, with instructions to pass them along to her boss.

"I'm sitting there, and I have the documents," Markopolos remembers.

> I'm going to hand them to him, but after the event, I give it to a woman to hand it to Eliot Spitzer because I can't get to him. He's just surrounded by people. Then he heads out the back door. I think he's going to go to the restroom and go to have dinner next door, all right? I'm not invited to the dinner. He's heading out the back door to get in a limo to the airport to catch the last shuttle flight to New York.... Eliot never got my package.

It is worth mentioning that at the time Markopolos was president of the Boston Security Analysts Society, a trade group with a membership of 4,000 professionals. He didn't have to show up incognito at Spitzer's speech, wearing a bulky overcoat and clutching a sheaf of documents wrapped inside two plain brown envelopes. He could have just called Spitzer's office directly and asked for a meeting.

I asked him about that:

> **Markopolos:** That's another regret of mine. I hold myself responsible for that. Spitzer was the guy. I should've just called him. Maybe I would've gotten through, maybe I wouldn't have, but I think I would have.
>
> **MG:** You had standing. You were—
>
> **Markopolos:** President of the Security Analysts.... If the past president or current president…calls the boss and says, "I have the biggest scheme ever. It's right in your backyard," I think I would've gotten in.
>
> **MG:** Why don't you think you did that?
>
> **Markopolos:** Woulda, coulda, shouldas. Regrets, you know. There's no perfect investigation and I made my share of mistakes, too. I should have.

Markopolos sees his mistake now, with the benefit of over a decade of hindsight. But in the midst of things, the same brilliant mind that was capable of unraveling Madoff's deceptions was incapable of getting people in positions of responsibility to take him seriously. That's the consequence of not defaulting to truth. If you don't begin in a state of trust, you can't have meaningful social encounters.

As Levine writes:

Being deceived once in a while is not going to prevent us from passing on our genes or seriously threaten the survival of the species. Efficient communication, on the other hand, has huge implications for our survival. The trade-off just isn't much of a trade-off.

Markopolos's communication at the library was, to put it mildly, not efficient. The woman he gave the envelope to, by the way? She wasn't one of Spitzer's aides. She worked for the JFK Library. She had no more special access to Spitzer than he did. And even if she had, she would've almost certainly seen it as her responsibility to protect a public figure like Spitzer from mysterious men in double-size overcoats clutching plain brown envelopes.

5.

After his failures with the SEC, Markopolos began carrying a Smith & Wesson handgun. He went to see the local police chief in the small Massachusetts town where he lived. Markopolos told him of his work against Madoff. His life was in danger, he said, but he begged him not to put that fact in the precinct log. The chief asked him if he wanted to wear body armor. Markopolos declined. He had spent seventeen years in the Army Reserves and knew something about lethal tactics. His assassins, he reasoned, would be professionals. They would give him two shots to the back of the head. Body armor wouldn't matter. Markopolos installed a high-tech alarm system in his house. He replaced the locks. He made sure to take a different route home every night. He checked his rearview mirror.

When Madoff turned himself in, Markopolos thought—for a moment—that he might finally be safe. But then he realized that he had only replaced one threat with another. Wouldn't the SEC now be after his files? After all, he had years of meticulously documented evidence of, at the least, their incompetence and, at the most, their criminal complicity. If they came for him, he concluded, his only hope would be to hold them off as long as possible, until he could get help. He loaded up a twelve-gauge shotgun and added six more rounds to the stock. He hung a bandolier of twenty extra rounds on his gun cabinet. Then he dug out his gas mask from his army days. What if they came in using tear gas? He sat at home, guns at the ready—while the rest of us calmly went about our business.

CHAPTER FIVE

Case Study: The Boy in the Shower

1.

Prosecution: When you were a graduate assistant in 2001, did something occur that was unusual?
McQueary: Yes.
P: Could you tell the jury about that occurrence?

March 21, 2017. Dauphin County Courthouse in Harrisburg, Pennsylvania. The witness is Michael Mc-Queary, former quarterback turned assistant coach of the Pennsylvania State University football team: strapping, self-confident, with close-cropped hair the color of paprika. His interrogator is the Deputy Attorney General for the state of Pennsylvania, Laura Ditka.

McQueary: One night I made my way to the football building—Lasch Football Building—and proceeded to one of the locker rooms in the building....I opened the locker room door. I heard showers running, heard slapping sounds, and entered another doorway that was already propped up open. My locker, in an aisle of lockers, was immediately to my right. Turned to my locker, and obviously I knew someone was in the locker room taking a shower. And the slapping sounds alerted me that something more than just a shower was going on.

At that point, Ditka stops him. What time of day was it? McQueary says, 8:30 at night on a Friday. That corner of the campus is quiet. The Lasch Building is all but deserted. The doors are locked.

P: OK. I interrupted you. I wanted to ask you another question. You've described something as slapping sounds. You aren't talking about like clapping, like applause?

McQueary: No, no.

P: You were talking about a different kind of sound?

McQueary: Yes.

McQueary said he looked over his right shoulder to a mirror on the wall, which allowed him to see, at an angle, into the shower. He saw a man, naked, standing behind someone he called a "minor individual."

P: Were you able to make—you say a minor individual.

Are we talking about a seventeen- or sixteen-year-old, or somebody who appeared younger?

McQueary: Oh, younger.

P: OK. What would be the estimation of the age of the boy you saw?

McQueary: Roughly ten to twelve years old.

P: OK. Were they clothed or unclothed?

McQueary: Unclothed, naked.

P: Did you see any movement?

McQueary: Slow, very subtle movement, but hardly any.

P: OK. But slow, subtle movement that you saw, what kind of movement was it? What was moving?

McQueary: It was Jerry behind the boy, right up against him.

P: Skin to skin?

McQueary: Yes, absolutely.

P: Stomach to back?

McQueary: Yes.

The "Jerry" McQueary was referring to was Jerry Sandusky, who had then just retired as defensive coordinator of the Penn State football team. Sandusky was a beloved figure at football-obsessed Penn State. McQueary had known him for years.

McQueary ran upstairs to his office and called his parents. "He's tall and he's a pretty strapping guy, and he's not a scaredy-cat. But he was shaken," McQueary's father told the court after his son finished his testimony. "He was clearly shaken. His voice wasn't right. Enough that his mom picked it up on the phone without ever seeing him. She said, 'There's something wrong, John.'"

After McQueary saw Sandusky in the shower in February 2001, he went to see his boss, Joe Paterno, the legendary head coach of the Penn State football team.

P: Did you explain to him that Jerry Sandusky was naked in the shower?

McQueary: Yes, absolutely.

P: Did you explain to him that there was skin-on-skin contact with the boy?

McQueary: I believe so, yes, ma'am.

P: And did you explain to him you heard these slapping sounds?

McQueary: Yes.

P: Okay. What was—I'm not asking you what he said. What was his reaction? What was his demeanor?

McQueary: Saddened. He kind of slumped back in his chair and put his hand up on his face, and his eyes just kind of went sad.

Paterno told his boss, the athletic director at Penn State, Tim Curley. Curley told another senior administrator at the university, Gary Schultz. Curley and Schultz then told the school's president, Graham Spanier. An investigation followed. In due course, Sandusky was arrested, and at his trial an extraordinary story emerged. Eight young men testified that Sandusky had abused them hundreds of times over the years, in hotel rooms and locker-room showers, and even in the basement of his home while his wife was upstairs. Sandusky was convicted of forty-five counts of child molestation. Penn State paid over $100 million in settlements to his victims.* He became—as the title of one book about the case reads—"the most hated man in America."

The most sensational fact about the Sandusky case, however, was that phrase "in due course." McQueary saw Sandusky in the shower in 2001. The investigation into Sandusky's behavior did not start until nearly a decade later, and Sandusky wasn't arrested until November 2011. Why did it take so long? After Sandusky was put behind bars, the spotlight fell on the leadership of Penn State University. Joe Paterno, the school's football coach, resigned in disgrace and died shortly thereafter. A statue of him that had been erected just a few years before was taken down. Tim Curley and Gary Schultz, the two senior university administrators McQueary had met with, were charged with conspiracy, obstruction of justice, and failure to report a case of child abuse.† Both went to jail. And in the scandal's final, devastating conclusion, prosecutors turned their attention to the university's president, Graham Spanier. He had led the school for sixteen years and had transformed its academic reputation. He was beloved. In November 2011, he was fired. Six years later, he was convicted of child endangerment.‡

---

* At the time, that was a record amount for a U.S. university in a sexual-abuse case. That record was soon broken, however, in the Larry Nassar case at Michigan State University, where damages paid by the school may end up being $500 million.
† Charges also included perjury (which was quickly dropped) and child endangerment. Eventually the two men pled guilty only to "child endangerment" so that all other charges could be dropped.
‡ Just as this book was going to press, Spanier's conviction was thrown out by a federal judge, the day before he was to finally report to prison. Whether or not the prosecution will appeal the ruling is—as we are going to press—unknown.

At the height of the controversy, Sandusky gave an interview to NBC sports anchor Bob Costas.

Costas: You say you're not a pedophile.
Sandusky: Right.
Costas: But you're a man who, by his own admission, has showered with young boys. Highly inappropriate.... Multiple reports of you getting into bed with young boys who stayed at your house in a room in the basement. How do you account for these things? And if you're not a pedophile, then what are you?
Sandusky: Well, I'm a person that has taken a strong interest...I'm a very passionate person in terms of trying to make a difference in the lives of some young people. I worked very hard to try to connect with them...
Costas: But isn't what you're just describing the classic M.O. of many pedophiles?...
Sandusky: Well—you might think that. I don't know.

Sandusky laughs nervously, launches into a long defensive explanation. And then:

Costas: Are you sexually attracted to young boys—to underage boys?
Sandusky: Am I sexually attracted to underage boys?

A pause.

Costas: Yes.

Another pause.

Sandusky: Sexually attracted, you know, I—I enjoy young people. I—I love to be around them. I—I—but no, I'm not sexually attracted to young boys.

Graham Spanier let *that* man roam free around the Penn State campus.

But here's my question, in light of Ana Montes and Bernie Madoff and Harry Markopolos and every bit of evidence marshaled by Tim Levine about how hard it is for us to overcome our default to truth: do you think that if you were the president of Penn State, confronted with the same set of facts and questions, you would have behaved any differently?

2.

Jerry Sandusky grew up in Washington, Pennsylvania. His father headed the local community recreation center, running sports programs for children. The Sanduskys lived upstairs. Their house was filled with baseball bats and basketballs and footballs. There were children everywhere. As an adult, Sandusky re-created the world of his childhood. Sandusky's son E.J. once described his father as "a frustrated playground director." Sandusky would organize kickball games in the backyard and, E.J. said, "Dad would get every single kid involved. We had the largest kickball games in the United States—kickball games with forty kids." Sandusky and his wife, Dottie, adopted six children and were foster parents to countless more. "They took in so many foster children that even their closest friends could not keep track of them all," Joe Posnanski wrote in a biography of Sandusky's boss, Joe Paterno. "Children constantly surrounded Sandusky, so much so that they became part of his persona."

Sandusky was a goofball and a cutup. Much of Sandusky's autobiography—titled, incredibly, *Touched*—is devoted to stories of his antics: the time he smeared charcoal over the handset of his chemistry teacher's phone, the time he ran afoul of a lifeguard for horseplay with his children in a public pool. Four and a half pages alone are devoted to water-balloon fights that he orchestrated while in college. "Wherever I went, it seemed like trouble was sure to follow," Sandusky wrote. "I live a good part of my life in a make-believe world," he continues. "I enjoyed pretending as a kid, and I love doing the same as an adult with these kids. Pretending has always been part of me."

In 1977, Sandusky founded a charity called the Second Mile. It was a recreational program for troubled boys. Over the years, thousands of children from impoverished and unsettled homes in the area passed through the program. Sandusky took his Second Mile kids to football games. He wrestled with them. He would give them gifts, write them letters, take them on trips, and bring them into his home. Many of the boys were being raised by single mothers. He tried to be the father they didn't have.

"If Sandusky did not have such a human side, there would be a temptation around [Penn State] to canonize him," a writer for *Sports Illustrated* said, upon Sandusky's retirement from the Penn State football-coaching staff.

Here, from the same era, is part of an article from the *Philadelphia Inquirer:*

> In more than one motel hallway, whenever you encountered him and offered what sounded like even the vaguest sort of compliment, he would blush and an engaging, lopsided grin of modesty would wrap its way around his face. He isn't in this business for recognition. His defense plays out in front of millions. But when he opens the door and invites in another stray, there is no audience. The ennobling measure of the man is that he has chosen the work that is done without public notice.

The first questions about Sandusky's conduct emerged in 1998. A Second Mile boy came home from a day with Sandusky, and his mother saw that he had wet hair. The boy said he had worked out with Sandusky, and then the two had taken a shower in the locker room. The boy said that Sandusky had wrapped his arms around him and said, "I'm gonna squeeze your guts out." Then he lifted him up to "get the soap out of his hair," with the boy's feet touching Sandusky's thigh.*

The mother told her son's psychologist, Alycia Chambers, about what happened. But she was unsure what to

---

* This was not unusual for Sandusky. He showered all the time after workouts with Second Mile boys, and loved playing locker-room games. "What happened is...the horsing around would lead to him starting like a soap battle," one former Second Miler testified at the Sandusky trial. "There was soap dispensers beside each one of the showers, and he would pump his hand full of soap and basically throw it."

make of the incident. "Am I overreacting?" she asked Chambers. Her son, meanwhile, saw nothing amiss. He described himself as the "luckiest boy in the world" because when he was with Sandusky he got to sit on the sidelines at Penn State football games.

The case was closed.

The next reported incident happened ten years later, involving a boy named Aaron Fisher, who had been in the Second Mile program since fourth grade. He came from a troubled home. He had gotten to know Sandusky well, and spent multiple nights at Sandusky's home. His mother thought of Sandusky as "some sort of angel." But in November 2008, when he was fifteen, Fisher mentioned to his mother that he felt uneasy about some of Sandusky's behavior. Sandusky would hold him tightly and crack his back. He would wrestle with him in a way that felt odd.

Fisher was referred to a child psychologist named Mike Gillum, a believer in the idea that victims of sexual abuse sometimes bury their experiences so deep that they can be retrieved only with great care and patience. He was convinced that Sandusky had sexually abused Fisher, but that Fisher couldn't remember it. Fisher met with his therapist repeatedly, sometimes daily, for months, with Gillum encouraging and coaxing Fisher. As one of the police investigators involved in the case would say later, "It took months to get the first kid [to talk] after it was brought to our attention. First it was, 'Yeah, he would rub my shoulders,' then it just took repetition and repetition, and finally we got to the point where he would tell us what happened." By March 2009, Fisher would nod in answer to the question of whether he had had oral sex with Sandusky. By June, he would finally answer, "Yes."

Here we have two complaints against Sandusky in the span of decade. Neither, however, led to Sandusky's apprehension. Why? Once again, because of default to truth.

Did doubt and suspicions rise to the level where they could no longer be explained away in the 1998 case of the boy in the shower? Not at all. The boy's psychiatrist wrote a report on the case arguing that Sandusky's behavior met the definition of a "likely pedophile's pattern of building trust and gradual introduction of physical touch, within a context of a 'loving,' 'special' relationship." Note the word *likely*. Then a caseworker assigned to the incident by the Department of Public Welfare in Harrisburg investigated, and he was even less certain. He thought the incident fell into a "gray" area concerning "boundary issues." The boy was then given a second evaluation by a counselor named John Seasock, who concluded, "There seems to be no incident which could be termed as sexual abuse, nor did there appear to be any sequential pattern of logic and behavior which is usually consistent with adults who have difficulty with sexual abuse of children." Seasock didn't see it at all. He said someone should talk to Sandusky about how to "stay out of such gray-area situations in the future."

The caseworker and a local police detective met with Sandusky. Sandusky told them he had hugged the boy but that there "wasn't anything sexual about it." He admitted to showering with other boys in the past. He said, "Honest to God, nothing happened." And remember, the boy himself also said nothing happened. So what do you do? You default to truth.

Aaron Fisher's story was just as ambiguous.* What Fisher remembered, during all those conversations with his therapist and sessions with the grand jury, kept changing. Once he said the oral sex stopped in November 2007; another time he said it started in the summer of 2007 and continued until September 2008; another time he said it started in 2008 and continued into 2009. He said that he had performed oral sex on Sandusky many times. A week later he said he had done it only once, and then five months later he denied ever having done it at all. Fisher testified about Sandusky before a grand jury twice in 2009, but it seems the grand jury didn't find him credible. They declined to indict Sandusky.

The police began systematically interviewing other boys who had been in the Second Mile program, looking for victims. They came up empty. This went on for *two years.* The prosecutor leading the case was ready to throw in the towel. You have a grown man who likes to horse around with young boys. Some people had doubts about Sandusky. But remember, doubts are not the enemy of belief; they are its companion.

Then, out of the blue, in November 2010, the prosecutor's office received an anonymous email: "I am contacting you regarding the Jerry Sandusky investigation," the email read. "If you have not yet done so, you need to contact

---

* The idea that traumatic memories are repressed and can be retrieved only under the direction of therapy is—to say the least—controversial. See the Notes for a further discussion of this.

and interview Penn State football assistant coach Mike McQueary. He may have witnessed something involving Jerry Sandusky and a child."

No more troubled teenagers with uncertain memories. With Michael McQueary, the prosecution finally had the means to make its case against Sandusky and the leadership of the university. A man sees a rape, tells his boss, and nothing happens—*for eleven years.* If you read about the Sandusky case at the time, that is the version you probably heard, stripped of all ambiguity and doubt.

"You know, there's a saying that absolute power corrupts absolutely," the prosecutor, Laura Ditka, said in her closing argument at Spanier's trial. "And I would suggest to you that Graham Spanier was corrupted by his own power and blinded by his own media attention and reputation; and he's a leader that failed to lead." At Penn State, the final conclusion was that blame for Sandusky's crimes went all the way to the top. Spanier made a choice, Ditka said: "We'll just keep it a secret," she imagined him saying to Curley and Schultz. "We won't report it. We won't tell any authorities."

If only things were that simple.

3.

Michael McQueary is six foot five. When he started as quarterback for Penn State, his weight was listed as 225 pounds. At the time of the shower incident, he was twenty-seven years old, in the physical prime of his life. Sandusky was thirty years older, with a laundry list of medical ailments.

First question: If McQueary was absolutely sure he witnessed a rape, why didn't he jump in and stop it?

In Part Three of *Talking to Strangers,* I'm going to tell the story of an infamous sexual-assault case at Stanford University. It was discovered when two graduate students were cycling at midnight through the campus and saw a young man and woman lying on the ground. The man was on top, making thrusting movements. The woman was still. The two students approached the couple. The man ran. The students gave chase. There were enough suspicious facts about that situation to trigger the grad students out of the default assumption that the encounter on the ground was innocent.

McQueary faced a situation that was—in theory, at least—a good deal more suspicious. It was not two adults. It was a man and a *boy,* both naked. But McQueary didn't step in. He backed away, ran upstairs, and called his father. His father told him to come home. Then his father asked a family friend, a medical doctor by the name of Jonathan Dranov, to come over and hear Michael's story.

This is Dranov, under oath, describing what McQueary told him:

He said that he heard sounds, sexual sounds. And I asked him what he meant. And he just said, "Well, you know, sounds, sexual sounds." Well, I didn't know exactly what he was talking [about]. He didn't become any more graphic or detail[ed than] that, but as I pressed him, it was obvious that he didn't have anything more he was going to say about it at the time. I asked him what he saw. He said he didn't see anything, but again he was shaken and nervous.

Dranov is a physician. He has a duty to report any child abuse he becomes aware of. Second question: So why doesn't Dranov go to the authorities when he hears McQueary's story? He was asked about this during the trial.

Defense: Now, you specifically pressed him that night and you wanted to know what specifically he had seen, but my understanding is he did not tell you what he had seen. Correct?

Dranov: That's correct.

D: All right. He told—but you left that meeting with the impression that he heard sexual sounds. Correct?

Dranov: What he interpreted as sexual sounds.

What *he interpreted* as sexual sounds.

D: And your—your plan that you presented to him or proposed to him was that he should tell his boss, Joe Paterno. Correct?

Dranov: That's correct.

D: You did not tell him to report to Children and Youth Services. Correct?

Dranov: That's correct.

Q: You did not tell him that he should report to the police. Correct?

Dranov: That's correct.

D: You did not tell him that he should report to campus security. Correct?

Dranov: That's correct…

D: You did not think it was appropriate for you to report it based on hearsay. Correct?

Dranov: That's correct.

D: And indeed, the reason that you did not tell Mike McQueary to report to Children and Youth Services or the police is because you did not think that what Mike McQueary reported to you was inappropriate enough for that sort of report. Correct?

Dranov: That's correct.

Dranov listens to McQueary's story, in person, *on the night it happened,* and he isn't convinced.

Things get even more complicated. McQueary originally said he saw Sandusky in the showers on Friday, March 1, 2002. It was spring break. He remembered the campus being deserted, and said that he went to see Paterno the following day—Saturday, March 2. But when investigators went back through university emails, they discovered that McQueary was confused. The date of his meeting with Paterno was actually a year earlier—Saturday, February 10, 2001—which would suggest the shower incident happened the evening before: Friday, February 9.

But this doesn't make sense. McQueary remembers the campus as being deserted the night he saw Sandusky in the showers. But on that Friday evening in February, the Penn State campus was anything but deserted. Penn State's hockey team was playing West Virginia at the Greenberg Pavilion next door, in a game that started at 9:15 p.m. There would have been crowds of people on the sidewalk, filing into the arena. And a five-minute walk away, at the Bryce Jordan Center, the popular Canadian rock band Barenaked Ladies was playing. On that particular evening, that corner of the Penn State campus was a madhouse.

John Ziegler, a journalist who has written extensively about the Penn State controversy, argues that the only plausible Friday night in that immediate time frame when the campus would have been deserted is Friday, December 29, 2000—during Christmas break. If Ziegler is right—and his arguments are persuasive—that leads to a third question: If McQueary witnessed a rape, why would he wait as long as five weeks—from the end of December to the beginning of February—to tell anyone in the university administration about it?*

The prosecution in the Sandusky case pretended that these uncertainties and ambiguities didn't exist. They told the public that everything was open-and-shut. The devastating 23-page indictment handed down in November of 2011 states that the "graduate assistant"—meaning McQueary—"saw a naked boy...with his hands up against the wall, being subjected to anal intercourse by a naked Sandusky." Then the next day McQueary "went to

---

* The evidence gathered by Ziegler on this point is compelling. For example, when Dranov testified in the Spanier trial, he said he had met with Gary Schultz on an entirely separate matter late that February, and had brought up the issue of Sandusky "since this was maybe three months after the incident and we hadn't heard any follow-up." Will we ever know the exact date? Probably not.

Ziegler is the most vociferous of those who believe that Sandusky was wrongfully accused. See also: Mark Pendergrast, *The Most Hated Man in America.* Some of Ziegler's arguments are more convincing than others. For a longer discussion of the Sandusky skeptics, see the Notes.

Paterno's home, where he reported what he had seen." But neither of those claims matches the facts, does it?

When McQueary read those words in the indictment, he emailed Jonelle Eshbach, the lead prosecutor in the case. He was upset. "I feel my words were slightly twisted and not totally portrayed accurately in the presentment," he wrote. "I want to make sure that you have the facts again in case I have not been clear." Then: "I cannot say 1000 percent sure that it was sodomy. I did not see insertion. It was a sexual act and / or way over the line in my opinion, whatever it was." He wanted to correct the record. "What are my options as far as a statement from me goes?" he asked Eshbach.

Think about how McQueary must have felt as he read the way Eshbach had distorted his words. He had seen something he thought was troubling. For five weeks, as he wrestled with his conscience, he must have been in agony. *What did I see? Should I say something? What if I'm wrong?* Then he read the indictment, and what did he find? That the prosecutors, in order to serve their own ends, had turned gray into black and white. And what did that make him? A coward who witnessed a rape, ran away to call his parents, and never told the police.

"My life has drastically, drastically changed," he wrote to Eshbach. The Sandusky who took showers with young boys late at night was a stranger to McQueary, and Eshbach had refused to acknowledge how difficult it is to make sense of a stranger. "My family's life has drastically changed," McQueary went on. "National media and public opinion has totally in every single way ruined me. For what?"

4.

It is useful to compare the Sandusky scandal to a second, even more dramatic child-molestation case that broke a few years later. It involved a doctor at Michigan State named Larry Nassar. Nassar served as the team physician for the USA Gymnastics women's national team. He was bespectacled, garrulous, a little awkward. He *seemed* harmless. He doted on his patients. He was the kind of person you could call on at 2 a.m., and he would come running. Parents loved him. He treated hips and shins and ankles and the myriad other injuries that result from the enormous stress that competitive gymnastics puts on young bodies.

Nassar's specialty was the treatment of what is known as "pelvic-floor dysfunction," which involved him inserting his fingers into the vagina of a patient to massage muscles and tendons that had been shortened by the physical demands of gymnastics training. He did the pelvic-floor procedure repeatedly and enthusiastically. He did it without consent, without wearing gloves, and when it wasn't necessary. He would massage his patients' breasts. He would penetrate them anally with his fingers for no apparent reason. He used a medical procedure as the cover for his own sexual gratification. He was convicted on federal charges in the summer of 2017 and will spend the rest of his life in prison.

As sexual-abuse scandals go, the Nassar case is remarkably clear-cut. This is not a matter of "he said, she said." The police retrieved the hard drive from Nassar's computer and found a library of child pornography— 37,000 images in all, some of them unspeakably graphic.

He had photographs of his young patients as they sat in his bathtub taking ice baths prior to treatment. He didn't have just one accuser, telling a disputed story. He had hundreds of accusers, telling remarkably similar stories. Here is Rachael Denhollander, whose allegations against Nassar proved critical to his conviction.

> At age fifteen, when I suffered from chronic back pain, Larry sexually assaulted me repeatedly under the guise of medical treatment for nearly a year. He did this with my own mother in the room, carefully and perfectly obstructing her view so she would not know what he was doing.

Denhollander had evidence, documentation.

> When I came forward in 2016, I brought an entire file of evidence with me....I brought medical records from a nurse practitioner documenting my graphic disclosure of abuse...I had my journals showing the mental anguish I had been in since the assault....I brought a witness I had disclosed it to...I brought the evidence of two more women unconnected to me who were also claiming sexual assault.

The Nassar case was open-and-shut. Yet how long did it take to bring him to justice? *Years.* Larissa Boyce, another of Nassar's victims, said that Nassar abused her in 1997, when she was sixteen. And what happened? Nothing. Boyce told the Michigan State gymnastics coach, Kathie Klages. Klages confronted Nassar. Nassar denied everything. Klages believed Nassar, not Boyce. The allegations raised doubts, but not enough doubts. The abuse went on. At Nassar's trial, in a heartrending moment, Boyce addressed Nassar directly: "I dreaded my next appointment with you because I was afraid that Kathie was going to tell you about my concerns," she said.

> And unfortunately, I was right. I felt ashamed, embarrassed, and overwhelmed that I had talked to Kathie about this. I vividly remember when you walked into that room, closed the door behind you, pulled up your stool and sat down in front of me, and said, "So, I talked to Kathie." As soon as I heard those words, my heart sank. My confidence had been betrayed. I wanted to crawl into the deepest, darkest hole and hide.

Over the course of Nassar's career as a sexual predator, there were as many as fourteen occasions in which people in positions of authority were warned that something was amiss with him: parents, coaches, officials. Nothing happened. In September 2016 the *Indianapolis Star* published a devastating account of Nassar's record, supported by Denhollander's accusations. Many people close to Nassar backed him even after this. Nassar's boss, the Dean of Osteopathic Medicine at Michigan State, allegedly told students, "This just goes to show that none of you learned the most basic lesson in medicine, Medicine 101....Don't trust your patients. Patients lie to get doctors in trouble." Kathie Klages had the gymnasts on her team sign a card for Nassar: "Thinking of you."

It took the discovery of Nassar's computer hard drive,

with its trove of appalling images, to finally change people's minds.

When scandals like this break, one of our first inclinations is to accuse those in charge of covering for the criminal—of protecting him, or deliberately turning a blind eye, or putting their institutional or financial interests ahead of the truth. We look for a conspiracy behind the silence. But the Nassar case reminds us how inadequate that interpretation is. Many of Nassar's chief defenders were the parents of his patients. They weren't engaged in some kind of conspiracy of silence to protect larger institutional or financial interests. *These were their children.*

Here is one gymnast's mother—a medical doctor herself, incidentally—in an interview for *Believed*, a brilliant podcast about the Nassar scandal. The woman was in the room while Nassar treated her daughter, sitting a few feet away.

> And I remember out of the corner of my eye seeing what looked to be potentially an erection. And I just remember thinking, "That's weird. That's really weird. Poor guy." Thinking, like, that would be very strange for a physician to get an erection in a patient's room while giving her an exam…
>
> But at the time, when you're in the room, and he's doing this procedure, you just think he's being a good doctor and doing his best for your child. He was that slick. He was that smooth.

In another instance, a young girl goes to see Nassar with her father. Nassar puts his fingers inside her, with her dad sitting in the room. Later that day, the gymnast tells her mother. Here is the mother looking back on the moment:

> I remember it like it was five seconds ago. I'm in the driver's seat, she's in the passenger seat, and she said, "Larry did something to me today that made me feel uncomfortable."
> And I said, "Well, what do you mean?"
> "Well, he...touched me."
> And I said, "Well, touched you where?"
> And she said, "Down there." And the whole time you know what she's saying but you're trying to rationalize that it can't be that.

She called her husband and asked him if he had left the room at any time during the appointment? He said he hadn't.

> And...God forgive me, I dropped it. I filed it back in the parenting filing cabinet until 2016.

After a while, the stories all start to sound the same. Here's another parent:

> And she's sitting in the car very quiet and depressed and saying, "Dad, he's not helping my back pain. Let's not go anymore." But this is Larry. This is the gymnastics doctor. If he can't cure her, nobody will cure her. Only God has more skills than Larry. "Be patient, honey. It's gonna take time. Good things take

time." That's what we always taught our kids. So, I would say, "OK. We're gonna go again next week. We're gonna go again the following week. And then you will start seeing the progress."

She said, "OK, Dad. You know. I trust your judgment."

The fact that Nassar was doing something monstrous is exactly what makes the parents' position so difficult. If Nassar had been rude to their daughters, they would have spoken up immediately. If their daughters had said to them on the way home that they had smelled liquor on Nassar's breath, most parents would have leapt to attention. It is not impossible to imagine that doctors are occasionally rude or drunk. Default to truth becomes an issue when we are forced to choose between two alternatives, one of which is likely and the other of which is impossible to imagine. Is Ana Montes the most highly placed Cuban spy in history, or was Reg Brown just being paranoid? Default to truth biases us in favor of the most likely interpretation. Scott Carmichael believed Ana Montes, right up to the point where believing her became absolutely impossible. The parents did the same thing, not because they were negligent but because this is how most human beings are wired.

Many of the women he had abused, in fact, defended Nassar. They couldn't see past default to truth either. Trinea Gonczar was treated 856 times by Nassar during her gymnastics career. When one of her teammates came to Gonczar and said that Nassar had put his fingers inside her, Gonczar tried to reassure her: "He does that to me all the time!"

When the *Indianapolis Star* broke the Nassar story,

Gonczar stood by him. She was convinced he would be exonerated. It was all a big mix-up. When did she finally change her mind? Only when the evidence against Nassar became overwhelming. At Nassar's trial, when Gonczar joined the chorus of his victims in testifying against him, she finally gave in to her doubts:

> I had to make an extremely hard choice this week, Larry. I had to choose whether [to] continue supporting you through this or to support them: the girls. I choose them, Larry. I choose to love them and protect them. I choose to stop caring for you and supporting you. I choose to look you in the face and tell you that you hurt us, you hurt me…I hope you will see it from me in my eyes today that I believed in you always until I couldn't anymore. I hope you cry like we cry. I hope you feel bad for what you've done. I hope more than anything, each day these girls can feel less pain. I hope you want that for us, but this is goodbye to you, Larry, and this time it's time for me to close the door. It's time for me to stand up for these little girls and not stand behind you anymore, Larry.
>
> Goodbye, Larry. May God bless your dark, broken soul.

I believed in you always until I couldn't anymore. Isn't that an almost perfect statement of default to truth?

Default to truth operates even in a case where the perpetrator had 37,000 child-porn images on his hard drive, and where he had been accused countless times, by numerous people, over the course of his career. The Nassar case was open-and-shut—and still there were doubts. Now imagine the same scenario, only in a case that *isn't* open-and-shut. That's the Sandusky case.

5.

After the accusations against Sandusky were made public, one of his staunchest defenders was a former Second Mile participant named Allan Myers. When the Pennsylvania police were interviewing former Second Mile kids in an attempt to corroborate the allegations against Sandusky, they contacted Myers, and he was adamant. "Myers said that he does not believe the allegations that have been made, and that the accuser…is only out to get some money," the police report read. "Myers continues to be in touch with Sandusky one to two times a week by telephone." Myers told the police that he had showered in the locker room with Sandusky many times after workouts and nothing untoward had ever happened.

Two months later, Myers went further. He walked into the offices of Sandusky's attorney and made a stunning revelation. After reading the details of McQueary's story, he realized that *he* had been the boy in the shower that night. Curtis Everhart, an investigator for Sandusky's lawyer, wrote a synopsis of his interview with Myers. It is worth quoting at length:

I asked the specific question: "Did Jerry ever touch you in a manner that you felt to be improper, or caused you to feel concern about his invading your personal space?" Myers answered with a very pronounced, "Never ever did anything like that ever occur."

Myers stated, "Never in my life while with Jerry did I ever [feel] uncomfortable or violated. I think of Jerry as the father I never had."...Myers stated on Senior Night at a West Branch High School football game, "I asked Jerry to walk onto the field with my mother. It was announced on the loudspeaker 'Father Jerry Sandusky' along with my mother's name.

"I invited Jerry and Dottie to my wedding. Why would I ask Jerry, my father figure at Senior Night, ask Jerry and Dottie to be at my wedding, and the school asked me to ask Jerry to speak at my graduation, which he did, if there was a problem....Why would I travel to games, go to his house, and make all the trips if Jerry had assaulted me? If that had happened, I would want to be as far away from him as possible."

Myers described the night in question clearly:

Myers stated he and Jerry had just finished a workout and went into the shower area to shower and leave. "I would usually work out one or two days a week, but this particular night is very clear in my mind. We were in the shower and Jerry and I were slapping towels at each other trying to sting each other. I would slap the walls and would slide on the shower floor, which I am sure you could have heard from the wooden locker area. While we were engaged in fun as I have described, I heard the sound of a wooden locker door close, a sound I have heard before. I never saw who closed the locker. The grand jury report says Coach McQueary said he observed Jerry and I engaged in sexual activity. This is not the truth and McQueary is not telling the truth. Nothing occurred that night in the shower."

A few weeks later, however, Myers signed up with a lawyer who represented a number of alleged Sandusky victims. Myers then made a statement to police in which he completely changed his tune. He *was* one of Sandusky's victims, he now said.

You can be forgiven if you find this confusing. The boy in the shower was the most important witness in the whole case. Prosecutors had been searching high and low for him, because he would be the final nail in Sandusky's coffin. So finally he surfaces, denies anything happened, then almost immediately flips, saying actually something *did* happen. So did Myers become the key prosecution witness in the Sandusky trial? That would make sense. He was the most important piece in the whole puzzle. No! The prosecution left him at home because they had no confidence in his story.*

The only time Myers ever appeared in court was to

---

* The prosecution's report on Allan Myers is a doozy. An investigator named Michael Corricelli spoke to Myers's lawyer, who told him that Myers now claimed to have been raped repeatedly by Sandusky. His lawyer produced a three-page account allegedly written by Myers detailing his abuse at the hands of Sandusky. The prosecution team read the account and suspected that it hadn't been written by Myers at all but rather by his lawyer. Finally the prosecution gave up, and walked away from one of the most important figures in the entire case.

testify at Sandusky's appeal. Sandusky had asked for him to testify, in the vain hope that Myers would revert to his original position and say that nothing happened in the shower. Myers did not. Instead, as Sandusky's lawyers read back to Myers each of the statements he had made less than a year before about Sandusky's innocence, Myers sat there stone-faced and shrugged at everything, including a picture of him standing happily next to Sandusky. Who are the people in the photo? he was asked.

Myers: That's myself and your client.
Defense: And when was that picture taken? If you know.
Myers: That I do not remember.

It was a picture of Myers and Sandusky at Myers's wedding. In all, he said he didn't recall thirty-four times.

Then there was Brett Swisher Houtz, a Second Mile child with whom Sandusky had been very close. He was probably the most devastating witness at Sandusky's trial. Houtz told of being repeatedly assaulted and abused—of dozens of lurid sexual encounters with Sandusky during his teenage years, in showers and saunas and hotel rooms.

Prosecution: Mr. Houtz, can you tell the ladies and gentlemen of the jury approximately how many times the defendant in either the East Area locker room or the Lasch Building shower... put his penis in your mouth?
Houtz: It would have to be forty times at least.
P: Did you want him to do it—
Houtz: No.

P: —on any of those occasions?
Houtz: No.

Then Sandusky's wife, Dottie, was called to the stand. She was asked when she and her husband last saw Brett Houtz.

D. Sandusky: I think it was three years ago, or two years ago. I'm not sure.

The stories Houtz told of his abuse were alleged to have happened in the 1990s. Dottie Sandusky was saying that two decades after being brutally and repeatedly victimized, Houtz decided to drop by for a visit.

Defense: Can you tell us about that?
D. Sandusky: Yeah. Jerry got a phone call. It was Brett. He said, I want to come over. I want to bring my girlfriend and my baby for you to see. The baby was like two years old. And they came over and my friend Elaine Steinbacher was there, and we went and got Kentucky Fried Chicken and had dinner. And it was a very pleasant visit.

This is a much more perplexing example than Trinea Gonczar in the Nassar case. Gonczar never denied that something happened in her sessions with Nassar. She chose to interpret his actions as benign—for entirely understandable reasons—up until the point when she listened to the testimony of her fellow gymnasts at Nassar's trial. Sandusky, by contrast, wasn't practicing some ambiguous medical procedure. He is supposed to have engaged in repeated acts of sexual violence. And his alleged victims didn't misinterpret what he was doing to them. They acted as if nothing had ever happened. They didn't confide in their friends. They didn't write anguished accounts in their journals. They dropped by, years later, to show off their babies to the man who raped them. They invited their rapist to their weddings. One victim showered with Sandusky and called himself the "luckiest boy in the world." Another boy emerged with a story, after months of prodding by a therapist, that couldn't convince a grand jury.

Sexual-abuse cases are *complicated,* wrapped in layers of shame and denial and clouded memories, and few high-profile cases were as complicated as Jerry Sandusky's. Now think about what that complication means for those who must make sense of all that swirling contradiction. There were always doubts about Sandusky. But how do you get to *enough* doubts when the victims are happily eating Kentucky Fried Chicken with their abuser?

6.

So: McQueary goes to see his boss, Joe Paterno on a Saturday. An alarmed Paterno sits down with Tim Curley and Gary Schultz the following day, Sunday. They immediately call the university's counsel and then brief the university president, Graham Spanier, on Monday. Then Curley and Schultz call in Mike McQueary.

You can only imagine what Curley and Schultz are thinking as they listen to him: If this really was a rape, why didn't you break it up? If what you saw was so troubling, why didn't anyone—including your family friend, who is a doctor—tell the police? And if you—Mike McQueary—were so upset about what you saw, why did you wait so long to tell us?

Curley and Schultz then call the university's outside counsel. But McQueary hasn't given them much. They instinctively reach—as we all do—for the most innocent of explanations: Maybe Jerry was just being goofy Jerry. Here is the Penn State lawyer, Wendell Courtney, recounting his conversation with Gary Schultz.

> **Courtney:** I asked at some point along the way whether this horseplay involving Jerry and a young boy, whether there was anything sexual in nature. And he indicated to me that there was not to his knowledge.... My vision, at least when it was being described to me and talking with Mr. Schultz, was that it was, you know, a young boy with the showers on, a lot of water in the shower area, group shower area just kinda, you know, running and sliding on the floor...
>
> **Prosecution:** Are you sure he didn't say slapping sound or anything sexual in nature at all?
>
> **Courtney:** I am quite positive he never said to me slapping sounds or anything sexual in nature that was reported going on in the shower.

Courtney said he thought about it and considered the worst-case scenario. This was, after all, a man and a boy in the shower after hours. But then he thought of what he knew of Jerry Sandusky "as someone that goofed around with Second Mile kids all the time in public," and he defaulted to that impression.[*]

Schultz and his colleague Tim Curley then go to see university president Spanier.

Prosecution: You did tell Graham Spanier it was "horseplay"?

Schultz: Yeah.

P: When did you tell him that?

Schultz: Well, the first—first report that we got that was passed on to us is "horsin' around." Jerry Sandusky was seen in the shower horsin' around with a kid....And I think that word was repeated to President Spanier that, you know...that he was horsin' around.

Spanier listened to Curley and Schultz and asked two questions. "Are you sure that's how it was described to you, as 'horsing around'?" They said yes. Then Spanier asked again: "Are you sure that's all that was said to you?"

---

[*] Courtney had doubts about Sandusky's innocence. But in the end Sandusky's cover story was just too convincing. *Someone that goofed around with Second Mile kids all the time in public.* Curley then called the executive director of the Second Mile, John Raykovitz. Raykovitz promised to have a word with Sandusky and tell him not to bring any more boys on campus. "I can only speak for myself, but I thought Jerry had a boundary issue, judgment issue, that needed to be addressed," Curley explained. Sandusky needed to be careful, he felt, or people would think he was a pedophile. "I told him," Raykovitz said, "that it would be more appropriate—if he was going to shower with someone after a workout—that he wear swim trunks. And I said that because...that was the time when there was a lot of stuff coming out about Boy Scouts and church and things of that nature."

They said yes. Spanier barely knew Sandusky. Penn State has thousands of employees. One of them—now retired—was spotted in a shower?

"I remember, for a moment, sort of figuratively scratching our heads and thinking about what's an appropriate way to follow up on 'horsing around,'" Spanier said later. "I had never gotten a report like that before."

If Harry Markopolos had been president of Penn State during the Sandusky case, of course, he would never have defaulted like this to the most innocent of explanations. A man in a shower? With a boy? The kind of person who saw through Madoff's deceit a decade before anyone else would have leaped at once to the most damning conclusion: *How old was the kid? What were they doing there at night? Wasn't there a weird case with Sandusky a couple of years ago?*

But Graham Spanier is not Harry Markopolos. He opted for the likeliest explanation—that Sandusky was who he claimed to be. Does he regret not asking one more follow-up question, not quietly asking around? Of course he does. But defaulting to truth is not a crime. It is a fundamentally human tendency. Spanier behaved no differently from the Mountain Climber and Scott Carmichael and Nat Simons and Trinea Gonczar and virtually every one of the parents of the gymnasts treated by Larry Nassar. Weren't those parents in the room when Nassar was abusing their own children? Hadn't their children said something wasn't right? Why did they send their child back to Nassar, again and again? Yet in the Nassar case no one has ever suggested that the parents of the gymnasts belong in jail for failing to protect their offspring from a predator. We accept the fact that being a parent requires a fundamental level of trust in the community of people around your child.

If every coach is assumed to be a pedophile, then no parent would let their child leave the house, and no sane person would ever volunteer to be a coach. We default to truth—even when that decision carries terrible risks—because we have no choice. Society cannot function otherwise. And in those rare instances where trust ends in betrayal, those victimized by default to truth deserve our sympathy, not our censure.

7.

Tim Curley and Gary Schultz were charged first. Two of the most important officials at one of the most prestigious state universities in the United States were placed under arrest. Spanier called his senior staff together for an emotional meeting. He considered Penn State to be a big family. These were his friends. When they told him the shower incident was probably just horseplay, he believed they were being honest.

"You're going to find that everyone is going to distance themselves from Gary and Tim," he said. But he would not.

Every one of you in here has worked with Tim and Gary for years. Some of you, for thirty-five or forty years, because that's how long Tim and Gary, respectively, were at the university. . . . You've worked with them every day of your life, and I have for the last sixteen years....If any of you operate according to how we have always agreed to operate at this university—honestly, openly, with integrity, always doing what's in the best interests of the university—if you were falsely accused of something, I would do the same thing for any of you in here. I want you to know that....None of [you] should ever fear doing the right thing, or being accused of wrongdoing when [you] knew [you] were doing the right thing...because this university would back them up.[*]

This is why people liked Graham Spanier. It's why he had such a brilliant career at Penn State. It's why you and I would want to work for him. We *want* Graham Spanier as our president—not Harry Markopolos, armed to the teeth, waiting for a squad of government bureaucrats to burst through the front door.

This is the first of the ideas to keep in mind when considering the death of Sandra Bland. We *think* we want our guardians to be alert to every suspicion. We blame them when they default to truth. When we try to send people like Graham Spanier to jail, we send a message to all of those in positions of authority about the way we want them to make sense of strangers—without stopping to consider the consequences of sending that message.

But we are getting ahead of ourselves.

---

[*] This is not a literal transcription of what Spanier said, but rather a paraphrase, based on his recollections.

Part Three

Transparency

CHAPTER SIX

The Friends *Fallacy*

1.

By its fifth season, *Friends* was well on its way to becoming one of the most successful television shows of all time. It was one of the first great "hang-out comedies." Six friends—Monica, Rachel, Phoebe, Joey, Chandler, and Ross—live in a chaotic jumble in downtown Manhattan, couple and decouple, flirt and fight but mostly just talk, endlessly and hilariously.

The season begins with Ross getting married to a non-*Friends* outsider. By midseason the relationship will be over, and by season's end he will be back in the arms of Rachel. Phoebe gives birth to triplets and takes up with a police officer. And, most consequentially, Monica and Chandler fall in love—a development that creates an immediate problem, because Monica is

Ross's sister and Chandler is Ross's best friend, and neither of them has the courage to tell Ross what is happening.

At the beginning of episode fifteen—titled "The One with the Girl Who Hits Joey"—Chandler and Monica's subterfuge falls apart. Ross looks out his window at the apartment across the way and spots his sister Monica in a romantic embrace with Chandler. He's thunderstruck. He runs to Monica's apartment and tries to barge in, but the chain is on her door. So he sticks his face into the six-inch gap.

"Chandler! Chandler! I saw what you were doing through the window. I saw what you were doing to my sister, now get out here!"

Chandler, alarmed, tries to escape out the window. Monica holds him back. "I can handle Ross," she tells him. She opens the door to her brother. "Hey, Ross. What's up, bro?"

Ross runs inside, lunges at Chandler, and starts to chase him around the kitchen table, shouting: "What the hell are you doing?!"

Chandler hides behind Monica. Joey and Rachel rush in.

Rachel: Hey, what's going on?
Chandler: Well, I think—I *think*—Ross knows about me and Monica.
Joey: Dude, he's right there.
Ross: I thought you were my best friend! This is my sister! My best friend, and my sister! I cannot believe this.

Did you follow all that? A standard *Friends* season had so many twists and turns of plot—and variations of narrative and emotion—that it seems as though viewers would need a flowchart to make sure they didn't lose their way. In reality, however, nothing could be further from the truth. If you've ever watched an episode of *Friends,* you'll know that it is almost impossible to get confused. The show is crystal clear. How clear? I think you can probably follow along even if you turn off the sound.

The second of the puzzles that began this book was the bail problem. How is it that judges do a worse job of evaluating defendants than a computer program, even though judges know a lot more about defendants than the computer does? This section of *Talking to Strangers* is an attempt to answer that puzzle, beginning with the peculiar fact of how transparent television shows such as *Friends* are.

2.

To test this idea about the transparency of *Friends,* I contacted a psychologist named Jennifer Fugate, who teaches at the University of Massachusetts at Dartmouth. Fugate is an expert in FACS, which stands for Facial Action Coding System.* In FACS, every one of the forty-three distinctive muscle movements in the face is assigned a number, called

---

* It was developed by legendary psychologist Paul Ekman, whom I wrote about in my second book, *Blink*. See the Notes for an explanation of how my views on Ekman's work have evolved since then.

an "action unit." People like Fugate who are trained in FACS can then look at someone's facial expressions and score them, just as a musician can listen to a piece of music and translate it into a series of notes on the page.

So, for example, take a look at this photo:

That's called a Pan-Am smile—the kind of smile a flight attendant gives you when he or she is trying to be polite. When you give that kind of smile, you pull up the corners of your lips, using what's called the zygomaticus major muscle, but leave the rest of your face impassive. That's why the smile looks fake: It's a smile without any kind of facial elaboration. In the FACS, the Pan-Am smile using the zygomaticus major is scored as AU 12.

Now take a look at this:

This is what's called a Duchenne smile. It's what a genuine smile looks like. In technical terms, it's AU 12 plus AU 6—meaning that it is a facial movement involving the outer portion of the orbicularis oculi muscle, raising the cheeks and creating those telltale crow's-feet around the eyes.

FACS is an extraordinarily sophisticated tool. It involves cataloging—in exacting detail—thousands of muscular movements, some of which may appear on the face for no more than a fraction of a second. The FACS manual is over five hundred pages long. If Fugate had done a FACS analysis of the entire "Girl Who Hits Joey" episode, it would have taken her days, so I asked her to focus just on that opening scene: Ross sees Chandler and Rachel embracing, then rushes over in anger.

Here's what she found.

When Ross looks through the cracked door and sees his sister in a romantic embrace with his best friend, his face shows action units 10 + 16 + 25 + 26: That's the upper-lip raiser (levator labii superioris, caput infraorbitalis), the lower-lip depressor (depressor labii), parted lips (depressor labii, relaxed mentalis or orbicularis oris), and jaw drop (relaxed temporal and internal pterygoid).

In the FACS system, muscular movements are also given an intensity measure from A to E, with A being mildest and E strongest. All of Ross's four muscle movements, in that moment, are Es. If you go back and watch that *Friends* episode, and freeze the screen at the moment when Ross looks through the door frame, you'll see exactly what the FACS coders are describing. He has an unmistakable look on his face of anger and disgust.

Ross then rushes into Monica's apartment. The tension in the scene is accelerating, and so are Ross's emotions. Now his face reads: 4C + 5D + 7C + 10E + 16E + 25E + 26E. Again, four Es!

"[AU] 4 is a brow-lowerer," Fugate explains.

That's what you do when you furrow your brow. Seven is an eye squint. It's called "lid-tightener." He's kind of scowling and closing his eyes at the same time, so that's a stereotypic anger. Then the 10 in this case is very classic for disgust. You kind of lift your upper lip, not really moving the nose, but it gives the appearance that the nose is being turned up. The 16 sometimes happens with that. That's a lower-lip depressor. That's when you push your bottom lip down so that you can see your bottom teeth.

Monica, at the door, tries to pretend nothing is amiss. She smiles at her brother. But it's a Pan-Am smile, not a Duchenne smile: some 12 and the barest, least-plausible whisper of 6.

Ross chases Chandler around the kitchen table. Chandler hides behind Monica, and as Ross approaches, he says: "Look, we're not just messing around. I love her. OK? I'm in love with her."

Then Monica reaches and takes Ross's hand. "I'm so sorry that you had to find out this way. I'm sorry. But it's true, I love him too."

There's a long silence as Ross stares at the two of them, processing a storm of competing emotions. Then he bursts into a smile, hugs them both, and repeats himself, only this time happily: "My best friend, and my sister! I'm so happy!"

As Monica breaks the news to her brother, Fugate scores her as 1C + 2D + 12D. The 1 and 2, in combination, are sadness: She's raised the inner and outer parts of her eyebrows. 12D, of course, is the emotionally incomplete Pan-Am smile.

"She kind of gives—as strange as that sounds—an indicator of sadness," Fugate said, "but then happiness. I think it kind of makes sense, because she's apologizing, but then she's showing Ross that she's actually okay with this."

Ross looks at his sister for a long beat. His face scores classic sadness. Then his face subtly shifts to 1E + 12D. He's giving back to his sister the exact same mix of emotions she gave to him: sadness combined with the beginnings of happiness. He's losing his sister. But at the same time, he wants her to know that he appreciates her joy.

Fugate's FACS analysis tells us that the actors in *Friends* make sure that every emotion their character is supposed to feel in their heart is expressed, perfectly, on their face. That's why you can watch the scene with the sound turned off and still follow along. The words are what make us laugh, or what explain particular nuances of narrative. But the facial displays of the actors are what carry the plot. The actors' performances in *Friends* are *transparent*.

Transparency is the idea that people's behavior and demeanor—the way they represent themselves on the *outside*—provides an authentic and reliable window into the way they feel on the *inside*. It is the second of the crucial tools we use to make sense of strangers. When we don't know someone, or can't communicate with them, or don't have the time to understand them properly, we believe we can make sense of them through their behavior and demeanor.

3.

The idea of transparency has a long history. In 1872, thirteen years after first presenting his famous treatise on evolution, Charles Darwin published *The Expression of the Emotions in Man and Animals.* Smiling and frowning and wrinkling our noses in disgust, he argued, were things that every human being did as part of evolutionary adaptation. Accurately and quickly communicating our emotions to one another was of such crucial importance to the survival of the human species, he argued, that the face had developed into a kind of billboard for the heart.

Darwin's idea is deeply intuitive. Children everywhere smile when they are happy, frown when they are sad, and giggle when they are amused, don't they? It isn't just people watching *Friends* in their living room in Cleveland, Toronto, or Sydney who can make sense of what Ross and Rachel are feeling; it's everyone.

The bail hearings described in Chapter Two are likewise an exercise in transparency. The judge does not correspond with the parties in a court case by email or call them up on the telephone. Judges believe that it's crucial to *look* at the people they are judging. A Muslim woman in Michigan was the plaintiff in a lawsuit a few years ago, and she came to court wearing the traditional niqab, a veil covering all but her eyes. The judge asked her to take it off. She refused. So the judge dismissed her case. He didn't think he could fairly adjudicate a disagreement between two parties when he couldn't see one of them. He told her:

> One of the things that I need to do as I am listening to testimony is I need to see your face and I need to see what's going on. And unless you take that off, I can't see your face and I can't tell whether you're telling me the truth or not, and I can't see certain things about your demeanor and temperament that I need to see in a court of law.*

---

* The plaintiff was Ginnah Muhammad. Her reply: "Well, first of all, I'm a practicing Muslim, and this is my way of life, and I believe in the Holy Koran, and God is first in my life. I don't have a problem with taking my veil off if it's a female judge, so I want to know, do you have a female that I could be in front of? Then I have no problem. But otherwise, I can't follow that order."

Do you think the judge was right? I'm guessing many of you do. We wouldn't spend as much time as we do looking at people's faces if we didn't think there was something valuable to be learned. In novels, we read that "his eyes widened in shock" or "her face fell in disappointment," and we accept without question that faces really do fall and eyes really do widen in response to the feelings of shock and disappointment. We can watch Ross's 4C + 5D + 7C + 10E + 16E + 25E + 26E and know what it means—with the sound off—because thousands of years of evolution have turned 4C + 5D + 7C+ 10E + 16E + 25E + 26E into the expression human beings make when filled with shock and anger. We believe someone's demeanor is a window into their soul. But that takes us back to Puzzle Number Two. Judges in bail hearings have a window into the defendant's soul. Yet they are much worse at predicting who will reoffend than Sendhil Mullainathan's computer, which has a window into no one's soul.

If real life were like *Friends,* judges would beat computers. But they don't. So maybe real life *isn't* like *Friends.*

4.

The cluster of islands known as the Trobriands lies 100 miles east of Papua New Guinea, in the middle of the Solomon Sea. The archipelago is tiny, home to 40,000 people. It's isolated and tropical. The people living there fish and farm much as their ancestors did thousands of years ago, and their ancient customs have proven remarkably durable, even in the face of the inevitable encroachments of the 21st century. In the same way that carmakers take new models to the Arctic to test them under the most extreme conditions possible, social scientists sometimes like to "stress test" hypotheses in places such as the Trobriands. If something works in London or New York *and* it works in the Trobriands, you can be pretty sure you're onto something universal—which is what sent two Spanish social scientists to the Trobriand Islands in 2013.

Sergio Jarillo is an anthropologist. He had worked in the Trobriands before and knew the language and culture. Carlos Crivelli is a psychologist. He spent the earliest part of his career testing the limits of transparency. Once he examined dozens of videotapes of judo fighters who had just won their matches to figure out when, exactly, they smiled. Was it at the moment of victory? Or did they win, *then* smile? Another time he watched videotapes of people masturbating to find out what their faces looked like at the moment of climax. Presumably an orgasm is a moment of true happiness. Is that happiness evident and observable in the moment? In both cases, it wasn't—which didn't make sense if our emotions are really a billboard for the heart. These studies made Crivelli a skeptic, so he and Jarillo decided to put Darwin to the test.

Jarillo and Crivelli started with six headshots of people looking happy, sad, angry, scared, and disgusted—with one final picture of someone with a neutral expression. Before they left for the Trobriands, the two men took their pictures to a primary school in Madrid and tried them out on a group of children. They put all six photos before a child and asked, "Which of these is the sad face?" Then they went to the second child and asked, "Which of these is the angry face?" and so on, cycling through all six pictures over and over again. Here are the results. The children had no difficulty with the exercise:

Emotion label	"Happy": Smiling	"Sad": Pouting	"Angry": Scowling	"Fear": Gasping	"Disgust": Nose-scrunching	Neutral
			Spaniards (n = 113)			
Happiness	**1.00**	.00	.00	.00	.00	.00
Sadness	.00	**.98**	.00	.00	.00	.02
Anger	.00	.00	**.91**	.00	.09	.00
Fear	.00	.07	.00	**.93**	.00	.00
Disgust	.00	.02	.00	.15	**.83**	.00

Then Jarillo and Crivelli flew to the Trobriand Islands and repeated the process.

The Trobrianders were friendly and cooperative. They had a rich, nuanced language, which made them an ideal test case for a study of emotion. Jarillo explained,

To say that something has really surprised you in a positive way, they say, it "has enraptured my mind," or it has "caught my mind." Then when you repeat that, you say, "Has this thing caught your mind?" And they say, "Well, no, this one is more like it has taken my stomach away."

These were not people, in other words, who would be flummoxed by being asked to make sense of the emotional truth of something. If Darwin was correct, the Trobrianders should be as good as the schoolchildren in Madrid at making sense of people's faces. Emotions are hardwired by evolution. That means people in the middle of the Solomon Sea must have the same operating system as people in Madrid. Right?

Wrong.

Take a look at the following chart, which compares the success rate of the Trobrianders with the success rate of the ten-year-olds at the Madrid school. The Trobrianders *struggled.*

Emotion label	"Happy": Smiling	"Sad": Pouting	"Angry": Scowling	"Fear": Gasping	"Disgust": Nose-scrunching	Neutral
			Trobrianders (n = 68)			
Happiness	**.58**	.08	.04	.08	.00	.23
Sadness	.04	**.46**	.04	.04	.23	.19
Anger	.20	.17	**.07**	.30	.20	.07
Fear	.08	.27	.04	**.31**	.27	.04
Disgust	.18	.11	.08	.29	**.25**	.11
			Spaniards (n = 113)			
Happiness	**1.00**	.00	.00	.00	.00	.00
Sadness	.00	**.98**	.00	.00	.00	.02
Anger	.00	.00	**.91**	.00	.09	.00
Fear	.00	.07	.00	**.93**	.00	.00
Disgust	.00	.02	.00	.15	**.83**	.00

The "emotional labels" down the left side of the chart are the pictures of people making different kinds of faces that Jarillo and Crivelli showed their subjects. The labels across the top are how the subjects identified those pictures. So 100 percent of the 113 Spanish schoolchildren identified the happiness face as a happiness face. But only 58 percent of the Trobrianders did, while 23 percent looked at a smiling face and called it "neutral." And happiness is the emotion where there is the most agreement between the Trobrianders and the Spanish children. On everything else, the Trobrianders' idea of what emotion looks like on the outside appears to be totally different from our own.

"I think the thing that surprised us the most is the fact that what we think of in western societies is a face of fear, of somebody who's scared, turns out to be recognized in the Trobriand Islands more as a threat," Crivelli said. To demonstrate, he mimed what is known as the gasping face: wide-open eyes, the face from Edvard Munch's famous painting, *The Scream*.

"In our culture, my face would be like, 'I'm scared; I'm scared of you.'" Crivelli went on. "In their culture, that…is the face of somebody who's trying to scare somebody else….It's the opposite [of what it means to us]."

The sensation of fear, for a Trobriand Islander, is not any different from the fear that you or I feel. They get the same sick feeling in the pit of their stomach. But for some reason they don't show it the same way we do.

Anger was just as bad. You would think—wouldn't you?—that everyone in the world would know what an angry face looks like. It's such a fundamental emotion.

This is anger, right?

The hard eyes. The tight mouth. But anger *baffled* the Trobrianders. Just look at the scores for the angry face. Twenty percent called it a happy face. Seventeen percent called it a sad face. Thirty percent called it a fearful face. Twenty percent thought it was a sign of disgust—and only seven percent identified it the way that nearly every Spanish schoolchild had. Crivelli said:

> They gave lots of different descriptors....They would just say, like, "They're frowning." Or they'd use one of these proverbs that say...it means his brow is dark, which obviously can translate as "He's frowning." They wouldn't infer that that means that this person is angry.

To make sure the Trobrianders weren't some kind of special case, Jarillo and Crivelli then traveled to Mozambique to study a group of isolated subsistence fishermen known as the Mwani. Once again, the results were dismal. The Mwani did marginally better than chance with the smiling faces, but they seemed baffled by sad faces and angry faces. Another group, led by Maria Gendron, traveled to the mountains of northwest Namibia to see whether the people there could accurately sort photographs into piles according to the emotional expression of the subject. They couldn't.

Even historians have now gotten into the act. If you could go into a time machine and show the ancient Greeks and Romans pictures of modern-day people grinning broadly, would they interpret that expression the same way we do? Probably not. As classicist Mary Beard writes in her book, *Laughter in Ancient Rome:*

This is not to say that Romans never curled up the edges of their mouths in a formation that would look to us much like a smile; of course they did. But such curling did not mean very much in the range of significant social and cultural gestures in Rome. Conversely, other gestures, which would mean little to us, were much more heavily freighted with significance.

If you staged a screening of that *Friends* episode for the Trobriand Islanders, they would see Ross confronting Chandler and think Chandler was angry and Ross was scared. They would get the scene completely wrong. And if you threw a *Friends* premiere in ancient Rome for Cicero and the emperor and a bunch of their friends, they would look at the extravagant grimaces and contortions on the faces of the actors and think: *What on earth?*

5.

OK. So what about *within* a culture? If we limit ourselves to the developed world—and forget about outliers and ancient Rome—do the rules of transparency now work? No, they don't.

Imagine the following scenario. You're led down a long, narrow hallway into a dark room. There you sit and listen to a recording of a Franz Kafka short story, followed by a memory test on what you've just heard. You finish the test and step back into the corridor. But while you were listening to Kafka, a team has been hard at work. The corridor was actually made of temporary partitions.

Now they've been moved to create a wide-open space. The room has bright-green walls. A single light bulb hangs from the ceiling, illuminating a bright red chair. And sitting in the chair is your best friend, looking solemn. You come out, thinking you're going to be heading down the same narrow hallway, and *BOOM*—a room where a room isn't supposed to be. And your friend, staring at you like a character in a horror film.

Would you be surprised? Of course you would. And what would your face look like? Well, you wouldn't look the same as a Trobriand Islander would in that situation, nor a citizen of ancient Rome. But within our culture, in this time and place, what surprise looks like is well established. There's a perfect example of it in that same *Friends* episode. Ross's roommate, Joey, rushes into Monica's apartment and discovers two of his best friends trying to kill each other, and his face tells you everything you need to know: AU 1 + 2 (eyebrows shooting up) plus AU 5 (eyes going wide) plus AU 25 + 26, which is your jaw dropping. You'd make the Joey face, right? Wrong.

Two German psychologists, Achim Schützwohl and Rainer Reisenzein, created this exact scenario and ran sixty people through it. On a scale of one to ten, those sixty rated their feelings of surprise, when they opened the door after their session with Kafka, at 8.14. They were stunned! And when asked, almost all of them were convinced that surprise was written all over their faces. But it wasn't. Schützwohl and Reisenzein had a video camera in the corner, and they used it to code everyone's expressions the same way Fugate had coded the *Friends* episode. In only *5 percent* of the cases did they find wide eyes, shooting eyebrows, and dropped jaws. In 17 percent of the cases they found two of those expressions. In the rest they found some combination of nothing, a little something, and things—such as knitted eyebrows—that you wouldn't necessarily associate with surprise at all.*

"The participants in all conditions grossly overestimated their surprise expressivity," Schützwohl wrote. Why? They "inferred their likely facial expressions to the surprising event from…folk-psychological beliefs about emotion-face associations." Folk psychology is the kind of crude psychology we glean from cultural sources such as sitcoms. But that is not the way things happen in real life. Transparency is a myth—an idea we've picked up from watching too much television and reading too many novels where the hero's "jaw dropped with astonishment" or "eyes went wide with surprise." Schützwohl went on: "The participants apparently reasoned that, since they felt surprised, and since surprise is associated with a characteristic facial display, they must have shown this display. In most cases, this inference was erroneous."

I don't think that this mistake—expecting what is happening on the outside to perfectly match what is going on inside—matters with our friends. Part of what it means to get to know someone is to come to understand how idiosyncratic their emotional expressions can be. My

---

* The 17 percent figure includes the three people (5 percent) who displayed all three expressions. Only seven people showed exactly two expressions. Also, although the vast majority of people believed they had expressed their surprise, one unusually self-aware person said he did not think his surprise had shown at all.

father was once in the shower in a vacation cottage that my parents had rented when he heard my mother scream. He came running to find a large young man with a knife to my mother's throat. What did he do? Keep in mind that this is a seventy-year-old man, naked and dripping wet. He pointed at the assailant and said in a loud, clear voice: "Get out NOW." And the man did.

On the inside, my father was terrified. The most precious thing in his life—his beloved wife of half a century—was being held at knifepoint. But I doubt very much that fear showed on his face. His eyes didn't go wide with terror, and his voice didn't jump an octave. If you knew my father, you would have seen him in other stressful situations, and you would have come to understand that the "frightened" face, for whatever reason, was simply not part of his repertoire. In crisis, he turned deadly calm. But if you *didn't* know him, what would you have thought? Would you have concluded that he was cold? Unfeeling? When we confront a stranger, we have to substitute an idea—a stereotype—for direct experience. And that stereotype is wrong all too often.

By the way, do you know how the Trobrianders show surprise? When Crivelli showed up, he had a little Apple iPod, and the islanders gathered around in admiration. "They were approaching me. I was showing them.... They were freaking out, but they were not doing it like, 'Gasp!'" He mimed a perfect AU 1 + 2 + 5. "No. They were doing this." He made a noise with his tongue against his palate. "They were going *click, click, click.*"

6.

This is the explanation for the second of the puzzles, in Chapter Two, about why computers do a much better job than judges at making bail decisions. The computer can't see the defendant. Judges can, and it seems logical that that extra bit of information ought to make them better decision-makers. Solomon, the New York State judge, could search the face of the person standing in front of him for evidence of mental illness—a glassy-eyed look, a troubled affect, aversion of the eyes. The defendant stands no farther than ten feet in front of him and Solomon has the chance to get a sense of the person he is evaluating. But all that extra information isn't actually useful. Surprised people don't necessarily look surprised. People who have emotional problems don't always look like they have emotional problems.

Some years ago there was a famous case in Texas in which a young man named Patrick Dale Walker put a gun to his ex-girlfriend's head—only to have the gun jam as he pulled the trigger. The judge in his case set bail at $1 million, then lowered it to $25,000 after Walker had spent four days in jail, on the grounds that this was long enough for him to "cool off." Walker, the judge explained later, had nothing on his record, "not even a traffic ticket." He was polite: "He was a real low-key, mild-mannered young man. The kid, from what I understand, is a real smart kid. He was valedictorian of his class. He graduated from college. This was supposedly his first girlfriend." Most important, according to the judge, Walker showed remorse.

The judge thought Walker was transparent. But what

does "showed remorse" mean? Did he put on a sad face, cast his eyes down, and lower his head, the way he had seen people show remorse on a thousand television shows? And why do we think that if someone puts on a sad face, casts their eyes down, and lowers their head, then some kind of sea change has taken place in their heart? Life is not *Friends.* Seeing Walker didn't help the judge. It hurt him. It allowed him to explain away the simple fact that Walker had put a gun to his girlfriend's head and failed to kill her only because the gun misfired. Four months later, while out on bail, Walker shot his girlfriend to death.

Team Mullainathan writes,

> Whatever these unobserved variables are that cause judges to deviate from the predictions—whether internal states, such as mood, or specific features of the case that are salient and over-weighted, such as the defendant's appearance—they are not a source of private information so much as a source of mis-prediction. The unobservables create noise, not signal.

Translation: The advantage that the judge has over the computer isn't actually an advantage.

Should we take the Mullainathan study to its logical conclusion? Should we hide the defendant from the judge? Maybe when a woman shows up in a courtroom wearing a niqab, the correct response isn't to dismiss her case—it's to require that everyone wear a veil. For that matter, it is also worth asking whether you should meet the babysitter in person before you hire her, or whether your employer did the right thing in scheduling a face-to-face interview before making you a job offer.

But of course we can't turn our backs on the personal encounter, can we? The world doesn't work if every meaningful transaction is rendered anonymous. I asked Judge Solomon that very question, and his answer is worth considering.

MG: What if you didn't see the defendant? Would it make any difference?

Solomon: Would I prefer that?

MG: Would you prefer that?

Solomon: There's a part of my brain that says I would prefer that, because then the hard decisions to put somebody in jail would feel less hard. But that's not right.... You have a human being being taken into custody by the state, and the state has to justify why it's taking liberty away from a human, right? But now I'll think of them as a widget.

The transparency problem ends up in the same place as the default-to-truth problem. Our strategies for dealing with strangers are deeply flawed, but they are also socially necessary. We need the criminal-justice system and the hiring process and the selection of babysitters to be human. But the requirement of humanity means that we have to tolerate an enormous amount of error. That is the paradox of talking to strangers. We need to talk to them. But we're terrible at it—and, as we'll see in the next two chapters, we're not always honest with one another about just how terrible at it we are.

Solomon: So while I guess there's a sliver of my brain that's saying, "Oh, yeah. Well, it'd be easier not to look," I have the person looking at me and me looking at them. Having their family in the audience waving to me during the defense argument, you know, and he has three family members back here. It should be.... You should know that you're impacting a person. It shouldn't be taken lightly.

CHAPTER SEVEN

A (Short) Explanation of the Amanda Knox Case

1.

On the night of November 1, 2007, Meredith Kercher was murdered by Rudy Guede. After a mountain of argumentation, speculation, and controversy, his guilt is a certainty. Guede was a shady character who had been hanging around the house in the Italian city of Perugia, where Kercher, a college student, was living during a year abroad. Guede had a criminal history. He admitted to being in Kercher's house the night of her murder—and could give only the most implausible reasons for why. The crime scene was covered in his DNA. After her body was discovered, he immediately fled Italy for Germany.

But Rudy Guede was not the exclusive focus of the police investigation—nor anything more than an afterthought in the tsunami of media attention that followed the discovery of Kercher's body. The focus was instead on Kercher's roommate. Her name was Amanda Knox. She came home one morning and found blood in the bathroom. She and her boyfriend, Raffaele Sollecito, called the police. The police came and found Kercher dead in her bedroom; within hours they added Knox and Sollecito to their list of suspects. The crime, the police believed, was a drug- and alcohol-fueled sex game gone awry, featuring Guede, Sollecito, and Knox. The three were arrested, charged, convicted, and sent to prison—with every step of the way chronicled obsessively by the tabloid press.

"A murder always gets people going. Bit of intrigue. Bit of mystery. A whodunit," British journalist Nick Pisa says in the documentary *Amanda Knox*—one of a vast library of books, academic essays, magazine articles, movies, and news shows spawned by the case. "And we have here this beautiful, picturesque hilltop town in the middle of Italy. It was a particularly gruesome murder. Throat slit, seminaked, blood everywhere. I mean, what more do you want in a story?"

Other signature crime stories, such as the O. J. Simpson and JonBenét Ramsey cases, are just as enthralling when you rediscover them five or ten years later. The Amanda Knox case is not. It is completely inexplicable in hindsight. There was never any physical evidence linking either Knox or her boyfriend to the crime. Nor was there ever a plausible explanation for why Knox—an immature, sheltered, middle-class girl from Seattle—would be interested in engaging in murderous sex games with a troubled drifter she barely knew. The police investigation against her was revealed as shockingly inept. The analysis of the DNA evidence supposedly linking her and Sollecito to the crime was completely botched. Her prosecutor was wildly irresponsible, obsessed with fantasies about elaborate sex crimes. Yet it took a ruling by the Italian Supreme Court, *eight* years after the crime, for Knox to be finally declared innocent. Even then, many otherwise intelligent, thoughtful people disagreed. When Knox was freed from prison, a large angry crowd gathered in the Perugia town square to protest her release. The Amanda Knox case makes no sense.

I could give you a point-by-point analysis of what was wrong with the investigation of Kercher's murder. It could easily be the length of this book. I could also refer you to some of the most comprehensive scholarly analyses of the investigation's legal shortcomings, such as Peter Gill's meticulous "Analysis and Implications of the Miscarriages of Justice of Amanda Knox and Raffaele Sollecito" in the July 2016 issue of the criminology journal *Forensic Science International,* which includes paragraphs like this:

> The amplified DNA product in sample B was also subjected to capillary gel electrophoresis. The electrophoretic graph showed peaks that were below the reporting threshold and allele imbalance at most loci. I counted only 6 alleles that were above the reporting threshold. The electrophoretic graph showed a partial DNA profile that was claimed to match Meredith Kercher. Consequently, sample B was borderline for interpretation.

But instead, let me give you the simplest and shortest of all possible Amanda Knox theories. Her case is about transparency. If you believe that the way a stranger looks and acts is a reliable clue to the way they feel—if you buy into the *Friends* fallacy—then you're going to make mistakes. Amanda Knox was one of those mistakes.

2.

Let's return, for a moment, to the theories of Tim Levine that I talked about in Chapter Three. Levine, as you will recall, set up a sting operation for college students. He gave them a trivia test to do. In the middle of it the instructor left the room, leaving the answers on her desk. Afterward, Levine interviewed the students and asked them point-blank whether they had cheated. Some lied. Some told the truth. Then he showed videos of those interviews to people and asked them if they could spot the students who were lying.

Social scientists have done versions of this kind of experiment for years. You have a "sender"—a subject—and a "judge," and you measure how accurate the judge is at spotting the sender's lies. What Levine discovered is what psychologists always find in these cases, which is that most of us aren't very good at lie detection. On average, judges correctly identify liars 54 percent of the time—just slightly better than chance. This is true no matter who does the judging. Students are terrible. FBI agents are terrible. CIA officers are terrible. Lawyers are terrible. There may be a handful of "super-detectors" who beat the odds. But if there are, they are rare. Why?

The first answer is the one we talked about in Chapter Three. We're truth-biased. For what turn out to be good reasons, we give people the benefit of the doubt and assume that the people we're talking to are being honest. But Levine wasn't satisfied with that explanation. The problem is clearly deeper than truth-default. In particular, he was struck by the finding that lies are most often detected only after the fact—weeks, months, sometimes years later.

For example, when Scott Carmichael said to Ana Montes during their first meeting, "Look, Ana. I have reason to suspect that you might be involved in a counterintelligence influence operation," she just sat there looking at him like a deer in the headlights. In retrospect, Carmichael believed that was a red flag. If she had been innocent, she would have said something—cried out, protested. But Montes? She "didn't do a freaking thing except sit there."

In the moment, however, Carmichael missed that clue. Montes was uncovered only by chance, four years later. What Levine found is that we nearly always miss the crucial clues in the moment—and it puzzled him. Why? What happens at the moment someone tells a lie that *specifically* derails us? To find an answer, Levine went back to his tapes.

Here is a snippet of another of the videos Levine showed me. It's of a young woman—let's call her Sally. Levine walked her through the straightforward questions without incident. Then came the crucial moment:

Interviewer: Now, did any cheating occur when Rachel left the room?
Sally: No.

Interviewer: Are you telling me the truth?
Sally: Yeah.
Interviewer: When I interview your partner, I'm going to ask her the same question. What is she going to say?

Sally pauses, looks uncertain.

Sally: Probably...the same answer.
Interviewer: Okay.

The moment Levine asks the question "Did any cheating occur?" Sally's arms and face begin to turn a bright red. Calling it an embarrassed blush doesn't quite do it justice. Sally gives a whole new meaning to the expression "caught red-handed." Then comes the critical question: What will your partner say? Blushing Sally can't even come up with a convincing "She'll agree with me." She hems and haws and says, weakly, "Probably...the same answer." *Probably?* Blushing Sally is lying, and *everyone* called in to judge the tape realizes she's lying.

Here's the next tape Levine showed me. It's of a woman who spent the entire interview obsessively playing with her hair. Let's call her Nervous Nelly.

Interviewer: Now, Rachel had to get called out of the room. Did any cheating occur when she was gone?
Nervous Nelly: Actually my partner did want to look at the scores, and I said no—was like, "I want to see how many we got right"—because I don't cheat. I think it's wrong, so I didn't. I told her no. I was like,

"I don't want to do that." But she did say, "Well, we'll just look at one." I was like, "No, I don't want to do that." I don't know if that was part of it or not, but no, we didn't do that.

Interviewer: OK, so are you telling me the truth about the cheating?

Nervous Nelly: Yeah, we didn't—she wanted…my partner honestly said, "We'll just look at one." I was like, "No, that's not cool, I don't want to do that." The only thing I said was, "I'm surprised they left all the money in here." I honestly don't steal or cheat, I'm a good person like that. I was just kind of surprised, because normally when people leave money behind, you are going to take it—that's just what everybody does. But no, we didn't cheat. We didn't steal anything.

The twirling of the hair never stops. Nor do the halting, overly defensive, repetitive explanations, nor the fidgeting and the low-level agitation.

Interviewer: OK, so when I call in your partner for an interview, what is she going to say to that question?

Nervous Nelly: I think she'll say that she wanted to look.

Interviewer: OK.

Nervous Nelly: If she says otherwise, then that's not cool at all, because I said, "No, I don't want to cheat at all." She just said, "Why not just look at one?" She said, "Well, the answers are right there," and I was like, "No, I'm not going to do that. That's not who I am. It's not what I do."

I was convinced Nervous Nelly was lying. You would conclude the same, if you saw her in action. *Everybody* thought Nervous Nelly was lying. But she wasn't! When her partner reported back to Levine, he confirmed everything Nervous Nelly said.

Levine found this pattern again and again. In one experiment, for instance, there was a group of interviewees whom 80 percent of the judges got wrong. And another group whom more than 80 percent got right.

So what's the explanation? Levine argues that this is the assumption of transparency in action. We tend to judge people's honesty based on their demeanor. Well-spoken, confident people with a firm handshake who are friendly and engaging are seen as believable. Nervous, shifty, stammering, uncomfortable people who give windy, convoluted explanations aren't. In a survey of attitudes toward deception conducted a few years ago, which involved thousands of people in fifty-eight countries around the world, 63 percent of those asked said the cue they most used to spot a liar was "gaze aversion." We think liars in real life behave like liars would on *Friends*—telegraphing their internal states with squirming and darting eyes.

This is—to put it mildly—nonsense. Liars don't look away. But Levine's point is that our stubborn belief in some set of nonverbal behaviors associated with deception explains the pattern he finds with his lying tapes. The people we all get right are the ones who *match*—whose level of truthfulness happens to correspond with the way they look. Blushing Sally matches. She acts like our stereotype of how a liar acts. *And* she also happens to be lying. That's why we all get her right. In the *Friends* episode, when Monica finally breaks the news to her brother Ross about her relationship, she takes Ross's hand and says, "I'm so sorry that you had to find out this way. I'm sorry. But it's true, I love him too." We believe her in that moment—that she is genuinely sorry and genuinely in love, because she's perfectly matched. She's being sincere and she looks sincere.

When a liar acts like an honest person, though, or when an honest person acts like a liar, we're flummoxed. Nervous Nelly is *mis*matched. She looks like she's lying, but she's not. She's just nervous! In other words, human beings are not bad lie detectors. We are bad lie detectors *in those situations when the person we're judging is mismatched.*

At one point in his pursuit of Bernie Madoff, Harry Markopolos approached a seasoned financial journalist named Michael Ocrant. Markopolos persuaded Ocrant to take Madoff seriously as a potential fraud, to the point that Ocrant made an appointment to interview Madoff in person. But what happened?

"It wasn't so much his answers that impressed me, but rather it was his entire demeanor," Ocrant said years later.

It was almost impossible to sit there with him and believe he was a complete fraud. I remember thinking to myself, *If [Markopolos's team] is right and he's running a Ponzi scheme, he's either the best actor I've ever seen or a total sociopath.* There wasn't even a hint of guilt or shame or remorse. He was very low-key, almost as if he found the interview amusing. His attitude was sort of "Who in their right mind could doubt me? I can't believe people care about this."

176

Madoff was mismatched. He was a liar with the demeanor of an honest man. And Ocrant—who knew, on an intellectual level, that something was not right—was so swayed by meeting Madoff that he dropped the story. Can you blame him? First there is default to truth, which gives the con artist a head start. But when you add mismatch to that, it's not hard to understand why Madoff fooled so many for so long.

And why did so many of the British politicians who met with Hitler misread him so badly? Because Hitler was mismatched as well. Remember Chamberlain's remark about how Hitler greeted him with a double-handed handshake, which Chamberlain believed Hitler reserved for people he liked and trusted? For many of us, a warm and enthusiastic handshake does mean that we feel warm and enthusiastic about the person we're meeting. But not Hitler. He's the dishonest person who acts honest.[*]

---

[*] Here's another example: Dzhokhar Tsarnaev, one of the two Chechen brothers who planted a series of deadly bombs at the Boston Marathon in 2013. The chief issue in Tsarnaev's trial was whether he would escape the death penalty. The prosecutor, Nadine Pellegrini, argued strongly that he shouldn't, because he felt no remorse for his actions. At one point Pellegrini showed the jury a photograph of Tsarnaev in his cell, giving the finger to the video camera in the corner. "He had one last message to send," she said, calling Tsarnaev "unconcerned, unrepentant, and unchanged." In *Slate* magazine, on the eve of the verdict, Seth Stevenson wrote:

> And though it's risky to read too deeply into slouches and tics, Tsarnaev certainly hasn't made much effort to appear chastened or regretful before the jury. The closed-circuit cameras that were broadcasting from the courtroom to the media room Tuesday were not high-resolution enough that I can 100 percent swear by this, but: I'm pretty sure that after Pellegrini showed that photo of him flipping the bird, Tsarnaev smirked.

Sure enough, Tsarnaev was found guilty and sentenced to death.

3.

So what was Amanda Knox's problem? She was mis-matched. She's the innocent person who acts guilty. She's Nervous Nelly.

Knox was—to those who did not know her—confusing. At the time of the crime she was twenty and beautiful, with high cheekbones and striking blue eyes. Her nickname was "Foxy Knoxy." The tabloids got hold of a list she had made of all the men she'd slept with. She was the femme fatale—brazen and sexual. The day after her roommate's brutal murder, she was spotted buying red underwear at a lingerie shop with her boyfriend.

In fact, the "Foxy Knoxy" nickname had nothing to do with sex. It was bestowed on her at age thirteen by soccer teammates for the deft way she moved the ball up and down

---

Afterward, ten members of the twelve-person jury said they believed he had felt no remorse.

But as psychologist Lisa Feldman Barrett points out, all of this discussion of whether Tsarnaev did or did not regret his actions is a perfect example of the pitfalls of transparency. The jury assumed that whatever Tsarnaev felt in his heart would be automatically posted on his face, in a way that matched American ideas about how emotions are supposed to be displayed. *But Tsarnaev wasn't American.* In her book *How Emotions Are Made,* Barrett writes:

> In the Boston Marathon Bombing case, if Tsarnaev felt remorse for his deeds, what would it have looked like? Would he have openly cried? Begged his victims for forgiveness? Expounded on the error of his ways? Perhaps, if he were following American stereotypes for expressing remorse, or if this were a trial in a Hollywood movie. But Tsarnaev is a young man of Muslim faith from Chechnya.... Chechen culture expects men to be stoic in the face of adversity. If they lose a battle, they should bravely accept defeat, a mindset known as the "Chechen wolf." So if Tsarnaev felt remorse, he might well have remained stony-faced.

the field. She was buying red underwear a few days after her roommate's murder because her house was a crime scene and she couldn't get access to her clothes. She wasn't a femme fatale.[*] She was an immature young woman only a few years removed from an awkward and pimply adolescence. Brazen and sexual? Amanda Knox was actually a bit of a misfit.

"I was the quirky kid who hung out with the sulky manga-readers, the ostracized gay kids, and the theater geeks," she writes in her memoir, published in 2011 after she was finally released from an Italian prison.

In high school she was the middle-class kid on financial aid, surrounded by well-heeled classmates. "I took Japanese and sang, loudly, in the halls while walking from one class to another. Since I didn't really fit in, I acted like myself, which pretty much made sure I never did."

Matched people conform with our expectations. Their intentions are consistent with their behavior. The mismatched are confusing and unpredictable: "I'd do things that would embarrass most teenagers and adults—walking down the street like an Egyptian or an elephant—but that kids found fall-over hilarious."

Kercher's murder changed the way Kercher's circle of friends behaved. They wept quietly, hushed their voices, murmured their sympathies. Knox didn't.

Just listen to a handful of quotations that I've taken—at random—from the British journalist John Follain's *Death*

---

[*] Knox's list of lovers wasn't what it seemed, either. In an effort to intimidate her, the Italian police lied to Knox and told her she was HIV positive. Knox, afraid and alone in her cell, wrote a list of her past sexual partners to work out how this could possibly be true.

in Perugia. Believe me, there are more like this. Here is Follain describing what happened when Kercher's friends met up with Knox and Sollecito at the police station the day after the murder.

> "Oh Amanda. I'm so sorry!" Sophie exclaimed, as she instinctively put her arms around her and gave her a bear hug.
>
> Amanda didn't hug Sophie back. Instead, she stiffened, holding her arms down by her sides. Amanda said nothing.
>
> Surprised, Sophie let go of her after a couple of seconds and stepped back. There was no trace of emotion on Amanda's face. Raffaele walked up to Amanda and took hold of her hand; the couple just stood there, ignoring Sophie and gazing at each other.

Then:

> Amanda sat with her feet resting on Raffaele's lap … the two caressed and kissed each other; sometimes they'd even laugh.
>
> *How could Amanda act like that?* Sophie asked herself. *Doesn't she care?*

Then:

> Most of Meredith's friends were in tears or looked devastated, but Amanda and Raffaele made smacking noises with their lips when they kissed or sent kisses to each other.

And then:

"Let's hope she didn't suffer," Natalie said.

"What do you think? They cut her throat, Natalie. She fucking bled to death!" Amanda retorted.

Amanda's words chilled Natalie; she was surprised both by Amanda talking of several killers, and by the coldness of her tone. Natalie thought it was as if Meredith's death didn't concern her.

In an interview with Knox, Diane Sawyer of ABC News brought up that last exchange in the police station, where Knox snapped at Kercher's friend and said, "She fucking bled to death."

Knox: Yeah. I was angry. I was pacing, thinking about what Meredith must have been through.
Sawyer: Sorry about that now?
Knox: I wish I could've been more mature about it, yeah.

In a situation that typically calls for a sympathetic response, Knox was loud and angry. The interview continues:

Sawyer: You can see that this does not look like grief. Does not read as grief.

The interview was conducted long after the miscarriage of justice in the Kercher case had become obvious. Knox had just been freed after spending four years in an Italian prison for the crime of not behaving the way we think people are supposed to behave after their roommate is murdered. Yet what does Diane Sawyer say to her? She scolds her for not behaving the way we think people are supposed to behave after their roommate is murdered.

In the introduction to the interview, the news anchor says that Knox's case remains controversial because, in part, "her pleas for innocence seemed to many people more cold and calculating than remorseful"—which is an even more bizarre thing to say, isn't it? Why would we expect Knox to be remorseful? We expect remorse from the guilty. Knox didn't do anything. But she's still being criticized for being "cold and calculating." At every turn, Knox cannot escape censure for her *weirdness*.

> **Knox:** I think everyone's reaction to something horrible is different.

She's right! Why can't someone be angry in response to a murder, rather than sad? If you were Amanda Knox's friend, none of this would surprise you. You would have seen Knox walking down the street like an elephant. But with strangers, we're intolerant of emotional responses that fall outside expectations.

While waiting to be interviewed by police, four days after Kercher's body was discovered, Knox decided to stretch. She'd been sitting, slumped, for hours. She touched her toes, held her arms over her head. The policeman on duty said to her, "You seem really flexible."

> I replied, "I used to do a lot of yoga." He said, "Can you show me? What else can you do?" I took

a few steps toward the elevator and did a split. It felt good to know I still could. While I was on the floor, legs splayed, the elevator doors opened. Rita Ficarra, the cop who had reprimanded Raffaele and me about kissing the day before, stepped out. "What are you doing?" she demanded, her voice full of contempt.*

The lead investigator in the case, Edgardo Giobbi, says he had doubts about Knox from the moment she walked with him through the crime scene. As she put on protective booties, she swiveled her hips and said, "Ta-dah."

"We were able to establish guilt," Giobbi said, "by closely observing the suspect's psychological and behavioral reaction during the interrogation. We don't need to rely on other kinds of investigation."

The prosecutor in the case, Giuliano Mignini, brushed off the mounting criticisms of the way his office had handled the murder. Why did people focus so much on the botched DNA analysis? "Every piece of proof has aspects of uncertainty," he said. The real issue was mismatched *Amanda.* "I have to remind you that her behavior

---

* There is an endless amount of this kind of thing. For the prosecutor in the case, the telling moment was when he took Knox into the kitchen to look at the knife drawer, to see if anything was missing. "She started hitting the palms of her hands on her ears. As if there was the memory of a noise, a sound, a scream. Meredith's scream. Undoubtedly, I started to suspect Amanda."

Or this: At dinner with Meredith's friends in a restaurant, Amanda suddenly burst into song. "But what drew laughs in Seattle got embarrassed looks in Perugia," she writes. "It hadn't dawned on me that the same quirks my friends at home found endearing could actually offend people who were less accepting of differences."

was completely inexplicable. Totally irrational. There's no doubt of this."*

From Bernard Madoff to Amanda Knox, we do not do well with the mismatched.

4.

The most disturbing of Tim Levine's findings was when he showed his lying videotapes to a group of seasoned law-enforcement agents—people with fifteen years or more of interrogation experience. He had previously used as his judges students and adults from ordinary walks of life. They didn't do well, but perhaps that's to be expected. If you are a real-estate agent or a philosophy major, identifying deception in an interrogation isn't necessarily something you do every day. But maybe, he thought, people whose job it was to do exactly the kind of thing he was measuring would be better.

In one respect, they were. On "matched" senders, the seasoned interrogators were perfect. You or I would probably come in at 70 or 75 percent on that set of tapes. But *every*one in Levine's group of highly experienced experts got *every* matched sender right. On mismatched senders,

---

* "What's compelling to me about Amanda Knox is that it was her slight offness that did her in, the everyday offness to be found on every schoolyard and in every workplace," the critic Tom Dibblee wrote in perceptive essays about the case. "This is the slight sort of offness that rouses muttered suspicion and gossip, the slight sort of offness that courses through our daily lives and governs who we choose to affiliate ourselves with and who we choose to distance ourselves from."

however, their performance was abysmal: they got 20 percent right. And on the subcategory of sincere-acting liars, they came in at 14 percent—a score so low that it ought to give chills to anyone who ever gets hauled into an interrogation room with an FBI agent. When they are confronted with Blushing Sally—the easy case—they are flawless. But when it comes to the Amanda Knoxes and Bernie Madoffs of the world, they are hapless.

This is distressing because we don't need law-enforcement experts to help us with matched strangers. We're all good at knowing when these kinds of people are misleading us or telling us the truth. We need help with mismatched strangers—the difficult cases. A trained interrogator ought to be adept at getting beneath the confusing signals of demeanor, at understanding that when Nervous Nelly overexplains and gets defensive, that's who she is— someone who overexplains and gets defensive. The police officer ought to be the person who sees the quirky, inappropriate girl in a culture far different from her own say "Ta-dah" and realize that she's just a quirky girl in a culture far different from her own. But that's not what we get. Instead, the people charged with making determinations of innocence and guilt seem to be as bad as *or even worse* than the rest of us when it comes to the hardest cases.

Is this part of the reason for wrongful convictions? Is the legal system constitutionally incapable of delivering justice to the mismatched? When a judge makes a bail decision and badly underperforms a computer, is this why? Are we sending perfectly harmless people to prison while they await trial simply because they don't look right? We all accept the flaws and inaccuracies of institutional judgment when we believe that those mistakes are random. But Tim Levine's research suggests that they aren't random—that we have built a world that systematically discriminates against a class of people who, through no fault of their own, violate our ridiculous ideas about transparency. The Amanda Knox story deserves to be retold not because it was a once-in-a-lifetime crime saga—a beautiful woman, a picturesque Italian hilltop town, a gruesome murder. It deserves retelling because it happens all the time.

"Her eyes didn't seem to show any sadness, and I remember wondering if she could have been involved," one of Meredith Kercher's friends said.

Amanda Knox heard *years* of this—perfect strangers pretending to know who she was based on the expression on her face.

"There is no trace of me in the room where Meredith was murdered," Knox says, at the end of the Amanda Knox documentary. "But you're trying to find the answer in my eyes.... You're looking at me. Why? These are my eyes. They're not objective evidence."

CHAPTER EIGHT

Case Study:
The Fraternity Party

1.

Prosecution: And at some point on your way over to Kappa Alpha house, did you observe anything unusual?

Jonsson: Yes.

P: What did you see?

Jonsson: We observed a man on top of a—or a person on top of another person, I should say.

P: And where was that?

Jonsson: Very close to the Kappa Alpha house.

Palo Alto, California. January 18, 2015. Sometime around midnight. Two Swedish graduate students are cycling across the campus of Stanford University on their way to a fraternity party. They see what looks like two people, lying on the ground, just outside a fraternity house where a party is full swing. They slow down so as not to disturb the couple. "We thought that it was their personal moment," one of the students, Peter Jonsson, would say when he testified in court. As they drew closer, they saw that the man was on top. And beneath the man was a young woman.

> **P:** What about the person on top? Did you see any movement or motion from that person?
>
> **Jonsson:** Yeah. So first, he was only moving a little bit. And then he started thrusting more intensely....
>
> **P:** And what could you see the person on the bottom doing?
>
> **Jonsson:** Nothing.

Jonsson and his friend, Carl-Fredrik Arndt, got off their bikes and walked closer. Jonsson called out, "Hey, is everything all right?" The man, on top, lifted his body and looked up. Jonsson came closer. The man stood up and began backing away.

Jonsson said, "Hey. What the fuck are you doing? She's unconscious." Jonsson said it a second time. "Hey. What the fuck are you doing?" The man began to run. Jonsson and his friend gave chase and tackled him.

The person Jonsson tackled was Brock Turner. He was nineteen, a freshman at Stanford and a member of the university's swim team. Less than an hour earlier, he had met a young woman at the Kappa Alpha party. Turner would later tell police that they had danced together, talked, gone outside, and lain down on the ground. The woman was a recent college graduate, known thereafter, under the protections of sexual-assault law, as Emily Doe. She had come to the party with a group of friends. Now she lay motionless under a pine tree, next to a dumpster. Her skirt was hiked up around her waist. Her underwear was on the ground next to her. The top of her dress was partially pulled down, revealing one of her breasts. When she came to in the hospital a few hours later that morning, a police officer told her she may have been sexually assaulted. She was confused. She got up, went to the bathroom, and found that her underwear was gone. It had been taken for evidence.

P: What happened after you used the bathroom?

Doe: I felt scratching on my neck and realized it was pine needles. And I thought that I may have fallen from a tree, because I didn't know why I was there.

P: Was there a mirror in the bathroom?

Doe: Yes.

P: Could you see your hair in the mirror?

Doe: Yes.

P: Can you describe what your hair—how your hair appeared?

Doe: Just disheveled and with little things poking out of it.

P: Do you have any idea how your hair ended up that way?

Doe: No idea.

P: What did you do after you finished using the restroom?

Doe: I went back to the bed. And they gave me a blanket, and I wrapped myself. And I went back to sleep.

2.

Every year, around the world, there are countless encounters just like the one that ended so terribly on the lawn outside the Kappa Alpha fraternity at Stanford University. Two young people who do not know each other well meet and have a conversation. It might be brief. Or go on for hours. They might go home together. Or things may end short of that. But at some point during the evening, things go badly awry. An estimated one in five American female college students say that they have been the victim of sexual assault. A good percentage of those cases follow this pattern.

The challenge in these kinds of cases is reconstructing the encounter. Did both parties consent? Did one party object, and the other party ignore that objection? Or misunderstand it? If the transparency assumption is a problem for police officers making sense of suspects, or judges trying to "read" defendants, it is clearly going to be an issue for teenagers and young adults navigating one of the most complex of human domains.

Take a look at the results of a 2015 *Washington Post*/Kaiser Family Foundation poll of one thousand college students. The students were asked whether they thought any of the following behaviors "establishes consent for *more* sexual activity."

1. Takes off their own clothes

	Yes	No	Depends	No opinion
All	47	49	3	1
Men	50	45	3	2
Women	44	52	3	1

2. Gets a condom

	Yes	No	Depends	No opinion
All	40	54	4	1
Men	43	51	4	2
Women	38	58	4	1

3. Nods in agreement

	Yes	No	Depends	No opinion
All	54	40	3	3
Men	58	36	3	3
Women	51	44	3	3

4. Engages in foreplay such as kissing or touching

	Yes	No	Depends	No opinion
All	22	74	3	*
Men	30	66	3	*
Women	15	82	3	*

5. Does not say "No"

	Yes	No	Depends	No opinion
All	18	77	3	1
Men	20	75	4	1
Women	16	80	2	1

Consent would be a straightforward matter if all college students agreed that getting a condom meant implicit consent to sex, or if everyone agreed that foreplay, such as kissing or touching, did *not* constitute an invitation to something more serious. When the rules are clear, each party can easily and accurately infer what the other wants from the way he or she behaves. But what the poll shows is that there are no rules. On every issue there are women who think one way and women who think another; men who think like some women but not others; and a perplexing number of people, of both sexes, who have no opinion at all.

29. For each of the following, please tell me if you think the situation IS sexual assault, IS NOT sexual assault, or is unclear.

Sexual activity when both people have not given clear agreement

	Is	Is not	Unclear	No opinion
All	47	6	46	*
Men	42	7	50	1
Women	52	6	42	–

What does it mean that half of all young men and women are "unclear" on whether clear agreement is necessary for sexual activity? Does it mean that they haven't thought about it before? Does it mean that they would rather proceed on a case-by-case basis? Does it mean they reserve the right to sometimes proceed without explicit consent, and at other times to insist on it? Amanda Knox confounded the legal system because there was a disconnect between the way she acted and the way she felt. But this is transparency failure on steroids. When one college student meets another—even in cases where both have the best of intentions—the task of inferring sexual intent from behavior is essentially a coin flip. As legal scholar Lori Shaw asks, "How can we expect students to respect boundaries when no consensus exists as to what they are?"

There is a second, complicating element in many of these encounters, however. When you read through the details of the campus sexual-assault cases that have become so depressingly common, the remarkable fact is how many involve an almost identical scenario. A young woman and a young man meet at a party, then proceed to tragically misunderstand each other's intentions—*and they're drunk.*

3.

D: What did you drink?
Turner: I had approximately five Rolling Rock beers.

Brock Turner began drinking well before he went to the Kappa Alpha party. He had been at his friend Peter's apartment earlier in the evening.

D: Other than the five Rolling Rock beers that you've mentioned, did you drink any other alcohol in Peter's room?

Turner: Yes. I had some Fireball Whiskey.

D: And how was that consumed?…

Turner: It was just out of the bottle.

When Turner got to the party, he kept drinking. In California the legal intoxication limit for drivers is a blood-alcohol concentration of .08; anything above that and you're considered drunk. By the end of the night Turner's blood-alcohol level was twice that.

Emily Doe arrived at the party in a group—with her sister and her friends Colleen and Trea. Earlier that evening, Trea had consumed an entire bottle of champagne, among other things. There they were joined by their friend Julia, who had also been drinking.

P: Did you have anything to drink at dinner?

Julia: Yes.

P: What did you drink?

Julia: A full bottle of wine.

And then:

P: What did you do after dinner?

Julia: After dinner [I] Ubered to a place called Griffin Suite.…

P: And what was going on there at Griffin Suite?

Julia: A pregame.

P: What's that?

Julia: Oh, sorry. It's a jargon. It's a pre-party that involves drinking.

After pregaming, Julia heads to the Kappa Alpha party, where she discovers an unopened bottle of vodka in the basement.

Julia: I opened it and we poured it into cups and took shots.

That leaves Emily Doe.

P: And so you started drinking with the shot of whiskey, and then how many—how many drinks did you have before you left your house?
Doe: Four.
P: And were they the same type of drink—a shot of whiskey—that you had the first time?
Doe: I had four shots of whiskey and one glass of champagne.
P: OK. So do you know approximately what time frame this was that you had the four shots of whiskey and one glass of champagne?
Doe: Probably between 10:00 and 10:45.

Then she and her friends go on to the party.

P: OK. And so after you guys kind of were goofing around, being the welcoming committee, what did you guys do?
Doe: Julia discovered a handle of vodka.

P: OK. And what is your description of a "handle of vodka"?

Doe: Probably, like, this big, Costco size…

P: And what happened when she presented the vodka?

Doe: I did a free pour into a red Solo cup.

P: OK. Were you measuring in any way how much vodka was in your cup?

Doe: I thought I was, but I was unsuccessfully measuring. I poured right below the second marking on the cup, which I thought was going to be two to three shots. It turned out to be maybe three to four shots, because that marking was five ounces.

P: And you're talking about a red Solo cup.

Doe: Yes.

P: Kind of something that you typically see at parties?

Doe: Yes…

P: OK. Now, when you were—after you poured the vodka, what did you do?

Doe: I drank it.

P: How did you drink it?

Doe: Just—for all.

P: Like, all at once?

Doe: Pretty much all at once. So I was already feeling drunk, because I was able to do that.

And then:

P: How—describe for us your level of intoxication at this point.

Doe: Umm, pretty much empty-minded. I become kind of just a dud, and I'm vacant, not articulating much. Just standing there.[*]

P: Do you have any idea what time this is in the night?

Doe: Maybe around midnight.

It was at that point that Brock Turner approached Emily Doe. He says she was dancing alone. He says he approached her and told her he liked the way she danced. He says she laughed. He says they chatted. He says he asked her to dance. He says she said yes. He says they danced for ten minutes. He says they started kissing.

D: OK. Did she appear to be responsive kissing you back?

Turner: Yes.

D: Did you have any further conversation with her that you remember?

Turner: Yes. I asked her if she wanted to go back to my dorm.

D: OK. And did she respond?

Turner: Yes.

D: What did she say?

Turner: She said, "Sure."

D: Approximately, this would have been after 12:30 then, right?

---

[*] At the time of the incident, her blood-alcohol concentration was .249. His BAC was .171. She was three times the legal limit. He was twice the legal limit. These BAC numbers are according to expert-witness testimony.

Turner: Yes.

D: Did you ever learn her name that night?

Turner: Yes. I asked her her name while we were dancing, but I didn't remember it.

He says he put his arm around her and the two of them
left the party. As they walked across the back lawn, he says
the two of them slipped.

Turner: She just lost her footing and kind of fell down.
And she grabbed onto me to try and prevent her fall
and that caused me to fall as well...

D: What happened then?

Turner: We laughed about it and I asked her if she
was OK.

D: Did she respond?

Turner: Yeah. She said she thought so.

D: What happened then?

Turner: We started kissing.

Normally, in a sexual-assault case, the prosecution
would present witnesses to raise questions about the
defendant's account. But that didn't happen in *People v.
Brock Turner.* By that point, Trea had become so drunk
that Emily's sister and her friend Colleen had taken her
back to Julia's dorm room. Turner's friend Peter never
made it to the party at all: he was too drunk, and
had to be taken back to his dorm by two of Turner's
other friends. Presumably there might have been other
people at the party who could corroborate or refute
Turner's story. But by this point it was after midnight,

the lights had been lowered, and people were dancing on the tables.

So we have only Turner's account:

D: What happened then?

Turner: We kissed for a little bit after that, and then I asked her if she wanted me to finger her.

D: Did she reply to you?

Turner: Yes.

D: What did she say?

Turner: She said yeah....

D: After you obtained her concurrence or permission to finger her, and you did finger her, what happened then?

Turner: I fingered her for a minute. And I thought she had an orgasm. And then I—well, during that time, I asked her if she liked it, and she said, "Uh huh."

And then:

D: And then after that, what did you do?

Turner: I started kissing with her again and then we started dry humping each other.

Under California law, someone is incapable of giving consent to sexual activity if they are either unconscious or so intoxicated that they are "prevented from resisting." Here is legal scholar Lori Shaw:

It is not enough that the victim was intoxicated to some degree, or that the intoxication reduced the

199

victim's sexual inhibitions....Instead, the level of intoxication and the resulting mental impairment must have been so great that the victim could no longer exercise reasonable judgment concerning that issue. As one California prosecutor explained, "the intoxicated victim must be so 'out of it' that she does not understand what she is doing or what is going on around her. It is not a situation where the victim just 'had too much to drink.'"

So was Doe a willing participant at the time of the sexual activity—and passed out afterward? Or was she *already* incapable of consent at the time Turner put his finger inside her? *People v. Brock Turner* is a case about *alcohol.* The entire case turned on the degree of Emily Doe's drunkenness.

In the end, the jury ruled against Turner. His version of events was simply unconvincing. If—as Turner suggests—they had a warm, consensual encounter, why did he run the moment he was challenged by the two grad students? Why was he "dry humping" her after she had passed out? Just after midnight, Doe left a voice mail for her boyfriend. The tape of that conversation was played for the jury. She's barely coherent. If the legal standard is "so 'out of it' that she does not understand what she is doing," then she sounded pretty close to that.

During the trial's closing arguments, the prosecutor showed the jury a picture of Doe, taken as she lay on the ground. Her clothes are half off. Her hair is disheveled. She's lying on a bed of pine needles. A dumpster is in the background. "No self-respecting woman who knows what's going on wants to get penetrated right there," the prosecutor said. "This photo alone can tell you that he took advantage of somebody who didn't know what was going on." Turner was convicted of three felony counts associated with the illegal use of his finger: assault with intent to commit rape of an intoxicated or unconscious person, sexual penetration of an intoxicated person, and sexual penetration of an unconscious person. He was sentenced to six months in prison and must register as a sex offender for the rest of his life.

The *who* of the Brock Turner case was never in doubt. The *what* was determined by the jury. But that still leaves the *why*. How did an apparently harmless encounter on a dance floor end in a crime? We know that our mistaken belief that people are transparent leads to all manner of problems between strangers. It leads us to confuse the innocent with the guilty and the guilty with the innocent. Under the best of circumstances, lack of transparency makes the encounter between a man and a woman at a party a problematic event. So what happens when alcohol is added to the mix?

4.

Dwight Heath was a graduate student in anthropology at Yale University in the mid-1950s when he decided to do the fieldwork for his dissertation in Bolivia. He and his wife, Anna Heath, flew to Lima with their baby boy, then waited five hours while mechanics put boosters on the plane's engines. "These were planes that the U.S. had dumped after

World War II," Heath recalls. "They weren't supposed to go above 10,000 feet. But La Paz, where we were headed, was at 12,000 feet." As they flew into the Andes, Anna Heath says, they looked down and saw the remnants of "all the planes where the boosters didn't work."

From La Paz they traveled 500 miles into the interior of eastern Bolivia, to a small frontier town called Montero. It was the part of Bolivia where the Amazon Basin meets the Chaco region—vast stretches of jungle and lush prairie. The area was inhabited by the Camba, a mestizo people descended from the indigenous Indian populations and Spanish settlers. The Camba spoke a language that was a mixture of the local Indian languages and seventeenth-century Andalusian Spanish. "It was an empty spot on the map," Heath says. "There was a railroad coming. There was a highway coming. There was a national government…coming."

They lived in a tiny house just outside of town. "There was no pavement, no sidewalks," Anna Heath recalls.

If there was meat in town, they'd throw out the hide in front, so you'd know where it was, and you would bring banana leaves in your hand, so it was your dish. There were adobe houses with stucco and tile roofs, and the town plaza, with three palm trees. You heard the rumble of oxcarts. The padres had a jeep. Some of the women would serve a big pot of rice and some sauce. That was the restaurant. The guy who did the coffee was German. The year we came to Bolivia, a total of eighty-five foreigners came into the country. It wasn't exactly a hot spot.

In Montero, the Heaths engaged in old-fashioned ethnography—"vacuuming up everything," Dwight says, "learning everything." They convinced the Camba that they weren't missionaries by openly smoking cigarettes. They took thousands of photographs. They walked around the town and talked to whomever they could, then Dwight went home and spent the night typing up his notes. After a year and a half, the Heaths packed up their photographs and notes and returned to New Haven. There, Dwight Heath sat down to write his dissertation—only to discover that he had nearly missed what was perhaps the most fascinating fact about the community he had been studying. "Do you realize," he told his wife as he looked over his notes, "that every weekend we were in Bolivia, we went out drinking?"

Every Saturday night the entire time they were there, the Heaths were invited to drinking parties. The host would buy the first bottle and issue the invitations. A dozen or so people would show up, and the party would proceed—often until everyone went back to work on Monday morning. The composition of the group was informal: sometimes people passing by would be invited. But the structure of the party was heavily ritualized. The group sat in a circle. Someone might play the drums or a guitar. A bottle of rum from one of the sugar refineries in the area and a small drinking glass were placed on a table. The host stood, filled the glass with rum, then walked toward someone in the circle. He stood before the "toastee," nodded, and raised the glass. The toastee smiled and nodded in return. The host then drank half the glass and handed it to the toastee, who finished it. The toastee eventually stood, refilled the glass, and repeated the ritual with someone else in the circle. When people got too tired or too drunk, they curled up on the ground and passed out, rejoining the party when they awoke.

"The alcohol they drank was awful," Anna recalled. "Literally, your eyes poured tears. The first time I had it, I thought, I wonder what will happen if I just vomit in the middle of the floor. Not even the Camba said they liked it. They say it tastes bad. It burns. The next day they are sweating this stuff. You can smell it." But the Heaths gamely persevered.

"The anthropology graduate student in the 1950s felt that he had to adapt," Dwight said. "You don't want to offend anyone, you don't want to decline anything. I gritted my teeth and accepted those drinks."

"We didn't get drunk that much," Anna went on, "because we didn't get toasted as much as the other folks around. We were strangers. But one night there was this really big party—sixty to eighty people. They'd drink. Then pass out. Then wake up and party for a while. And I found, in their drinking patterns, that I could turn my drink over to Dwight. The husband is obliged to drink for his wife. And Dwight is holding a Coleman lantern with his arm wrapped around it, and I said, 'Dwight, you are burning your arm.'" She mimed her husband peeling his forearm off the hot surface of the lantern. "And he said— very deliberately—'So I am.'"

When the Heaths came back to New Haven, they had a bottle of the Camba's rum analyzed and learned that it was 180 proof. It was *laboratory* alcohol—the concentration that scientists use to preserve tissue. No one drinks laboratory alcohol. This was the first of the astonishing findings of the Heaths' research—and, predictably, no one believed it at first.

"One of the world's leading physiologists of alcohol was at the Yale center," Heath recalled. "His name was Leon Greenberg. He said to me, 'Hey, you spin a good yarn. But you couldn't really have drunk that stuff.' And he needled me just enough that he knew he would get a response. So I said, 'You want me to drink it? I have a bottle.' So one Saturday I drank some under controlled conditions. He was taking blood samples every twenty minutes, and, sure enough, I did drink it, the way I said I'd drunk it."

Greenberg had an ambulance ready to take Heath home. But Heath decided to walk. Anna was waiting up for him in the third-floor walkup they rented in an old fraternity house. "I was hanging out the window waiting for him, and there's the ambulance driving along the street, very slowly, and next to it is Dwight. He waves, and he looks fine. Then he walks up the three flights of stairs and says, 'Ahh, I'm drunk,' and falls flat on his face. He was out for three hours."

Here we have a community of people, in a poor and undeveloped part of the world, who hold drinking parties with 180-proof alcohol *every weekend*, from Saturday night until Monday morning. The Camba must have paid dearly for their excesses, right? Wrong.

"There was no social pathology—none," Dwight Heath said. "No arguments, no disputes, no sexual aggression, no verbal aggression. There was pleasant conversation or silence." He went on: "The drinking didn't interfere with work....It didn't bring in the police. And there was no alcoholism either."

Heath wrote up his findings in a now-famous article for the *Quarterly Journal of Studies on Alcohol.* In the years that followed, countless other anthropologists chimed in to report the same thing. Alcohol sometimes led people to raise their voices and fight and say things they would otherwise regret. But a lot of other times, it didn't. The Aztec called pulque—the traditional alcoholic beverage of central Mexico—"four hundred rabbits" because of the seemingly infinite variety of behaviors it could create. Anthropologist Mac Marshall traveled to the South Pacific island of Truk and found that, for young men there, drunkenness created aggression and mayhem. But when the islanders reached their mid-thirties, it had the opposite effect.

In Oaxaca, Mexico, the Mixe Indians were known to engage in wild fistfights when drunk. But when anthropologist Ralph Beals started watching the fights, they didn't seem out of control at all. They seemed as though they all followed the same script:

Although I probably saw several hundred fights, I saw no weapon used, although nearly all men carried machetes and many carried rifles. Most fights start with a drunken quarrel. When the pitch of voices reaches a certain point, everyone expects a fight. The men hold out their weapons to the onlookers, and then begin to fight with their fists, swinging wildly until one falls down, [at which point] the victor helps his opponent to his feet and usually they embrace each other.

None of this makes sense. Alcohol is a powerful drug. It *disinhibits*. It breaks down the set of constraints that hold our behavior in check. That's why it doesn't seem surprising that drunkenness is so overwhelmingly linked with violence, car accidents, and sexual assault.

But if the Camba's drinking bouts had so few social side effects, and if the Mixe Indians of Mexico seem to be following a script even during their drunken brawls, then our perception of alcohol as a disinhibiting agent can't be right. It must be something else. Dwight and Anna Heath's experience in Bolivia set in motion a complete rethinking of our understanding of intoxication. Many of those who study alcohol no longer consider it an agent of disinhibition. They think of it as an agent of myopia.

5.

The myopia theory was first suggested by psychologists Claude Steele and Robert Josephs, and what they meant by *myopia* is that alcohol's principal effect is to narrow our emotional and mental fields of vision. It creates, in their words, "a state of shortsightedness in which superficially understood, immediate aspects of experience have a disproportionate influence on behavior and emotion." Alcohol makes the thing in the foreground even more salient and the thing in the background less significant. It makes short-term considerations loom large, and more cognitively demanding, longer-term considerations fade away.

Here's an example. Lots of people drink when they are feeling down because they think it will chase their troubles away. That's inhibition-thinking: alcohol will unlock my good mood. But that's plainly not what happens. *Sometimes* alcohol cheers us up. But at other times, when an anxious person drinks they just get more anxious. Myopia theory has an answer to that puzzle: it depends on what the anxious, drunk person is doing. If he's at a football game surrounded by rabid fans, the excitement and drama going on around him will temporarily crowd out his pressing worldly concerns. The game is front and center. His worries are not. But if the same man is in a quiet corner of a bar, drinking alone, he will get more depressed. Now there's nothing to distract him. Drinking puts you at the mercy of your environment. It crowds out everything except the most immediate experiences.*

Here's another example. One of the central observations of myopia theory is that drunkenness has its greatest effect in situations of "high conflict"—where there are two sets

---

* A group of Canadian psychologists led by Tara MacDonald recently went into a series of bars and asked the patrons to read a short vignette. They were to imagine that they had met an attractive person at a bar, walked him or her home, and ended up in bed—only to discover that neither of them had a condom. The subjects were then asked to respond on a scale of 1 (very unlikely) to 9 (very likely) to the proposition: "If I were in this situation, I would have sex." You'd think that the subjects who had been drinking heavily would be more likely to say they would have sex—and that's exactly what happened. The drunk people came in at 5.36, on average, on the 9-point scale. The sober people came in at 3.91. The drinkers couldn't sort through the long-term consequences of unprotected sex. But then MacDonald went back to the bars and stamped the hands of some of the patrons with the phrase "AIDS kills." Drinkers with the hand stamp were slightly *less likely than the sober people* to want to have sex in that situation: they couldn't sort through the rationalizations necessary to set aside the risk of AIDS. Where norms and standards are clear and obvious, the drinker can become more rule-bound than his sober counterpart.

of considerations, one near and one far, that are in oppo-sition. So, suppose that you are a successful professional comedian. The world thinks you are very funny. You think you are very funny. If you get drunk, you don't think of yourself as even funnier. There's no conflict over your hilariousness that alcohol can resolve. But suppose you think you are very funny and the world generally doesn't. In fact, whenever you try to entertain a group with a funny story, a friend pulls you aside the next morning and gently discourages you from ever doing it again. Under normal circumstances, the thought of that awkward conversation with your friend keeps you in check. But when you're drunk? The alcohol makes the conflict go away. You no longer think about the future corrective feedback regard-ing your bad jokes. Now it is possible for you to believe that you are actually funny. When you are drunk, *your understanding of your true self changes.*

This is the crucial implication of drunkenness as myopia. The old disinhibition idea implied that what was revealed when someone got drunk was a kind of stripped-down, distilled version of their sober self—without any of the muddying effects of social nicety and propriety. You got the real you. As the ancient saying goes, *In vino veritas:* "In wine there is truth."

But that's backward. The kinds of conflicts that normally keep our impulses in check are a crucial part of how we form our character. All of us construct our personality by managing the conflict between immediate, near consider-ations and more complicated, longer-term considerations. That is what it means to be ethical or productive or responsible. The good parent is someone who is willing to temper their own immediate selfish needs (to be left alone, to be allowed to sleep) with longer-term goals (to raise a good child). When alcohol peels away those longer-term constraints on our behavior, it obliterates our true self.

So who were the Camba, in reality? Heath says their society was marked by a singular lack of "communal expression." They were itinerant farmworkers. Kinship ties were weak. Their daily labor tended to be solitary, the hours long. There were few neighborhood or civic groups. The daily demands of their lives made socializing difficult. So on the weekends, they used the transformative power of alcohol to create the "communal expression" so sorely lacking from Monday to Friday. They used the myopia of alcohol to temporarily create a different world for themselves. They gave themselves strict rules: one bottle at a time, an organized series of toasts, all seated around the circle, only on the weekends, never alone. They drank only within a structure, and the structure of those drinking circles in the Bolivian interior was a world of soft music and quiet conversation: order, friendship, predictability, and ritual. This was a new Camba society, manufactured with the assistance of one of the most powerful drugs on earth.

Alcohol isn't an agent of revelation. It is an agent of transformation.

6.

In 2006, England had its own version of the Brock Turner trial, a high-profile case involving a twenty-five-year-old software designer named Benjamin Bree and a woman

210

identified by the court only as "M." It is a textbook example of the complications created by alcohol myopia.

The two met for the first time at Bree's brother's apartment and went out that same night. Over the course of the evening, M had two pints of cider and between four and six drinks of vodka mixed with Red Bull. Bree, who had been drinking earlier in the day, matched her round for round. Footage from closed-circuit cameras showed the two of them walking back to her apartment, arm in arm, around one in the morning. They had sex. Bree thought it was consensual. M said it wasn't. He was convicted of rape and sentenced to five years in prison—only to have the verdict thrown out on appeal. If you have read any other accounts of these kinds of cases, the details will be depressingly familiar: pain, regret, misunderstanding, and anger.

Here is Bree, describing his side of the story.

I was hoping to avoid sleeping on the floor and thought that maybe I could share her bed, which in hindsight seems such a stupid thing to do.

I wasn't looking for sex, just a mattress and some human company. She woke up and I lay down next to her and eventually we started hugging, and then kissing.

It was a bit unexpected, but nice. We were indulging in foreplay for about thirty minutes and it sounded like she was enjoying it.

And then, from the court's decision:

He insisted that M appeared to welcome his advances, which progressed from stroking of a comforting nature to sexual touching. She said and did nothing to stop him. He told the jury that one needed to be sure about consent which is why he stroked her for so long. The complainant could not gainsay that this foreplay lasted for some time. Eventually he put the top of his fingers inside the waistband of her pyjama trousers, which would have given her an opportunity to discourage him. She did not. She seemed particularly responsive when he put his hand inside her pyjama trousers. After sexual touching, he motioned for her to remove her pyjama trousers. He pulled them down slightly, then she removed them altogether.

Bree thought he could infer M's inner state from her behavior. He assumed she was transparent. She wasn't. Here, from the court's filings, is how M was actually feeling:

She had no idea how long intercourse lasted. When it ended she was still facing the wall. She did not know whether the appellant had in fact used a condom or not, nor whether he ejaculated or not. Afterwards he asked if she wanted him to stay. She said "no." In her mind she thought "get out of my room," although she did not actually say it. She didn't know "what to say or think, whether he would turn and beat me. I remember him leaving, the door shutting." She got up and locked the door and then returned to lie on her bed curled up in a ball, but she could not remember for how long.

At 5 a.m., M called her best friend, in tears. Bree, meanwhile, was still so oblivious to her inner state that he knocked on M's door a few hours later and asked M if she wanted to go and get fish and chips for lunch.

After several months in prison, Bree was freed when an appeals court concluded that it was impossible to figure out what the two of them did or did not consent to in M's bedroom that night. "Both were adults," the judge wrote:

> Neither acted unlawfully in drinking to excess. They were both free to choose how much to drink, and with whom. Both were free, if they wished, to have intercourse with each other. There is nothing abnormal, surprising, or even unusual about men and women having consensual intercourse when one, or the other, or both have voluntarily consumed a great deal of alcohol....The practical reality is that there are some areas of human behaviour which are inapt for detailed legislative structures.*

---

* Is drunken consent still consent? It has to be, the ruling goes on. Otherwise the vast majority of people happily having sex while drunk belong in jail alongside the small number of people for whom having sex while drunk constituted a criminal act. Besides, if M can say that she was not responsible for her decisions because she was drunk, why couldn't Benjamin Bree say the same thing? The principle that "drunken consent is still consent," the ruling points out, "also acts as a reminder that a drunken man who intends to commit rape, and does so, is not excused by the fact that his intention is a drunken intention." Then the Bree ruling comes to the question taken up by California's consent. What if one of the parties is *really* drunk? Well, how on earth can we decide what "*really* drunk" means? We don't really want our lawmakers to create some kind of elaborate, multivariable algorithm governing when we can or can't have sex in the privacy of our bedrooms. The judge concludes: "The problems do not arise from the legal principles. They lie with infinite circumstances of human behavior, usually taking place in private without independent evidence, and the consequent difficulties of proving this very serious offence."

You may or may not agree with that final ruling. But it is hard to disagree with the judge's fundamental complaint—that adding alcohol to the process of understanding another's intentions makes a hard problem downright impossible. Alcohol is a drug that reshapes the drinker according to the contours of his immediate environment. In the case of the Camba, that reshaping of personality and behavior was benign. Their immediate environment was carefully and deliberately constructed: they wanted to use alcohol to create a temporary—and, in their minds, better—version of themselves. But when young people today drink to excess, they aren't doing so in a ritualized, predictable environment carefully constructed to create a better version of themselves. They're doing so in the hypersexualized chaos of fraternity parties and bars.

Defense: What was your observation that you've made of the kind of atmosphere that existed at parties at Kappa Alpha before?

Turner: A lot of grinding and—

D: What do you mean by grinding?

Turner: Girls dancing...facing away from a guy, and the guy behind them dancing with them.

D: All right. So you're describing a position where—are you both facing in the same direction?

Turner: Yes.

D: But the boy's behind the girl?

Turner: Yes.

D: And how close are their bodies during this grinding dancing?

Turner: They're touching.

214

D: Is that common at these parties that you noticed?

Turner: Yes.

D: Did people dance on tables? Was that a common thing, too?

Turner: Yes.

Consent is something that two parties negotiate, on the assumption that each side in a negotiation is who they say they are. But how can you determine consent when, at the moment of negotiation, both parties are so far from their true selves?

7.

What happens to us when we get drunk is a function of the particular path the alcohol takes as it seeps through our brain tissue. The effects begin in the frontal lobes, the part of our brain behind our forehead that governs attention, motivation, planning, and learning. The first drink "dampens" activity in that region. It makes us a little dumber, less capable of handling competing complicated considerations. It hits the reward centers of the brain, the areas that govern euphoria, and gives them a little jolt. It finds its way into the amygdala. The amygdala's job is to tell us how to react to the world around us. Are we being threatened? Should we be afraid? Alcohol turns the amygdala down a notch. The combination of those three effects is where myopia comes from. We don't have the brainpower to handle more complex, long-term considerations. We're distracted by the unexpected pleasure of the alcohol. Our neurological burglar alarm is turned off. We become altered versions of ourselves, beholden to the moment. Alcohol also finds its way to your cerebellum, at the very back of the brain, which is involved in balance and coordination. That's why you start to stumble and stagger when intoxicated. These are the predictable effects of getting drunk.

But under certain very particular circumstances—especially if you drink a lot of alcohol very quickly—something else happens. Alcohol hits the hippocampus—small, sausage-like regions on each side of the brain that are responsible for forming memories about our lives. At a blood-alcohol level of roughly 0.08—the legal level of intoxication—the hippocampus starts to struggle. When you wake up the morning after a cocktail party and remember meeting someone but cannot for the life of you remember their name or the story they told you, that's because the two shots of whiskey you drank in quick succession reached your hippocampus. Drink a little more and the gaps get larger—to the point where maybe you remember pieces of the evening but other details can be summoned only with the greatest difficulty.

Aaron White, at the National Institutes of Health outside Washington, DC, is one of the world's leading experts on blackouts, and he says that there is no particular logic to which bits get remembered and which don't. "Emotional salience doesn't seem to have an impact on the likelihood that your hippocampus records something," he says. "What that means is you might, as a female, go to a party and you might remember having a drink downstairs, but you don't remember getting raped. But then you do remember getting in the taxi." At the next level—roughly around a blood-alcohol level of 0.15—the hippocampus simply shuts down entirely.

"In the true, pure blackout," White said, "there's just nothing. Nothing to recall."

In one of the earliest studies of blackouts, an alcohol researcher named Donald Goodwin gathered ten men from an unemployment line in St. Louis, gave them each the better part of a bottle of bourbon over a four-hour period, then had them perform a series of memory tests. Goodwin writes:

One such event was to show the person a frying pan with a lid on it, suggest that he might be hungry, take off the lid, and there in the pan are three dead mice. It can be said with confidence that sober individuals will remember this experience, probably for the rest of their lives.

But the bourbon drinkers? Nothing. Not thirty minutes later, and not the next morning. The three dead mice never got recorded at all.

In a blackout state—in that window of extreme drunkenness before their hippocampus comes back online—drunks are like ciphers, moving through the world without retaining anything.

Goodwin once began an essay on blackouts with the following story:

A thirty-nine-year-old salesman awoke in a strange hotel room. He had a mild hangover but otherwise felt normal. His clothes were hanging in the closet; he was clean-shaven. He dressed and went down to the lobby. He learned from the clerk that he was in Las Vegas and that he had checked in two days previously. It had been obvious that he had been drinking, the clerk said, but he had not seemed very drunk. The date was Saturday the 14th. His last recollection was of sitting in a St. Louis bar on Monday the 9th. He had been drinking all day and was drunk, but could remember every-thing perfectly until about 3 p.m., when "like a curtain dropping," his memory went blank. It remained blank for approximately five days. Three years later, it was still blank. He was so frightened by the experience that he abstained from alcohol for two years.

The salesman had left the bar in St. Louis, gone to the airport, bought a plane ticket, flown to Las Vegas, found a hotel, checked in, hung up his suit, shaved, and apparently functioned perfectly well in the world, all while in black-out mode. That's the way blackouts work. At or around the 0.15 mark, the hippocampus shuts down and memories stop forming, but it is entirely possible that the frontal lobes, cerebellum, and amygdala of that same drinker—at the same time—can continue to function more or less normally.

"You can do anything in a blackout that you can do when you're drunk," White said.

You're just not going to remember it. That could be ordering stuff on Amazon. People tell me this all the time….People can do very complicated things. Buy tickets, travel, all kinds of things, and not remember.

It follows that it's really hard to tell, just by looking at someone, whether they've blacked out. It's like trying to figure out if someone has a headache exclusively from the expression on their face. "I might look a little drunk, I might look wasted, but I can talk to you," White said.

> I can have a conversation with you. I can go get us drinks. I can do things that require short-term storage of information. I can talk to you about our growing up together.... Even wives of hardcore alcoholics say they can't really tell when their spouse is or is not in a blackout.[*]

When Goodwin was doing his pioneering work in the 1960s, he assumed that only alcoholics got blackout drunk. Blackouts were rare. Scientists wrote about them in medical journals the way they would about a previously unknown disease. Take a look at the results of one of the

---

[*] It is also, by the way, surprisingly hard to tell if someone is just plain drunk. An obvious test case is police sobriety checkpoints. An officer stops a number of people on a busy road late on a Friday night, talks to each driver, looks around each car—and then gives a Breathalyzer to anyone they think is drunk enough to be over the legal limit. Figuring out who seems drunk enough to qualify for a Breathalyzer turns out to be *really* hard. The best evidence is that well over half of drunk drivers sail through sobriety checkpoints with flying colors. In one study in Orange County, California, over 1,000 drivers were diverted to a parking lot late one night. They were asked to fill out a questionnaire about their evening, then interrogated by graduate students trained in intoxication detection. How did the driver talk? Walk? Was there alcohol on their breath? Were there bottles or beer cans in their car? After the interviewers made their diagnoses, the drivers were given a blood-alcohol test. Here's how many drunk drivers were correctly identified by the interviewers: 20 percent.

first comprehensive surveys of college drinking habits. It was conducted in the late 1940s and early 1950s, at twenty-seven colleges around the United States. Students were asked how much they drank, on average, "at a sitting." (For the purposes of the question, drinking amounts were divided into three groups. "Smaller" meant no more than two glasses of wine, two bottles of beer, or two mixed drinks. "Medium" was from three to five beers or glasses of wine, or three to four mixed drinks. And "Larger" was anything above that.)

	Beer	
	Male (%)	Female (%)
Smaller	46	73
Medium	45	26
Larger	9	1

	Wine	
	Male (%)	Female (%)
Smaller	79	89
Medium	17	11
Larger	4	0

	Spirits	
	Male (%)	Female (%)
Smaller	40	60
Medium	31	33
Larger	29	7

At these consumption levels, very few people are drinking enough to reach blackout.

Today, two things about that chart have changed. First, the heavy drinkers of today drink far more than the heavy drinkers of fifty years ago. "When you talk to students [today] about four drinks or five drinks, they just sort of go, 'Pft, that's just getting started,'" reports alcohol researcher Kim Fromme. She says the heavy binge-drinking category now routinely includes people who have had *twenty* drinks in a sitting. Blackouts, once rare, have become common. Aaron White recently surveyed more than 700 students at Duke University. Of the drinkers in the group, over half had suffered a blackout at some point in their lives, 40 percent had had a blackout in the previous year, and almost one in ten had had a blackout in the previous two weeks.*

Second, the consumption gap between men and women, so pronounced a generation ago, has narrowed

---

* In a remarkable essay in the *New York Times*, Ashton Katherine Carrick, a student at the University of North Carolina, describes a drinking game called "cuff and chug." Two people are handcuffed together until they can down a fifth of liquor. She writes, "For the supercompetitive, Sharpie pens were used to tally the number of drinks on your arm, establishing a ratio of drinks to the time it takes to black out—a high ratio was a source of pride among the guys." She continues:

The way we as students treat the blacking out of our peers is also partly responsible for its ubiquity. We actually think it's funny. We joke the next day about how ridiculous our friends looked passed out on the bathroom floor or Snapchatting while dancing and making out with some random guy, thus validating their actions and encouraging them to do it again. Blacking out has become so normal that even if you don't personally do it, you understand why others do. It's a mutually recognized method of stress relief. To treat it as anything else would be judgmental.

considerably—particularly among white women. (The same trends aren't nearly as marked among Asians, Hispanics, or African Americans.)

"I think it's an empowerment issue," Fromme argues:

> I do a lot of consulting work in the military, and it's easier for me to see it there because in the military the women are really put to the same standards as men in terms of their physical boot camps and training and all of that. They have worked very hard to try to say, "We're like the men and therefore we can drink like the men."

For physiological reasons, this trend has put women at greatly increased risk for blackouts. If an American male of average weight has eight drinks over four hours—which would make him a moderate drinker at a typical frat party—he would end up with a blood-alcohol reading of 0.107. That's too drunk to drive, but well below the 0.15 level typically associated with blackouts. If a woman of average weight has eight drinks over four hours, by contrast, she's at a blood-alcohol level of 0.173. She's blacked out.[*]

It gets worse. Women are also increasingly drinking wine and spirits, which raise blood-alcohol levels much faster than beer. "Women are also more likely to skip meals when they drink than men," White says.

---

[*] Nor is it just a matter of weight. There are also meaningful differences in the way the sexes metabolize alcohol. Women have much less water in their bodies than men, with the result that alcohol enters their bloodstream much more quickly. If a 195.7-pound female matches a 195.7-pound male drink for drink over four hours, he'll be at 0.107. She'll be at 0.140.

Having a meal in your stomach when you drink reduces your peak BAC [blood-alcohol concentration] by about a third. In other words, if you drink on an empty stomach you're going to reach a much higher BAC and you're going to do it much more quickly, and if you're drinking spirits and wine while you're drinking on an empty stomach, again higher BAC much more quickly. And if you're a woman, less body water [yields] higher BAC much more quickly.

And what is the consequence of being blacked out? It means that women are put in a position of vulnerability. Our memory, in any interaction with a stranger, is our first line of defense. We talk to someone at a party for half an hour and weigh what we learned. We use our memory to make sense of who the other person is. We collect things they've told us, and done, and those shape our response. That is not an error-free exercise in the best of times. But it is a necessary exercise, particularly if the issue at hand is whether you are going to go home with the person. Yet if you can't remember anything you've just learned, you are necessarily not making the same-quality decision you would have if your hippocampus were still working. You have ceded control of the situation.

"Let's be totally clear: Perpetrators are the ones responsible for committing their crimes, and they should be brought to justice," critic Emily Yoffe writes in *Slate:*

But we are failing to let women know that when they render themselves defenseless, terrible things can be done to them. Young women are getting a distorted message that their right to match men drink for drink is a feminist issue. The real feminist message should be that when you lose the ability to be responsible for yourself, you drastically increase the chances that you will attract the kinds of people who, shall we say, don't have your best interest at heart. That's not blaming the victim; that's trying to prevent more victims.

And what of the stranger talking to you? He may not know you are blacked out. Maybe he leans in and tries to touch you, and you stiffen. Then ten minutes later he circles back, a little more artfully. Normally you would stiffen again, because you would recognize the stranger's pattern. But you don't this second time, because you don't remember the first time. And the fact that you don't stiffen in quite the same way makes the stranger think, under the assumption of transparency, that you are welcoming his advances. Normally he would be cautious in acting on that assumption: friendliness is not the same thing as an invitation to intimacy. But he's drunk too. He's in the grip of alcohol myopia, and the kind of longer-term considerations that might otherwise constrain his behavior (what happens to me tomorrow if I have misread this situation?) have faded from view.

Does alcohol turn every man into a monster? Of course not. Myopia resolves high conflict: it removes the higher-order constraints on our behavior. The reserved man, normally too shy to profess his feelings, might blurt out some intimacy. The unfunny man, normally aware that the world does not find his jokes funny, might start playing comedian. Those are harmless. But what of the sexually aggressive teenager—whose impulses are normally kept in check by an understanding of how inappropriate those behaviors are? A version of the same admonition that Emily Yoffe gave to women can also be given to men:

> But we are failing to let men know that when they render themselves myopic, they can do terrible things. Young men are getting a distorted message that drinking to excess is a harmless social exercise. The real message should be that when you lose the ability to be responsible for yourself, you drastically increase the chances that you will commit a sexual crime. Acknowledging the role of alcohol is not excusing the behavior of perpetrators. It's trying to prevent more young men from becoming perpetrators.

It is striking how underappreciated the power of myopia is. In the *Washington Post*/Kaiser Family Foundation study, students were asked to list the measures they thought would be most effective in reducing sexual assault. At the top of that list they put harsher punishment for aggressors, self-defense training for victims, and teaching men to respect women more. How many thought it would be "very effective" if they drank less? Thirty-three percent. How many thought stronger restrictions on alcohol on campus would be very effective? Fifteen percent.*

These are contradictory positions. Students think it is a good idea to be trained in self-defense, and *not* such

---

* Adults feel quite differently. Fifty-eight percent of adults think "drinking less" would be very effective in reducing sexual assault.

a good idea to clamp down on drinking. But what good is knowing the techniques of self-defense if you're blind drunk? Students think it's a really good idea if men respect women more. But the issue is not how men behave around women when they are sober. It is how they behave around women when they are drunk, and have been transformed by alcohol into a person who makes sense of the world around them very differently. Respect for others requires a complicated calculation in which one party agrees to moderate their own desires, to consider the longer-term consequences of their own behavior, to think about something other than the thing right in front of them. And that is exactly what the myopia that comes with drunkenness makes it so hard to do.

The lesson of myopia is really very simple. If you want people to be themselves in a social encounter with a stranger—to represent their own desires honestly and clearly—they cannot be blind drunk. And if they *are* blind drunk, and therefore at the mercy of their environment, the worst possible place to be is an environment where men and women are grinding on the dance floor and jumping on the tables. A Kappa Alpha fraternity party is not a Camban drinking circle.

"Persons learn about drunkenness what their societies import to them, and comporting themselves in consonance with these understandings, they become living confirmations of their society's teachings," Craig MacAndrew and Robert Edgerton conclude in their classic 1969 work *Drunken Comportment*. "Since societies, like individuals, get the sorts of drunken comportment that they allow, they deserve what they get."

8.

So: At the Kappa Alpha party at Stanford, sometime just after midnight, Emily Doe suffered a blackout. That's what happens when you begin your evening with a light dinner and four quick shots of whiskey and a glass of champagne—followed by three or four shots of vodka in a red Solo cup.

P: And at some point, do you recall your sister leaving the party?

Doe: I do not.

P: What is your next memory after going to the bathroom outside, coming back to the patio, having the beers, and seeing some of the guys shotgun some beers?

Doe: I woke up in the hospital.

Emily Doe has no memory of meeting Brock Turner, no memory of whether she did or didn't dance with him, no memory of whether she did or didn't kiss him, did or didn't agree to go back to his dorm, and no memory of whether she was a willing or unwilling participant in their sexual activity. Did she resist when they left the party? Did she struggle? Did she flirt with him? Did she just stumble, blindly, after him? We'll never know. After the fact, when she was sober, Doe was adamant that she would never have willingly left the party with another man. She was in a committed relationship. But it wasn't the real Emily Doe who met Brock Turner. It was drunk and blacked-out Emily Doe, and our drunken, blacked-out selves are not the same as our sober selves.

Brock Turner claimed to remember what happened that night, and that at every step of the way Emily Doe was a willing participant. But that is the story he told at his trial, after months of prepping and strategizing with his lawyers. On the night of his arrest, as he sat in shock in the interview room of the local police station, he had none of that certainty about Emily Doe.

> **Q:** Were you guys hooking up there before or—before you even moved over?
> **Turner:** I think so. But I'm not sure when we started kissing, honestly.

Then the police officer asks him why he ran when the two graduate students discovered him and Emily Doe on the ground.

> **Turner:** I don't think I ran.
> **Q:** You don't remember running?
> **Turner:** No.

Keep in mind that the event in question *just* happened earlier that night, and that even as he is speaking, Turner is nursing an injured wrist from when he was tackled as he tried to escape. But it's all gone.

> **Q:** Did you get a look at her while she—this was going on, while the guys were approaching you and talking to you?
> **Turner:** No.
> **Q:** Is it possible she was unresponsive at that point?

228

Turner: Honestly, I don't know, because I—like, I really don't remember. Like, I—I think I was kind of blacked out after, uh, like, from the point of me going—like, hooking up to her, to, like, me being on the ground with the other guys. Like, I really don't remember how that happened.

I think I was kind of blacked out. So the whole story about flirting and kissing and Emily Doe agreeing to go back to his dorm was a fiction: it was what he hoped had happened. What actually happened will be forever a mystery. Maybe Turner and Emily Doe just stood there on the dance floor, repeating the same things to each other, over and over again, without realizing that they were trapped in an infinite, blacked-out loop.

At the end of the trial, Emily Doe read a letter out loud to the court, addressed to Brock Turner. Every young man and woman who goes to a bar or a fraternity party should read Emily Doe's letter. It is brave and eloquent and a powerful reminder of the consequences of sexual assault: that what happens between two strangers, in the absence of real consent, causes genuine pain and suffering.

What happened that night, she said, shattered her:

My independence, natural joy, gentleness, and steady lifestyle I had been enjoying became distorted beyond recognition. I became closed off, angry, self-deprecating, tired, irritable, empty. The isolation at times was unbearable.

At work she would show up late, then go and cry in the stairwell. She would cry herself to sleep at night and in the morning hold refrigerated spoons to her eyes to lessen the swelling.

I can't sleep alone at night without having a light on, like a five-year-old, because I have nightmares of being touched where I cannot wake up. I did this thing where I waited until the sun came up and I felt safe enough to sleep. For three months, I went to bed at six o'clock in the morning.

I used to pride myself on my independence; now I am afraid to go on walks in the evening, to attend social events with drinking among friends where I should be comfortable being. I have become a little barnacle always needing to be at someone's side, to have my boyfriend standing next to me, sleeping beside me, protecting me. It is embarrassing how feeble I feel, how timidly I move through life, always guarded, ready to defend myself, ready to be angry.

Then she comes to the question of alcohol. Was it a *factor* in what happened that night? Of course. But then she says:

Alcohol was not the one who stripped me, fingered me, had my head dragging against the ground, with me almost fully naked. Having too much to drink was an amateur mistake that I admit to, but it is not criminal. Everyone in this room has had a night where they have regretted drinking too much, or knows someone

230

close to them who has had a night where they have regretted drinking too much. Regretting drinking is not the same as regretting sexual assault. We were both drunk. The difference is I did not take off your pants and underwear, touch you inappropriately, and run away. That's the difference.

In his own statement to the court, Turner had said he was hoping to set up a program for students to "speak out against the campus drinking culture and the sexual promiscuity that goes along with that." Doe was scathing:

Campus drinking culture. That's what we're speaking out against? You think that's what I've spent the past year fighting for? Not awareness about campus sexual assault, or rape, or learning to recognize consent. Campus drinking culture. Down with Jack Daniels. Down with Skyy Vodka. If you want to talk to people about drinking, go to an AA meeting. You realize, having a drinking problem is different than drinking and then forcefully trying to have sex with someone? Show men how to respect women, not how to drink less.

But that's not quite right, is it? That last line should be "Show men how to respect women *and* how to drink less," because the two things are connected. Brock Turner was asked to do something of crucial importance that night—to make sense of a stranger's desires and motivations. That is a hard task for all of us under the best circumstances, because the assumption of transparency we rely on in those encounters is so flawed. Asking a drunk and immature nineteen-year-old to do that, in the hypersexualized chaos of a frat party, is an invitation to disaster.

The outcome of *People v. Brock Turner* brought a measure of justice to Emily Doe. But so long as we refuse to acknowledge what alcohol does to the interaction between strangers, that evening at Kappa Alpha will be repeated again. And again.

P: You've heard that voice mail of [Emily], haven't you?
Turner: Yes.

Turner is being cross-examined by the prosecutor. She's referring to the slurred phone call Emily Doe made to her boyfriend sometime after she blacked out.

P: You would agree with me that in that voice mail, she sounds super intoxicated?
Turner: Yes.
P: That's how she was with you that night, wasn't she?
Turner: Yes.
P: She was very drunk, wasn't she?
Turner: Not more than anybody else that I had been with.

Part Four

Lessons

CHAPTER NINE

KSM: What Happens When the Stranger Is a Terrorist?

1.

"My first thought was that he looked like a troll," James Mitchell remembers. "He was angry, he was belligerent, he was glaring at me. I'm doing a neutral probe, so I'm talking to him basically like I'm talking to you. I took the hood off and I said, 'What would you like me to call you?'"

The man answered in accented English, "Call me Mukhtar. *Mukhtar* means *the brain*. I was the emir of the 9/11 attacks."

It was March 2003, in a CIA black site somewhere "on the other side of the world," Mitchell said. Mukhtar was Khalid Sheikh Mohammed, or KSM, as he was otherwise known—one of the most senior Al Qaeda officials ever captured. He was naked, hands and feet shackled, yet defiant.

"They had shaved his head by that point and shaved his beard," Mitchell said. "But he just was the hairiest person I'd ever seen in my life, and little, real little. He had a huge, like Vietnamese pot-bellied pig belly. I thought—this guy killed all those Americans?"

Mitchell has a runner's build, tall and slender, with longish white hair parted in the middle and a neatly trimmed beard. He speaks with a mild Southern accent. "I look like some guy's uncle," is how he describes himself, which is perhaps overly self-deprecating. He gives off a sense of unshakable self-confidence, as if he always gets a good night's sleep, no matter what he did to anyone that day, or what anyone did to him.

Mitchell is a psychologist by training. After 9/11, he and a colleague, Bruce Jessen, were brought in by the CIA because of their special skills in "high stakes" interrogation. Jessen is bigger than Mitchell, quieter, with a cropped military haircut. Mitchell says he looks like "an older [Jean-]Claude van Damme." Jessen does not speak publicly. If you hunt around online, you can find portions of a videotaped deposition he and Mitchell once gave in a lawsuit arising from their interrogation practices. Mitchell is unruffled, discursive, almost contemptuous of the proceedings. Jessen is terse and guarded: "We were soldiers doing what we were instructed to do."

Their first assignment, after the towers fell, was to help interrogate Abu Zubaydah, one of the first high-level Al Qaeda operatives to be captured. They would go on to personally question many other "high value" suspected terrorists over eight years in a variety of black sites around the world. Of them all, KSM was the biggest prize.

"He just struck me as being brilliant," Mitchell recalled. During their sessions, Mitchell would ask him a question, and KSM would answer: "That's not the question I would ask. You'll get an answer and you'll find it useful and you'll think that's all you need. But really the question I would ask is this question." Mitchell says he would then ask KSM's question of KSM himself, "and he would give a much more detailed, much more global answer." KSM would hold forth on the tactics of terrorist engagement, on his strategic vision, on the goals of jihad. Had he not been captured, KSM had all manner of follow-ups to 9/11 planned. "His descriptions of the low-tech, lone-wolf attacks were horrifying," Mitchell said. "The fact that he sits around and thinks about economy of scale when it comes to killing people..." He shook his head.

"He completely creeped me out when he was talking about Daniel Pearl. That was the most...I cried and still do, because it was horrific." Daniel Pearl was the *Wall Street Journal* reporter kidnapped—and then killed—in Pakistan in January 2002. KSM brought up the subject of Pearl without being asked, then got out of his chair and demonstrated—with what Mitchell thought was a touch of relish—the technique he had used in beheading Pearl with a knife. "What was horrific about it was he acted like he had some sort of an intimate relationship with Daniel. He kept calling him 'Daniel' in that voice like they were not really lovers, but they were best friends or something. It was just the creepiest thing."

But all that was later—after KSM opened up. In March 2003, when Mitchell and Jessen first confronted him, tiny and hairy and potbellied, things were very different.

"You've got to remember at that particular time [we] had credible evidence that Al Qaeda had another big wave of attacks coming," Mitchell said.

There was a lot of chatter. We knew that Osama bin Laden had met with the Pakistani scientists who were passing out nuclear technology, and [we] knew that the Pakistani scientists had said to Bin Laden, "The biggest problem is getting the nuclear material." Bin Laden had said, "What if we've already got it?" That just sent chills through the whole intelligence community.

The CIA had people walking around Manhattan with Geiger counters, looking for a dirty bomb. Washington was on high alert. And when KSM was first captured, the feeling was that if anyone knew anything about the planned attacks, it would be him. But KSM wasn't talking, and Mitchell wasn't optimistic. KSM was a hard case.

The first set of interrogators sent to question KSM had tried to be friendly. They made him comfortable and brewed him some tea and asked respectful questions. They'd gotten nowhere. He had simply looked at them and rocked back and forth.

Then KSM had been handed over to someone Mitchell calls the "new sheriff in town," an interrogator who Mitchell says crossed the line into sadism—contorting KSM into a variety of "stress" positions, like taping his hands together behind his back, then raising them up over his head, so that his shoulders almost popped out. "This guy told me that he had learned his interrogation approaches in South America from the communist rebels,"

Mitchell said. "He got into a battle of wills with KSM. The new sheriff had this idea that he wanted to be called sir. That's all he focused on." KSM had no intention of calling anyone sir. After a week of trying, the new sheriff gave up. The prisoner was handed over to Mitchell and Jessen.

What happened next is a matter of great controversy. The methods of interrogation used on KSM have been the subject of lawsuits, congressional investigations, and endless public debate. Those who approve refer to the measures as "enhanced interrogation techniques"—EITs. Those on the other side call them torture. But let us leave aside those broader ethical questions for a moment, and focus on what the interrogation of KSM can tell us about the two puzzles.

The deceptions of Ana Montes and Bernie Madoff, the confusion over Amanda Knox, the plights of Graham Spanier and Emily Doe are all evidence of the underlying problem we have in making sense of people we do not know. Default to truth is a crucially important strategy that occasionally and unavoidably leads us astray. Transparency is a seemingly commonsense assumption that turns out to be an illusion. Both, however, raise the same question: once we accept our shortcomings, what should we do? Before we return to Sandra Bland—and what exactly happened on that roadside in Texas—I want to talk about perhaps the most extreme version of the talking-to-strangers problem: a terrorist who wants to hold on to his secrets, and an interrogator who is willing to go to almost any lengths to pry them free.

2.

Mitchell and Jessen met in Spokane, Washington, where they were both staff psychologists for the Air Force's SERE program—Survival, Evasion, Resistance, Escape. All branches of the U.S. military have their own versions of SERE, which involves teaching key personnel what to do in the event that they fall into enemy hands.

The exercise would begin with the local police rounding up Air Force officers, unannounced, and bringing them to a detention center mocked up as an enemy POW camp. "They just stop them and arrest them," Mitchell said. "Then they hand them over to whoever's going to do the operational-readiness test."

One exercise involved crews of the bombers that carry nuclear weapons. Everything about their mission was classified. If they were to crash in hostile territory, you can imagine how curious their captors would be about the contents of their planes. The SERE program was supposed to prepare a flight crew for what might happen.

The subjects would be cold, hungry, forced to stand—awake—inside a box for days. Then came the interrogation. "You would see if you could try and extract that information from them," Mitchell said. He says it was "very realistic." One particularly effective technique developed at SERE was "walling." You wrap a towel around someone's neck to support their head, then bang them up against a specially constructed wall.

"You do it on a fake wall," Mitchell explained:

It's got a clapper behind it and it makes a tremendous amount of noise and there's a lot of give, and your ears start swirling. You don't do it in a way to cause damage to the person. I mean, it's like a wrestling mat, only louder. It's not painful, it's just confusing. It's disruptive to your train of thought, and you're off balance. Not only physically off balance—I mean, you're just off balance.

Mitchell's responsibility was to help design the SERE program, and that meant he occasionally went through the training protocol himself. Once, he says, he was part of a SERE exercise involving one of the oldest tricks in the interrogation business: the interrogator threatens not the subject, but a colleague of the subject's. In Mitchell's experience, men and women react very differently to this scenario. The men tend to fold. The women don't.

"If you are a female pilot and they said they were going to do something to the other airman, the attitude of a lot of them was, 'It sucks to be you,'" he said. "'You do your job, I'm going to do mine. I'm going to protect the secrets. I'm sorry this has happened to you, but you knew this when you signed up.'" Mitchell first saw this when he debriefed women who had been held as POWs during Desert Storm.

They would drag those women out and threaten to beat them every time the men wouldn't talk. And [the women] were angry at the men for not holding out, and they said, "Maybe I would have gotten a beating, maybe I would have got sexually molested, but it would have happened one time. By showing them that the way to get the keys to the kingdom was to drag me out, it happened every time. So let me do my job. You do your job."

In the SERE exercise, Mitchell was paired with a woman, a senior-ranking Air Force officer. Her interrogators said they would torture Mitchell unless she talked. True to form, she said, "I'm not talking." Mitchell said:

> They put me in a fifty-five-gallon drum that was buried in the ground, put a lid on it, covered it up with dirt. At the top of the drum, protruding through the lid, was a hose spewing cold water....Unbeknownst to me because of the way they positioned me, the drain holes were at the very top, at the level of my nose.

Slowly the barrel filled with water.

Mitchell: I'm pretty sure they wouldn't kill the next psychologist to come to the school, I was pretty sure of that, but I wasn't convinced of that. You know what I mean?

MG: How did you feel when that was happening?

Mitchell: I wasn't happy, because your knees are up against your chest and you can't get out. Your arms are down beside you. You can't move. They put a strap underneath you and lower you into the thing.

MG: At what point were you removed?

Mitchell: An hour or so later.

MG: How high was the water?

Mitchell: It comes right up to your nose. It comes right up so you really don't know. I mean, the thing's coming up around your neck, it's coming up around your ears.

MG: You're in darkness?

Mitchell: Oh yeah.... Maybe it wasn't an hour, maybe it was less than that. I'm sure it was, otherwise I'd have some hypothermia. It felt like an hour. Anyway I'm in this thing, and they lower you down, and I think, "Oh, they're going to put me in a barrel, see if I'm claustrophobic. I'm not. No big deal to me." Oh no. They stick the hose in, put that little metal lid on, and then cover it up with rocks.

MG: Do they tell you beforehand what they're going to do?

Mitchell: They tell you as they're doing it.

MG: Everything they were doing to the trainees at SERE they did to you as well?

Mitchell: Oh yeah.

As Mitchell put it, "A lot of people spent time in that barrel." At the time, that was part of the standard course.

Mitchell: I also took the advanced course. If you think the basic course is rough.... Dude.

3.

This is where the CIA's "Enhanced Interrogation" program came from. The CIA came to Mitchell and Jessen and asked for their advice. The two of them had been working for years, designing and implementing what they believed to be the most effective interrogation technique imaginable, and the agency wanted to know what worked. So Mitchell and Jessen made a list, at the top of which was sleep deprivation, walling, and waterboarding. Waterboarding is where you're placed on a gurney with your head lower than your feet, a cloth is placed over your face, and water is poured into your mouth and nose to produce the sensation of drowning. As it happened, waterboarding was one of the few techniques Mitchell and Jessen *didn't* use at SERE. From the Air Force's perspective, waterboarding was too good. They were trying to teach their people that resisting torture was possible, so it made little sense to expose them to a technique that, for most people, made resistance impossible.* But to use on suspected terrorists? To many in the CIA, it made sense. As a precautionary step, he and Jessen tried it out on themselves first, each waterboarding the other—two sessions in total for each of them, using the most aggressive protocol, the forty-second continuous pour.

"We wanted to be sure the physicians could develop

---

* There was plenty of experience with waterboarding at the Navy SERE school, however. There, the training philosophy was a little different. "The Navy's view was that people go into that situation expecting that they can hold out, that they can be cocky. When that happens to you [not holding out], you're devastated and you don't bounce back," Mitchell said. "So, part of what they try to do in the Navy school is show people that you really will capitulate at some point. But your job as an American soldier is to resist to the best of your ability." The Navy wanted to show their trainees how bad things could get. The Air Force felt their trainees were better off not knowing that.

safety procedures and the guards knew what they were going to do, and we wanted to know what [the detainees] were going to experience," he said.

MG: So describe what it was like.

Mitchell: You ever been on a super tall building and thought you might jump off? Knowing you wouldn't jump off, but thought you might jump off? That's what it felt like to me. I didn't feel like I was going to die, I felt like I was afraid I was going to die.

When the Justice Department sent two senior attorneys to the interrogation site to confirm the legality of the techniques under consideration, Mitchell and Jessen waterboarded them too. One of the lawyers, he remembers, sat up afterward, dried her hair, and said simply, "Well, that sucked."

Mitchell and Jessen developed a protocol. If a detainee was reluctant to answer questions, they would start with the mildest of "enhanced measures." If the detainee persisted, they would escalate. Walling was a favorite, as was sleep deprivation. The Justice Department's rules were that seventy-two hours of sleep deprivation was the maximum, but Mitchell and Jessen found that unnecessary. What they preferred to do was to let someone sleep, but not sleep enough; to systematically break up their REM cycles.

Waterboarding was the technique of last resort. They used a hospital gurney, tilted at 45 degrees. The Justice Department allowed them to pour at twenty- to forty-second intervals, separated by three breaths, for a total of twenty minutes. They preferred one forty-second pour, two twenty-second pours, and the remainder at three to ten seconds. "The main point," Mitchell said,

> is you don't want it to go in their lungs, you just want it to go in their sinuses. We had no interest in drowning the person. We originally used water out of a one-liter bottle, but the physicians wanted us to use saline because some people swallowed the water and they didn't want [them] to have water intoxication.

Before the first pour, they took a black T-shirt and lowered it over the subject's face, covering their nose. "The cloth goes like this," Mitchell said, miming the lowering of the shirt.

> And then you lift the cloth up, and then you put the cloth down, and then you lift the cloth up, and then you put the cloth down, and you lift the cloth up, and you put the cloth down.
>
> Literally, when you lift the cloth up, the pourer stops pouring. There's a guy up there with a stopwatch and he's counting the seconds so I know how many seconds it's going on. We've got a physician right there.

The room was crowded. Typically, the chief of base would be there, the intelligence analyst responsible for the case, and a psychologist, among others. Another group was outside, watching the proceedings on a large TV monitor: more CIA experts, a lawyer, guards—a big group.

No questions were asked during the process. That was for later.

Mitchell: You're not screaming at the guy. Literally, you're pouring the water, and you're saying to him in a not-quite-conversational tone, but not an aggressive tone, "It doesn't have to be this way. We want information to stop operations inside the United States. We know you don't have all of it, but we know you have some of it...." I'm saying it to him as it's happening, "It doesn't have to be this way. This is your choice."

MG: How do you know—in general, with EITs—how do you know when you've gone as far as you need to go?

Mitchell: They start talking to you.

Talking meant specifics—details, names, facts.

Mitchell: You'd give him a picture and say, "Who's this guy?" He'd say, "Well, this guy is this guy, but you know, the guy in the back, that guy in the back is this guy, and this is where he's at..." and you know—so he would go beyond the question.

Mitchell and Jessen focused on compliance. They wanted their subjects to talk and volunteer information and answer questions. And from the beginning with KSM, they were convinced they would need every technique in their arsenal to get him to talk. He wasn't a foot soldier on the fringes of Al Qaeda, someone ambivalent about his participation in terrorist acts. Foot soldiers are easy. They have little to say—and little to lose by saying it. They'll cooperate with their interrogators because they realize it is their best chance of winning their freedom.

But KSM knew he wasn't seeing daylight again, ever. He had no incentive to cooperate. Mitchell knew all the psychological interrogation techniques used by the people who didn't believe in enhanced interrogation, and he thought they would work just fine on what he called "common terrorists that you catch on the battlefield, like the everyday jihadists that were fighting Americans." But not on "the hard-core guys."

And KSM was a hard-core guy. Mitchell and Jessen could use only walling and sleep deprivation to get him to talk because, incredibly, waterboarding did not work on him. Somehow KSM was able to open his sinuses, and the water that flowed into his nose would simply flow out his mouth. No one understood how he did it. Mitchell calls it a magic trick. After a few sessions, KSM grasped the cadence of the pours. He would mock the room by counting down the remaining seconds on his fingers—then making a slashing gesture with his hand when it was over. Once, in the middle of a session, Mitchell and Jessen ducked out of the room to confer with a colleague; when they came back inside, KSM was snoring. "He was asleep," Mitchell said, laughing at the memory. "I know I'm laughing at this potentially horrific image that people have, but there is a piece of this…" He shook his head in wonderment. "I'd never heard of it," he said. "I'm telling you, when the CIA was doing due diligence, they called JPRA." JPRA is a Pentagon agency that monitors the various SERE programs run by the service branches. They had a file on waterboarding. "The person they talked to there said it's 100 percent effective on our students. We have never had anyone not capitulate."

Mitchell and Jessen gave KSM the full treatment for

three weeks. Finally, he stopped resisting. But KSM's hard-won compliance didn't mean his case was now open-and-shut. In fact, the difficulties were just beginning.

4.

A few years before 9/11, a psychiatrist named Charles Morgan was at a military neuroscience conference. He was researching post-traumatic stress syndrome, trying to understand why some veterans suffer from PTSD and why others, who go through exactly the same experiences, emerge unscathed. Morgan was talking to his colleagues about how hard it was to study the question, because what you really wanted to do was to identify a group of people *before* they had a traumatic experience and track their reactions in real time. But how could you do that? There was no war going on at the time, and it wasn't as though he could arrange for all his research subjects to simultaneously get robbed at gunpoint, or suffer some devastating loss. Morgan jokes that the best idea he could come up with was to study couples on the eve of their wedding day.

But afterward, an Army colonel came to Morgan and said, "I think I can solve your problem." The colonel worked at a SERE school at Fort Bragg, North Carolina. He invited Morgan to come and visit. It was the Army's version of the Air Force school in Spokane where Jessen and Mitchell worked. "It was kind of surreal," Morgan says. The Army had built a replica of a prisoner-of-war camp—the kind you might find in North Korea or some distant corner of the old Soviet Union. "I had a tour of the whole compound when nothing was running, so it was this really foggy, gray morning. It reminded me of some war movie you've seen, showing up in this concentration camp, but no one's there."

Morgan went on:

Each cycle of training always ended with a former POW talking to the class and saying, "This happened to me. You spent three hours in a little tiny cage. I lived in one for four years. Here's how they tried to play tricks on me."

Morgan was fascinated, but skeptical. He was interested in traumatic stress. SERE school was a realistic simulation of what it meant to be captured and interrogated by the enemy, but it was still just a simulation. At the end of the day, all the participants were still in North Carolina, and they could still go and get a beer and watch a movie with their friends when they were done: "They know they're in a course and they know they're in training. How could this possibly be stressful?" he asked. The SERE instructors just smiled at that. "Then they invited me to come and said I could monitor it for about a six-month period. So every month, for two weeks, I'd go, and I was like a little anthropologist taking notes."

He started with the interrogation phase of the training, taking blood and saliva samples from the soldiers after they had been questioned. Here is how Morgan describes the results, in the scientific journal *Biological Psychiatry:*

The realistic stress of the training laboratory produced rapid and profound changes in cortisol, testosterone, and thyroid hormones. These alterations were of a magnitude that . . . [is] comparable to those documented in individuals undergoing physical stressors such as major surgery or actual combat.

This was a pretend interrogation. The sessions lasted half an hour. A number of the subjects were Green Berets and Special Forces—the cream of the crop. *And they were reacting as if they were in actual combat.* Morgan watched in shock as one soldier after another broke down in tears. "I was amazed at that," Morgan said. "It was hard for me to figure out."

Well, I [had] thought, these are all really tough people—that it'll be kind of like a game. And I hadn't anticipated seeing people that distressed or crying. And it wasn't because of a physical pressure. It's not because somebody's manhandling you.

These were soldiers—organized, disciplined, motivated—and Morgan realized that it was the uncertainty of their situation that was unsettling to them.

Many [of them had] always operated by, "I should know the rules of the book so I know what to do." And I think much of the stress, as I got to know it over time, was largely driven by an internal sense of real alarm, like, "I don't know what the right answer is."

Then he decided to have the SERE students do what is called the Rey-Osterrieth Complex Figure drawing test. You're given this:

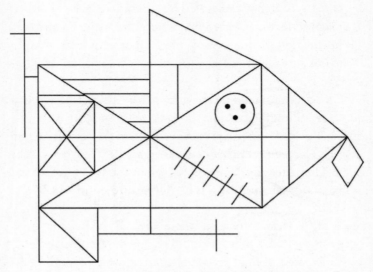

First you have to copy it. Then the original is taken away and you have to draw it from memory. Most adults are pretty good at this task, and they use the same strategy: they start by drawing the outlines of the figure, then fill in the details. Children, on the other hand, use a piecemeal approach: they randomly do one chunk of the drawing, then move on to another bit. Before interrogations, the SERE students sailed through the test with flying colors. Being able to quickly memorize and reproduce a complex visual display, after all, is the kind of thing Green Beret and Special Operations soldiers are trained to do. Here's a typical example of a Rey-Osterrieth figure drawn from memory by one of the soldiers before interrogation. These guys are good.

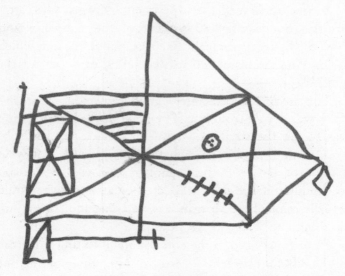

But just look at what the soldier drew fifteen minutes after interrogation:

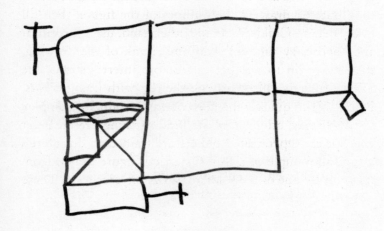

In one version of the experiment, Morgan says, after stressful questioning, 80 percent of the sample would draw the figure piecemeal, "like a prepubescent kid, which means your prefrontal cortex has just shut down for the while."

For anyone in the interrogation business, Morgan's work was deeply troubling. The point of the interrogation was to get the subject to talk—to crack open the subject's memory and access whatever was inside. But what if the process of securing compliance proved so stressful to the interviewee that it affected what he or she could actually remember? Morgan was watching adults turn into children.

"I had just been in the compound collecting spit from all the different students," Morgan says, remembering one incident from early at his time at SERE:

And I went back out because they had now opened the gates, the family [members] are there. They all say hello. And I walked up to a couple of students: "So, it's nice to see you when no longer under those conditions."

And I remember some of them went, "When did you get here?" And I was like, "What do you mean, when did I get here? I actually collected spit from you twenty minutes ago. I had you fill out—"

"I don't remember that."

And I said, "And I saw you the other night when you were being interrogated."

And they're like, "No, got nothing."

I looked at one of the instructors and I said, "That's

crazy." And he said, "Happens all the time." He goes, "They don't even remember me, and I'm the guy who was yelling at them thirty minutes ago."

Morgan was so astonished that he decided to run a quick field test. He put together the equivalent of a police lineup, filling it with instructors, officers, and a few stray outsiders.

"The physician for the unit had come back. He'd been on vacation....I said, 'You're going in the lineup today.' We put him in."

Then Morgan gave his instructions to the soldiers: "We're really interested in the person who ran the camp and ordered all your punishments. If they're there, please indicate who they are. If they're not, just say, 'Not here.'" He wanted them to identify the commandant—the man in charge.

"Out of the fifty-two students, twenty of them picked this doctor....And he goes, 'But I wasn't here! I was in Hawaii!'"*

If one of the soldiers had gotten it wrong, it would have been understandable. People make mistakes. So would two misidentifications, or even three. But *twenty* got it wrong. In any court of law, the hapless physician would end up behind bars.

After 9/11, Morgan went to work for the CIA. There

---

* In another, larger study, Morgan found that 77 out of 114 soldiers falsely identified their interrogators in a photo lineup—and this was 24 hours *after* interrogation! When these soldiers were asked how confident they were in their responses, there was no relationship between confidence and accuracy.

he tried to impress upon his colleagues the significance of his findings. The agency had spies and confidential sources around the world. They had information gathered from people they had captured or coerced into cooperating. These sources were people who often spoke with great confidence. Some were highly trusted. Some gave information that was considered very credible. But Morgan's point was that if the information they were sharing had been obtained under stress—if they had just been through some nightmare in Iraq or Afghanistan or Syria—what they said might be inaccurate or misleading, and the sources wouldn't know it. They would say, *It's the doctor! I know it was the doctor,* even though the doctor was a thousand miles away. "I said to the other analysts, 'You know, the implication of this is really alarming.'"

So what did Charles Morgan think when he heard what Mitchell and Jessen were up to with KSM in their faraway black site?

> I told people—this was before I was at the CIA, and I told people while I was there—"Trying to get information out of someone you are sleep-depriving is sort of like trying to get a better signal out of a radio that you are smashing with a sledgehammer.... It makes no sense to me at all."

5.

KSM made his first public confession on the afternoon of March 10, 2007, just over four years after he was captured by the CIA in Islamabad, Pakistan. The occasion was a tribunal hearing held at the U.S. Naval Base in Guantánamo Bay, Cuba. There were eight people present in addition to KSM—a "personal representative" assigned to the prisoner, a linguist, and officers from each of the four branches of the U.S. military service.

KSM was asked if he understood the nature of the proceedings. He said he did. A description of the charges against him was read out loud. Through his representative, he made a few small corrections: "My name is misspelled in the Summary of Evidence. It should be *S-h-a-i-k-h* or *S-h-e-i-k-h*, but not *S-h-a-y-k-h*, as it is in the subject line." He asked for a translation of a verse from the Koran. A few more matters of administration were discussed. Then KSM's personal representative read his confession:

> I hereby admit and affirm without duress to the following:
>
> I swore Bay'aat [i.e., allegiance] to Sheikh Usama Bin Laden to conduct Jihad...
>
> I was the Operational Director for Sheikh Usama Bin Laden for the organizing, planning, follow-up, and execution of the 9/11 Operation....
>
> I was directly in charge, after the death of Sheikh Abu Hafs Al-Masri Subhi Abu Sittah, of managing and following up on the Cell for the Production of Biological Weapons, such as anthrax and others, and following up on Dirty Bomb Operations on American soil.

Then he listed every single Al Qaeda operation for which he had been, in his words, either "a responsible participant, principal planner, trainer, financier (via the Military Council Treasury), executor, and/or a personal participant." There were thirty-one items in that list: the Sears Tower in Chicago, Heathrow Airport, Big Ben in London, countless U.S. and Israeli embassies, assassination attempts on Bill Clinton and Pope John Paul II, and on and on, in horrifying detail. Here, for example, are items 25 to 27:

25. I was responsible for surveillance needed to hit nuclear power plants that generate electricity in several U.S. states.

26. I was responsible for planning, surveying, and financing to hit NATO Headquarters in Europe.

27. I was responsible for the planning and surveying needed to execute the Bojinka Operation, which was designed to down twelve American airplanes full of passengers. I personally monitored a round-trip, Manila-to-Seoul, Pan Am flight.

The statement ended. The judge turned to KSM: "Before you proceed, Khalid Sheikh Muhammad, the statement that was just read by the Personal Representative, were those your words?" KSM said they were, then launched into a long, impassioned explanation of his actions. He was simply a warrior, he said, engaged in combat, no different from any other soldier:

War start from Adam when Cain he killed Abel until now. It's never gonna stop killing of people. This is the way of the language. American start the Revolutionary War then they starts the Mexican then Spanish War then World War One, World War Two. You read the history. You know never stopping war. This is life.

KSM's extraordinary confession was a triumph for Mitchell and Jessen. The man who had come to them in 2003, angry and defiant, was now willingly laying his past bare.

But KSM's cooperation left a crucial question unanswered: was what he said *true*? Once someone has been subjected to that kind of stress, they are in Charles Morgan territory. Was KSM confessing to all those crimes just to get Mitchell and Jessen to stop? By some accounts, Mitchell and Jessen had disrupted and denied KSM's sleep for a week. After all that abuse, did KSM know what his real memories were anymore? In his book *Why Torture Doesn't Work*, neuroscientist Shane O'Mara writes that extended sleep deprivation "might induce some form of surface compliance"—but only at the cost of "long-term structural remodeling of the brain systems that support the very functions that the interrogator wishes to have access to."

Former high-ranking CIA officer Robert Baer read the confession and concluded that KSM was "making things up." One of the targets he listed was the Plaza Bank building in downtown Seattle. But Plaza Bank wasn't founded as a company until years after KSM's arrest. Another longtime CIA veteran, Bruce Reidel, argued that the very thing that made it hard to get KSM to cooperate in the first place—the fact that he was never getting out of prison—

is also what made his claims suspect. "He has nothing else in life but to be remembered as a famous terrorist," Reidel said. "He wants to promote his own importance. It's been a problem since he was captured." If he was going to spend the rest of his days in a prison cell, why not make a play for the history books? KSM's confession went on and on:

9. I was responsible for planning, training, survey-ing, and financing for the Operation to bomb and destroy the Panama Canal.

10. I was responsible for surveying and financing for the assassination of several former American Presidents, including President Carter.

Was there anything KSM did *not* claim credit for?

None of these critics questioned the need to interrogate KSM. The fact that strangers are hard to understand doesn't mean we shouldn't try. Ponzi schemers and pedophiles can't be allowed to roam free. The Italian police had a responsibility to understand Amanda Knox. And why did Neville Chamberlain make such an effort to meet Hitler? Because with the threat of world war looming, trying to make peace with your enemy is essential.

But the harder we work at getting strangers to reveal themselves, the more elusive they become. Chamberlain would have been better off never meeting Hitler at all. He should have stayed home and read *Mein Kampf*. The police in the Sandusky case searched high and low for his victims for two years. What did their efforts yield? Not clarity, but confusion: stories that changed; allegations that surfaced and then disappeared; victims who were bringing their own children to meet Sandusky one minute, then accusing him of terrible crimes the next.

James Mitchell was in the same position. The CIA had reason to believe that Al Qaeda was planning a second round of attacks after 9/11, possibly involving nuclear weapons. He *had* to get KSM to talk. But the harder he worked to get KSM to talk, the more he compromised the quality of their communication. He could deprive KSM of sleep for a week, at the end of which KSM was confessing to every crime under the sun. But did KSM *really* want to blow up the Panama Canal?

Whatever it is we are trying to find out about the strangers in our midst is not robust. The "truth" about Amanda Knox or Jerry Sandusky or KSM is not some hard and shiny object that can be extracted if only we dig deep enough and look hard enough. The thing we want to learn about a stranger is fragile. If we tread carelessly, it will crumple under our feet. And from that follows a second cautionary note: we need to accept that the search to understand a stranger has real limits. We will never know the whole truth. We have to be satisfied with something short of that. The right way to talk to strangers is with caution and humility. How many of the crises and controversies I have described would have been prevented had we taken those lessons to heart?

We are now close to returning to the events of that day in Prairie View, Texas, when Brian Encinia pulled over Sandra Bland. But before we do, we have one last thing to consider—the strangely overlooked phenomenon of coupling.

Part Five

Coupling

CHAPTER TEN

Sylvia Plath

1.

In the fall of 1962, the American poet Sylvia Plath left her cottage in the English countryside for London. She needed a fresh start. Her husband, Ted Hughes, had abandoned her for another woman, leaving her alone with their two small children. She found an apartment in London's Primrose Hill neighborhood—the top two floors of a townhouse. "I am writing from London, so happy I can hardly speak," she told her mother. "And guess what, it is W.B. Yeats' house. With a blue plaque over the door saying he lived there!"

At Primrose Hill she would write in the early-morning hours while her children slept. Her productivity was extraordinary. In December she finished a poetry collection, and her publisher told her it should win the Pulitzer

Prize. She was on her way to becoming one of the most celebrated young poets in the world—a reputation that would only grow in the coming years.

But in late December, a deadly cold settled on England. It was one of the most bitter winters in 300 years. The snow began falling and would not stop. People skated on the Thames. Water pipes froze solid. There were power outages and labor strikes. Plath had struggled with depression all her life, and the darkness returned. Her friend, literary critic Alfred Alvarez, came to see her on Christmas Eve. "She seemed different," he remembered in his memoir *The Savage God:*

> Her hair, which she usually wore in a tight, school-mistressy bun, was loose. It hung straight to her waist like a tent, giving her pale face and gaunt figure a curiously desolate, rapt air, like a priestess emptied out by the rites of her cult. When she walked in front of me down the hall passage...her hair gave off a strong smell, sharp as an animal's.

Her apartment was spare and cold, barely furnished and with little in the way of Christmas decorations for her children. "For the unhappy," Alvarez wrote, "Christmas is always a bad time: the terrible false jollity that comes at you from every side, braying about good-will and peace and family fun, makes loneliness and depression particularly hard to bear. I had never seen her so strained."

They each had a glass of wine, and following their habit she read to him her latest poems. They were dark. The new year came and the weather grew even worse. Plath feuded with her ex-husband. She fired her au pair. She gathered her children and went to stay at the house of Jillian and Gerry Becker, who lived nearby. "I feel terrible," she said. She took some antidepressants, fell asleep, then woke up in tears. That was a Thursday. On Friday she wrote her ex-husband, Ted Hughes, what he would later call a "farewell note." On Sunday she insisted that Gerry Becker drive her and her children back to their apartment. He left her in the early evening, after she had put her children to bed. At some point over the next few hours, she left some food and water for her children in their room and opened their bedroom window. She wrote out the name of her doctor, with a telephone number, and stuck it to the baby carriage in the hallway. Then she took towels, dishcloths, and tape and sealed the kitchen door. She turned on the gas in her kitchen stove, placed her head inside the oven, and took her own life.

2.

Poets die young. That is not just a cliché. The life expectancy of poets, as a group, trails playwrights, novelists, and non-fiction writers by a considerable margin. They have higher rates of "emotional disorders" than actors, musicians, composers, and novelists. And of every occupational category, poets have far and away the highest suicide rates—as much as five times higher than the general population. Something about writing poetry appears either to attract the wounded or to open new wounds—and few have so perfectly embodied that image of the doomed genius as Sylvia Plath.*

Plath was obsessed with suicide. She wrote about it, thought about it. "She talked about suicide in much the same tone as she talked about any other risky, testing activity: urgently, even fiercely, but altogether without self-pity," Alvarez wrote. "She seemed to view death as a physical challenge she had, once again, overcome. It was an experience of much the same quality as...careering down a dangerous snow slope without properly knowing how to ski."

She fulfilled every criterion of elevated suicide risk. She had tried it before. She was a former mental patient. She was an American living in a foreign culture—dislocated from family and friends. She was from a broken home. She'd just been rejected by a man she idolized.†

---

* "A poet has to adapt himself, more or less consciously, to the demands of his vocation," Stephen Spender, himself an accomplished poet, once wrote, "and hence the peculiarities of poets and the condition of inspiration which many people have said is near to madness."

† "When she killed herself at age thirty," Ernest Shulman wrote, "Sylvia fit several categories for which suicide odds are increased. Although former suicide attempters constitute about 5 percent of the population, a third of completed suicides have previously attempted suicide; this includes Sylvia. Ex–mental patients comprise a significant proportion of suicides; this also includes Sylvia. Divorcees have a suicide rate several times higher than that of married women; Sylvia was getting a divorce. Foreigners everywhere have elevated suicide rates; Sylvia was living in England, far from familiar places and people. Suicides tend to be isolated people under severe stress; this was true of Sylvia. Broken homes produce a disproportionate number of suicides; Sylvia came from a broken home." He goes on: "She could never again be inter-twined with a man from whose alleged greatness she could feed her own dreams of glory." Not to mention Plath's earlier, aborted grieving for her father, who died when she was eight. "If a child's development

On the night of her death, Plath left her coat and her keys behind at the Beckers'. In her book on Plath (everyone who knew Plath, even tangentially, has written at least one book about her), Jillian Becker interprets that as a sign of the finality of Plath's decision:

> Had she supposed that Gerry or I would come after her during the night with her coat and keys? No. She had not expected or wanted to be saved at the last moment from self-inflicted death.

The coroner's report stated that Plath had placed her head as far inside the oven as she could, as if she were determined to succeed. Becker continued:

> She'd blocked the cracks at the bottom of the doors to the landing and the sitting room, turned all the gas taps full on, neatly folded a kitchen cloth and placed it on the floor of the oven, and laid her cheek on it.

Can there be any doubt about her intentions? Just look at what she was writing in the days before she took her own life.

> *The woman is perfected.*
> *Her dead*

---

is impeded because of incomplete mourning of a loss, that child will be handicapped in acquiring the mutuality necessary for building an integrated identity and maintaining strong emotional ties," Shulman continues. "Sylvia's narcissism was ultimately her undoing."

Body wears the smile of accomplishment...
Her bare
Feet seem to be saying:
We have come so far, it is over.

We look at Sylvia Plath's poetry and her history and catch glimpses of her inner life, and we think we understand *her*. But there's something we're forgetting—the third of the mistakes we make with strangers.

3.

In the years after the First World War, many British homes began to use what was called "town gas" to power their stoves and water heaters. It was manufactured from coal and was a mixture of a variety of different compounds: hydrogen, methane, carbon dioxide, nitrogen, and, most important, the odorless and deadly carbon monoxide. That last fact gave virtually everyone a simple means of committing suicide right inside their home. "The victims in the great majority of cases are found with their heads covered with coats or blankets, and with the tube from a gas tap brought under the edge of the covering article," a physician wrote in 1927, in one of the first accounts of the lethal properties of town gas:

> In several instances persons have been found sitting in
> a chair with the gas tube close to or in the mouth, and
> still held in position by the hand; or they have been
> found lying on the floor with the head in a gas oven.

In one case a woman was found with a mask which she had made out of a tea cozy tied over her face, the gas tube having been introduced through a hole in the top of the cozy.

In 1962, the year Sylvia Plath took her own life, 5,588 people in England and Wales committed suicide. Of those, 2,469—44.2 percent—did so as Sylvia Plath did. Carbon-monoxide poisoning was by then the leading cause of lethal self-harm in the United Kingdom. Nothing else—not over-dosing on pills or jumping off a bridge—came close.

But in that same period, the 1960s, the British gas industry underwent a transformation. Town gas was in-creasingly expensive—and dirty. Large reserves of natural gas were discovered in the North Sea, and the decision was made to convert the country from town gas to natural gas. The scale of the project was immense. Natural gas had markedly different chemical properties than town gas: it required twice as much oxygen to burn cleanly, the flame moved far more slowly, and the pressure of the gas needed to be greater. Those facts, in combination, meant the size and shape of the gas ports and burners on the stoves inside virtually every English household were now obso-lete. Every gas appliance in England had to be upgraded or replaced: meters, cookers, water heaters, refrigerators, portable heaters, boilers, washing machines, solid-fuel grates, and on and on. New refineries had to be built, new gas mains constructed. One official at the time, without exaggeration, called it "the greatest peacetime operation in this nation's history."

The long process began in 1965 with a pilot project

on a tiny island thirty miles from London, with 7,850 gas customers. Yorkshire and Staffordshire were next. Then Birmingham—and slowly every apartment, house, office, and factory in the country was converted, one by one. It took a decade. By the fall of 1977, the process was finally complete. Town gas—hydrogen, methane, carbon dioxide, nitrogen, and carbon monoxide—was replaced with natural gas: methane, ethane, propane, small amounts of nitrogen, carbon dioxide, hydrogen sulphide, and no carbon monoxide at all. After 1977, if you stuck your head in an oven and turned on the gas, the worst that could happen to you was a mild headache and a crick in your neck.

Take a look at how the number of gas suicides changed as town gas was slowly phased out over the 1960s and 1970s.

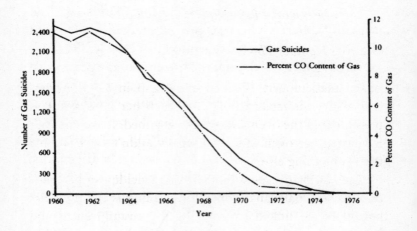

So here is the question: once the number-one form of suicide in England became a physiological impossibility, did the people who wanted to kill themselves switch to other methods? Or did the people who would have put their heads in ovens now not commit suicide at all?

The assumption that people would simply switch to another method is called displacement. Displacement assumes that when people think of doing something as serious as committing suicide, they are very hard to stop. Blocking one option isn't going to make much of a difference. Sylvia Plath, for example, had a long history of emotional instability. She was treated with electroshock therapy for depression while still in college. She made her first suicide attempt in 1953. She spent six months in psychiatric care at McLean Hospital outside Boston. A few years later, she deliberately drove her car into a river—then, in typical fashion, wrote a poem about it:

And like the cat I have nine times to die.

This is Number Three.

She meticulously blocked every gap in the doorway, turned the gas taps full on, and stuck her head as far as possible into the oven. She was determined. If she couldn't have used her oven to kill herself, wouldn't she have just tried something else?

The alternative possibility is that suicide is a behavior *coupled* to a particular context. Coupling is the idea that behaviors are linked to very specific circumstances and conditions. My father read Charles Dickens's *A Tale of Two Cities* to me and my brothers when we were children, and at the very end, when Sydney Carton dies in Charles

Darney's place, my father wept. My father was not a weeper. He was not someone whose emotions bubbled over in every emotionally meaningful moment. He didn't cry in sad movies. He didn't cry when his children left for college. Maybe he got stealthily misty-eyed from time to time, but not so anyone other than maybe my mother would notice. In order to cry, he needed his children on the sofa listening, and he needed one of history's most sentimental novelists. Take away either of those two factors and no one would ever have seen his tears. That's coupling. If suicide is coupled, then it isn't simply the act of depressed people. It's the act of depressed people at a particular moment of extreme vulnerability and in combination with a particular, readily available lethal means.

So which is it—displacement or coupling? The modernization of British gas is an almost perfect way to test this question. If suicide follows the path of displacement—if the suicidal are so determined that when you block one method, they will simply try another—then suicide rates should have remained pretty steady over time, fluctuating only with major social events. (Suicides tend to fall in wartime, for example, and rise in times of economic distress.) If suicide is coupled, on the other hand, then it should vary with the availability of particular methods of committing suicide. When a new and easy method such as town gas arrives on the scene, suicides should rise; when that method is taken away, they should fall. The suicide curve should look like a roller coaster.

Take a look.

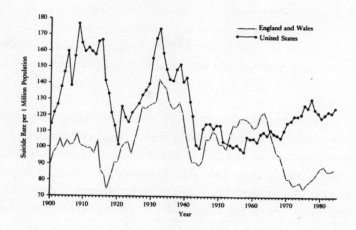

It's a roller coaster.

It goes way up when town gas first makes its way into British homes. And it comes plunging down as the change-over to natural gas begins in the late 1960s. In that ten-year window, as town gas was being slowly phased out, thousands of deaths were prevented.

"[Town] gas had unique advantages as a lethal method," criminologist Ronald Clarke wrote in his classic 1988 essay laying out the first sustained argument in favor of coupling:

> It was widely available (in about 80 percent of British homes) and required little preparation or specialist knowledge, making it an easy choice for less mobile people and for those coming under sudden extreme stress. It was painless, did not result in disfigurement, and did not produce a mess (which women in particular will try to avoid).... Deaths by hanging, asphyxiation,

or drowning all usually demand more planning, while more courage would be needed with the more violent methods of shooting, cutting, stabbing, crashing one's car, and jumping off high places or in front of trains or buses.

There is something awfully matter-of-fact about that paragraph, isn't there? Nowhere in Clarke's article does he speak empathetically about the suicidal, or dwell on the root causes of their pain. He analyzes the act the way an engineer would look at a mechanical problem. "The whole idea wasn't very popular at all amongst psychiatrists and social workers," Clarke remembers:

They thought it was very superficial, that these people were so upset and demoralized that it was sort of insulting to think you could deal with it by simply making it harder to commit suicide. I got quite a lot of pushback here and there from people about that idea.*

---

* I haven't even mentioned the biggest example of how our inability to understand suicide costs lives: roughly 40,000 Americans commit suicide every year, half of whom do so by shooting themselves. Handguns are the suicide method of choice in the United States—and the problem with that, of course, is that handguns are uniquely deadly. Handguns are America's town gas. What would happen if the U.S. did what the British did, and somehow eradicated its leading cause of suicide? It's not hard to imagine. It would uncouple the suicidal from their chosen method. And those few who were determined to try again would be forced to choose from far-less-deadly options, such as overdosing on pills, which is fifty-five times less likely to result in death than using a gun. A very conservative estimate is that banning handguns would save 10,000 lives a year, just from thwarted suicides. That's a lot of people.

This simply isn't the way we talk about suicide. We act as if the method were irrelevant. When gas was first introduced into British homes in the 1920s, two government commissions were created to consider the new technology's implications. Neither mentioned the possibility that it might lead to increased suicides. When the official British government report on the gas-modernization program came out in 1970, it stated that one of the positive side effects of the transition to natural gas would be a decline in fatal accidents. It didn't even mention suicide— even though the number of people who killed themselves deliberately with gas dwarfed the number who died from it accidentally. In 1981, the most comprehensive academic work on the subject, *A History of the British Gas Industry,* was published. It goes into extraordinary detail about every single aspect of the advent and growth of gas heating and gas stoves in English life. Does it mention suicide, even in passing? No.

Or consider the inexplicable saga of the Golden Gate Bridge in San Francisco. Since it opened in 1937, it has been the site of more than 1,500 suicides. No other place in the world has seen as many people take their lives in that period.[*]

---

[*] Suicides happen on the Golden Gate with such devastating regularity that in 2004 filmmaker Eric Steel put a video camera at either end of the bridge and wound up filming twenty-two suicides over the course of the year. In the death that served as the signature case study in Steel's subsequent documentary, *The Bridge,* his camera followed a thirty-four-year-old man named Gene Sprague for ninety-three minutes as he paced back and forth across the bridge before jumping to his death. If you stand on the bridge long enough, you can *expect* to see someone try to jump off.

What does coupling theory tell us about the Golden Gate Bridge? That it would make a big difference if a barrier prevented people from jumping, or a net was installed to catch them before they fell. The people prevented from killing themselves on the bridge wouldn't go on to jump off something else. Their decision to commit suicide is *coupled* to that particular bridge.

Sure enough, this is exactly what seems to be the case, according to a very clever bit of detective work by psychologist Richard Seiden. Seiden followed up on 515 people who had tried to jump from the bridge between 1937 and 1971, but had been unexpectedly restrained. Just 25 of those 515 persisted in killing themselves some other way. Overwhelmingly, the people who want to jump off the Golden Gate Bridge at a given moment want to jump off the Golden Gate Bridge only at that given moment.

So when did the municipal authority that runs the bridge finally decide to install a suicide barrier? In 2018, more than *eighty* years after the bridge opened. As John Bateson points out in his book *The Final Leap*, in the intervening period, the bridge authority spent millions of dollars building a traffic barrier to protect cyclists crossing the bridge, even though no cyclist has ever been killed by a motorist on the Golden Gate Bridge. It spent millions building a median to separate north- and southbound traffic, on the grounds of "public safety." On the southern end of the bridge, the authority put up an eight-foot cyclone fence to prevent garbage from being thrown onto Fort Baker, a former army installation on the ground below. A protective net was even installed during the initial construction of the bridge—at enormous cost—to prevent workers from falling to their deaths. The net saved nineteen lives. Then it was taken down. But for suicides? Nothing for more than eighty years.

Now, why is this? Is it because the people managing the bridge are callous and unfeeling? Not at all. It's because it is really hard for us to accept the idea that a behavior can be so closely coupled to a place. Over the years, the bridge authority periodically asked the public to weigh in on whether it supported the building of a suicide barrier. The letters generally fell into two categories: Those in favor tended to be people whose loved ones had committed suicide, who had some understanding of the psychology of the suicidal. The balance—in fact, the majority—simply dismissed the idea of coupling out of hand.

Here is a small sample:

"If a physical barrier on the bridge were to be erected, it would not surprise me if after three months, a suicide prone individual would walk to the north tower with a pistol and put the gun to his head in frustration of not being able to jump. What then of the millions to erect a physical suicide barrier?"

"People bent on suicide will find many ways to do away with themselves—pills, hanging, drowning, cutting arteries, jumping from any other bridge or building. Wouldn't it be much better to spend the money on mental health care for many people instead of worrying about the few that jump off bridges?"

"I oppose the construction of a suicide barrier because it would waste money and achieve nothing. Anyone who was prevented from jumping off the

Golden Gate Bridge would find another, more destructive, way of killing himself or herself. Someone who jumps off a tall building would be much more likely to kill someone who is walking in the street than someone who jumps off the bridge into the water."

"All it will do is cost money and deface the bridge. There are many ways to commit suicide. You take one away from someone it will only be replaced by another."

In one national survey, three quarters of Americans predicted that when a barrier is finally put up on the Golden Gate Bridge, most of those who wanted to take their life on the bridge would simply take their life some other way.[*] But that's absolutely wrong. *Suicide is coupled.*

The first set of mistakes we make with strangers—the default to truth and the illusion of transparency—has to do with our inability to make sense of the stranger as an individual. But on top of those errors we add another, which pushes our problem with strangers into crisis. We do not understand the importance of the *context* in which the stranger is operating.

4.

Brooklyn's 72nd Precinct covers the neighborhood surrounding Greenwood Cemetery, from Prospect Express-

---

[*] Thirty-four percent, in fact, predicted that *everyone* thwarted at the bridge would simply switch to another method.

way in the north to Bay Ridge in the south. In the narrow strip between the western perimeter of the cemetery and the waterfront, a series of streets run downhill toward the water. A crumbling, elevated freeway meanders down the middle. Today, it is a gentrifying neighborhood. Thirty years ago, when David Weisburd spent a year walking up and down those streets, it was not.

"This was a different world," Weisburd remembers. "This was a scary place. You'd go into an apartment building, there'd be refrigerators in the hall, garbage would be in the halls. Apartment buildings would have backyards five feet deep in garbage. There were people on the streets who would scare the hell out of you."

Weisburd was a criminologist by training. He had done his dissertation at Yale University on violent behavior among settlers in the West Bank in Israel. He was born in Brooklyn. After leaving Yale, he got a job working on a research project back in his old borough.

The study was based out of the precinct house on Fourth Avenue, a squat, modernist box that looked as if it were designed to repel an invading army. There were nine officers involved, each assigned to a beat of ten to thirty blocks. "Their job was to walk around those beat areas and to interact with the public, and to develop ways of doing something about the problems," Weisburd said. He was the observer and note-taker, responsible for writing up what was learned. Four days a week, for a year, he tagged along. "I would always wear a suit and tie, and I had a police identification card. People in the street thought I was the detective and I would say, 'Oh no.'"

He had been studying crime in a library. Now he was

at ground level, walking side by side with beat cops. And right from the beginning, something struck him as odd. Common sense had always held that crime was connected to certain neighborhoods. Where there were problems such as poverty, drugs, and family dysfunction, there was crime: The broad conditions of economic and social disadvantage bred communities of lawlessness and disorder.

In Los Angeles, that neighborhood was South Central. In Paris, it was the outer suburbs. In London, places like Brixton. Weisburd was in New York's version of one of those neighborhoods—only the neighborhood wasn't at all what he had imagined: "What I found was, quite quickly, that after we got to know the area, we spent all our time on one or two streets," he says. "It was the bad neighborhood of town, [but] most of the streets didn't have any crime."

After a while it seemed almost pointless to walk every street in his patrol area, since on most of them nothing ever happened. He didn't understand it. Criminals were people who operated outside social constraint. They were driven by their own dark impulses: mental illness, greed, despair, anger. Weisburd had been taught that the best way to understand why criminals did what they did was to understand *who* they were. "I call it the Dracula model," Weisburd said. "There are people and they're like Dracula. They have to commit crime. It's a model that says that people are so highly motivated to commit crime, nothing else really matters."

Yet if criminals were like Dracula, driven by an insatiable desire to create mayhem, they should have been roaming throughout the 72nd. The kinds of social conditions that Draculas feed on were everywhere. But the Draculas weren't everywhere. They were only on particular streets. And by "streets" Weisburd meant a single block—a street segment. You could have one street segment with lots of crime and the next, literally across an intersection, was fine. It was that specific. Didn't criminals have legs? Cars? Subway tokens?

"So that then begins a sort of rethinking of my idea of criminology," Weisburd said. "Like most other people, my studies were about *people*. I said, maybe we ought to be more concerned with *places*."

5.

When he finished his stint in Brooklyn, Weisburd decided to team up with Larry Sherman, another young criminologist. Sherman had been thinking along these lines as well. "I was inspired, at the time, by the AIDS map of the country," Sherman remembers, "which showed that fifty census tracks out of fifty thousand had over half of the AIDS cases in the United States." AIDS didn't look to him like a contagious disease roaming wildly and randomly across the land. It looked to him like an interaction between certain kinds of people and certain very specific places, an epidemic with its own internal logic.

Gathering the kind of data necessary to study the geographical component of crime wasn't easy. Crime had always been reported by precinct—by the general geographical area where it occurred. But Weisburd had just walked the 72nd Precinct, and he knew an area that nonspecific wouldn't help them. They needed *addresses*. Luckily, Sherman knew the police chief in Minneapolis, who was willing to help. "We chose Minneapolis because how could you find someone crazy enough to allow us to do what we wanted to do?" Weisburd said with a laugh.

Sherman crunched the numbers and found something that seemed hard to believe: 3.3 percent of the street segments in the city accounted for more than 50 percent of the police calls. Weisburd and his graduate students at Rutgers University then put a map of Minneapolis on the wall, and pasted little strips of paper wherever they found there had been a crime. The unbelievable finding was now impossible to dismiss. From his days walking the 72nd, Weisburd had expected some concentration of crime, but not this. "When Larry and I were talking about it, it was like, 'Oh my God!'"

In Boston right around the same time, another criminologist did a similar study: Half the crime in the city came from 3.6 percent of the city's blocks. That made two examples. Weisburd decided to look wherever he could: New York. Seattle. Cincinnati. Sherman looked in Kansas City, Dallas. Anytime someone asked, the two of them would run the numbers. And every place they looked, they saw the same thing: Crime in every city was concentrated in a tiny number of street segments. Weisburd decided to try a foreign city, somewhere entirely different—culturally, geographically, economically. His family was Israeli, so he thought Tel Aviv. Same thing. "I said, 'Oh my God. Look at that! Why should it be that five percent of the streets in Tel Aviv produce fifty percent of the crime? There's this thing going on, in places that are so different.'" Weisburd

284

refers to this as the Law of Crime Concentration.* Like suicide, crime is tied to very specific places and contexts. Weisburd's experiences in the 72nd Precinct and in Minneapolis are not idiosyncratic. They capture something close to a fundamental truth about human behavior. And that means that when you confront the stranger, you have to ask yourself where and when you're confronting the stranger—because those two things powerfully influence your interpretation of who the stranger is.

6.

So: Sylvia Plath. In her thinly disguised autobiography, *The Bell Jar*, Plath's protagonist, Esther Greenwood, describes her descent into madness. And she thinks about suicide precisely as Ronald Clarke (who made the link between town gas and suicide) suggests she would. She is incredibly sensitive to the question of how she'll take her own life. "If you were going to kill yourself, how would

---

* Take a look at a map Weisburd made of Seattle (page 369). Those dots are Seattle's crime "hot spots." If you talk to someone from Seattle, they will tell you their city has some bad areas. But the map tells you that statement is false. Seattle does not have bad *neighborhoods;* it has a handful of problematic *blocks* scattered throughout the city. What distinguishes those problematic blocks from the rest of the city? A jumble of factors, acting in combination. Hot spots are more likely to be on arterial roads, more likely to have vacant lots, more likely to have bus stops, more likely to have residents who don't vote, more likely to be near a public facility such as a school. The list of variables—some of which are well understood and many of which are not—goes on. And because most of those variables are pretty stable, those blocks don't change much over time.

you do it?" Esther asks Cal, a young man she's lying next to on a beach.

> Cal seemed pleased. "I've often thought of that. I'd blow my brains out with a gun." I was disappointed. It was just like a man to do it with a gun. A fat chance I had of laying my hands on a gun. And even if I did, I wouldn't have a clue as to what part of me to shoot at.

That very morning Esther had tried to hang herself with the silk cord of her mother's bathrobe, and it hadn't worked. "But each time I would get the cord so tight I could feel a rushing in my ears and a flush of blood in my face, my hands would weaken and let go, and I would be all right again." She and Cal swim for the shore. She decides to try to drown herself—and dives for the bottom of the sea.

> I dived and dived again, and each time popped up like a cork.
> The gray rock mocked me, bobbing on the water easy as a lifebuoy.
> I knew when I was beaten.
> I turned back.

Plath's protagonist wasn't looking to kill herself. She was looking for a *way* to kill herself. And not just any method would do. That's the point of coupling: behaviors are specific. She needed to find a method that fit. And on that cold February night, the method that fit for Sylvia Plath happened to be right there in her kitchen.

If you only knew how the veils were killing my days.
To you they are only transparencies, clear air.

This is "A Birthday Present," written in September 1962, at the beginning of Plath's anguished final months in London:

But my god, the clouds are like cotton.
Armies of them. They are carbon monoxide.
Sweetly, sweetly I breathe in,
Filling my veins with invisibles...

Take a look at the following graph showing suicide rates from 1958 to 1982 for British women ages twenty-five to forty-four. (Plath was thirty when she died.)

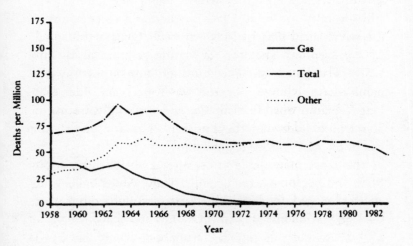

In the early 1960s, when Plath committed suicide, the suicide rate for women of her age in England reached a staggering 10 per 100,000—driven by a tragically high number of deaths by gas poisoning. That is as high as the suicide rate for women in England has ever been. By 1977, when the natural-gas changeover was complete, the suicide rate for women of that age was roughly half that. Plath was really unlucky. Had she come along ten years later, there would have been no clouds like "carbon monoxide" for her to "sweetly, sweetly...breathe in."

7.

In the fall of 1958, two years after their wedding, Sylvia Plath and her husband, Ted Hughes, moved to Boston. The poetry that would make her famous was still several years away. Plath worked as a receptionist at the psychiatric unit of Massachusetts General Hospital. In the evenings, she took a writing seminar at Boston University. There she met another young poet by the name of Anne Sexton. Sexton was four years older than Plath—glamorous, charismatic, and strikingly beautiful. She would later win the Pulitzer Prize for poetry for her book *Live or Die,* establishing her reputation as one of the most formidable contemporary American poets. Plath and Sexton became friends. They would linger after class, then go out for drinks with another young poet, George Starbuck.

"We would pile into the front seat of my old Ford, and I would drive quickly through the traffic to, or near, the Ritz," Sexton recalled, in an essay written after Plath's death:

> I would park illegally in a LOADING ONLY ZONE telling them gaily, "It's okay, because we are only going to get loaded!" Off we'd go, each on George's arm, into the Ritz and drink three or four or two martinis.

Sexton and Plath were both young, preternaturally gifted, and obsessed with death:

> Often, very often, Sylvia and I would talk at length about our first suicides; at length, in detail, and in depth between the free potato chips. Suicide is, after all, the opposite of the poem. Sylvia and I often talked opposites. We talked death with a burned-up intensity, both of us drawn to it like moths to an electric light bulb.

Sexton came from a family with a history of mental illness. She suffered from wild mood swings, anorexia, depression, and alcoholism. She attempted suicide at least five times. She stole a bottle of the barbiturate Nembutal—deadly in large enough doses—from her parents' medicine cabinet and carried it around in her purse. As her biographer Diane Wood Middlebrook explains, Sexton wanted "to be prepared to kill herself anytime she was in the mood."

In her early forties, she went into decline. Her drinking got worse. Her marriage failed. Her writing deteriorated.

On the morning of October 4, 1974, Sexton had breakfast with an old friend, then lunch with another friend, as if saying goodbye.

Middlebrook writes:

> She stripped her fingers of rings, dropping them into her big purse, and from the coat closet she took her mother's old fur coat. Though it was a sunny afternoon, a chill was in the air. The worn satin lining must have warmed quickly against her flesh; death was going to feel something like an embrace, like falling asleep in familiar arms.

She poured herself a vodka and took her own life. Like her friend Sylvia Plath, Sexton will forever be in the category of doomed genius. "No one who knew Anne Sexton well was surprised by her suicide," Middlebrook writes.

I hope by now, however, that you aren't satisfied with this account of Sexton's death. If suicide is a coupled act, then Sexton's character and pathology should be only part of the explanation for what happened to her. The same is true for Plath. Her friend Alfred Alvarez believed that too many people have painted her as "the poet as a sacrificial victim, offering herself up for the sake of her art," and he's absolutely right. That distorts who she is: it says her identity was tied up entirely in her self-destructiveness. Coupling forces us to see the stranger in her full ambiguity and complexity.

Weisburd has a map that, I think, makes this point even more powerfully. It's from Jersey City, just across the Hudson River from Manhattan.

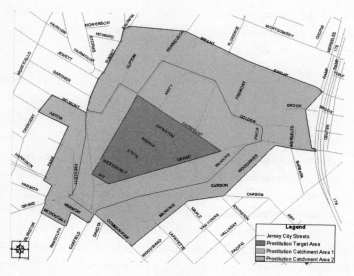

The dark area in the middle—bounded by Corneli-son Avenue, Grand Street, and Fairmount Avenue—is a prostitution hot spot and has been for some time. A few years ago, Weisburd conducted an experiment in which he assigned ten extra police officers—an extraordinarily high number—to patrol those few blocks. Not surprisingly, the amount of prostitution in the area fell by two-thirds.

Weisburd was most interested, though, in what happened in the lighter part of the map, just outside the triangle. When the police cracked down, did the sex workers simply move one or two streets over? Weisburd had trained observers stationed in the area, talking to the sex workers. Was there displacement? There was not. It turns out that most would rather try something else—leave the field entirely, change their behavior—than shift their location. They weren't just coupled to place. They were *anchored* to place.

> We found people would say to us, "I'm in this area. I don't want to move because it'll make it hard on my customers." Or, "No, I have to build up a business again." There are all these objective reasons why they're not moving. Another reason would be, "If I go someplace else, it's good for drugs, to sell drugs. There's already people there, they'll kill me."

The easiest way to make sense of a sex worker is to say that she is someone compelled to turn tricks—a prisoner of her economic and social circumstances. She's someone different from the rest of us. But what is the first thing the sex workers said, when asked to explain their behavior? That moving was really stressful—which is the same thing that *everyone* says about moving.

Weisburd continues:

> They talked about how hard it would be for business. They'd have to reestablish themselves. They talked about danger, people they don't know. What do they mean by *people they don't know*? "Here, I know who's going to call the police and who won't call the police." That's a big issue for them....When they're in the same place, they begin to have a high level of correct prediction about people. Going to a new place? You don't know who these people are. Someone who looks bad could be good. Someone who looks good, from their perspective, could be bad.

The interviewer said, "Well, why don't you just go four blocks away? There's another prostitution site." Her response: "Those are not my type of girls. I don't feel comfortable there." That hit me....Even people with these tremendous problems, with these tremendous difficulties in life, they respond to many of the same things as you or I.

Some of them may have children in nearby schools, and grocery stores where they shop, and friends they like to be close to, and parents they need to look in on—and as a result have all kinds of reasons not to move their business. Their job, at that moment, is sex work. But they are mothers and daughters and friends and citizens first. Coupling forces us to see the stranger in her full ambiguity and complexity.

Was Sexton determined to take her own life, by any means possible? Not at all. She would never use a gun. "For Ernest Hemingway to shoot himself with a gun in the mouth is the greatest act of courage I can think of," she told her therapist. "I worry about the minutes before you die, that fear of death. I don't have it with the pills, but with a gun there'd be a minute when you'd know, a terrible fear. I'd do anything to escape that fear."

Her chosen method was pills, downed with alcohol, which she considered the "woman's way out." Take a look at the following chart, comparing different suicide methods by fatality rate.

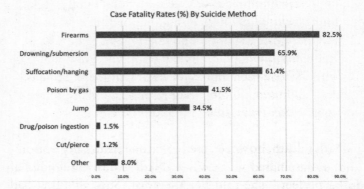

Case Fatality Rates (%) By Suicide Method

Firearms	82.5%
Drowning/submersion	65.9%
Suffocation/hanging	61.4%
Poison by gas	41.5%
Jump	34.5%
Drug/poison ingestion	1.5%
Cut/pierce	1.2%
Other	8.0%

People who overdose on pills die 1.5 percent of the time. Sexton was coupled to a method of suicide that was highly unlikely to kill her. That is not a coincidence. Like many people with suicidal tendencies, she was profoundly ambivalent about taking her own life. She took sleeping pills nearly every night, tiptoeing up to the line between dose and overdose but never crossing it. Just listen to her rationale, in her poem "The Addict":

Sleepmonger,
deathmonger,
with capsules in my palms each night,
eight at a time from sweet pharmaceutical bottles
I make arrangements for a pint-sized journey.
I'm the queen of this condition.
I'm an expert on making the trip
and now they say I'm an addict.
Now they ask why.
Why!

Don't they know
that I promised to die!
I'm keeping in practice.
I'm merely staying in shape.
The pills are a mother, but better,
every color and as good as sour balls.
I'm on a diet from death.

Plath's death, however, made Sexton rethink her options. "I'm so fascinated with Sylvia [Plath]'s death: the idea of dying perfect," she told her therapist. She felt Plath had chosen an even better "woman's way." She had gone out as "a Sleeping Beauty," immaculate even in death. Sexton needed suicide to be painless and leave her unmarked. And by 1974, she had become convinced that dying from car-exhaust fumes fit that set of criteria. It would be her town gas. She thought about it, spoke about it with friends.

So that's how Sexton took her life, after taking off her rings and putting on her mother's fur coat. She went to her garage, closed the door, sat in the front seat of her red 1967 Mercury Cougar, and turned on the engine. The difference between her original choice of sleeping pills and carbon-monoxide poisoning, of course, is that whereas the former are rarely lethal, carbon monoxide invariably is. She was dead within fifteen minutes.

But here Sexton's story converges with Plath's once again. Beginning in 1975—the year after her suicide—automobiles sold in the United States were required to have catalytic converters installed on their exhaust systems. A catalytic converter is a secondary combustion chamber that burns off carbon monoxide and other impurities before they leave the exhaust pipe. The fumes from Sexton's 1967 Cougar would have been thick with carbon monoxide. That's why she could sit in a closed garage with the engine running and be dead within fifteen minutes. The exhaust from the 1975 version of that car would have had half as much carbon monoxide—if that. Today's cars emit so little carbon monoxide that the gas barely registers in automobile exhaust. It is much more difficult to commit suicide today by turning on your car and closing the door of the garage.

Like her friend Sylvia Plath, Sexton was unlucky. She had an impulse coupled with a lethal method, just a year before that method stopped being so lethal. Had her difficult 1974 been instead her difficult 1984, she too might have lived much longer.

We overhear those two brilliant young poets in the bar at the Ritz, eagerly exchanging stories about their first suicide attempts, and we say that these two do not have long to live. Coupling teaches us the opposite. Don't look at the stranger and jump to conclusions. Look at the stranger's world.

CHAPTER ELEVEN

Case Study: The Kansas City Experiments

1.

A century ago, a legendary figure in American law enforcement named O. W. Wilson came up with the idea of "preventive patrol."* Wilson believed that having police cars in constant, unpredictable motion throughout a city's streets would deter crime. Any would-be criminal would always have to wonder if a police car was just around the corner.

But think about it. When you walk down the street of your neighborhood, do *you* feel like the police are just around the corner? Cities are vast, sprawling places. It's

---

* Wilson first experimented with preventive patrol when he was the chief of police in Wichita, Kansas. He would later hold the same post in Chicago.

not obvious that a police force—even a large police force—could ever create the feeling that they were everywhere.

This was the question facing the Kansas City Police Department in the early 1970s. The department was about to hire extra police officers, but it was divided over how to deploy them. Should they follow Wilson's advice—and have them drive randomly around the city? Or assign them to specific locations—such as schools or difficult neighborhoods? To resolve the question, the city hired a criminologist named George Kelling.

"One group said riding around in cars doesn't improve anything, it doesn't do anything," Kelling remembers. "Another group said it's absolutely essential. That was the standoff. Then I was brought in."

Kelling's idea was to select fifteen beats from the southern part of the city and divide them into three groups. It was a big area: thirty-two square miles, 150,000 people, good neighborhoods and bad neighborhoods, and even a little farmland on the fringes. One of the three groups would be the control group. Police work would continue there as it always had. In the second neighborhood, Kelling would have no preventive patrol at all; police officers would respond only when called. In the third neighborhood, he would double and in some cases triple the number of squad cars on the streets.

"Nothing like this had ever been done in policing," Kelling remembers. "This was 1970. Nothing had been written about police tactics.... This was at a very primitive stage in policing." People like O. W. Wilson had ideas and hunches. But police work was considered an art, not a science that could be evaluated like a new drug.

Kelling says that many people told him his experiment would fail, "that the police simply weren't ready for research. I wouldn't be able to do it. They'd sabotage it." But Kelling had the backing of the city's police chief. The chief had spent the bulk of his career in the FBI, and he was shocked to learn how little police departments seemed to know about what they did. "Many of us in the department," the chief would later admit, "had the feeling we were training, equipping, and deploying men to do a job neither we, nor anyone else, knew much about." He told Kelling to go ahead.

Kelling ran the experiment for a year, meticulously collecting every statistic he could on crime in the three areas of the study. The result? Nothing. Burglaries were the same in all three neighborhoods. So were auto thefts, robberies, and vandalism. The citizens in the areas with beefed-up patrols didn't feel any safer than the people in the areas with no patrols. They didn't even seem to notice what had happened. "The results were all in one direction and that was, it doesn't make any difference," Kelling said. "It didn't matter to citizen satisfaction, it didn't matter to crime statistics, it just didn't seem to matter."

Every police chief in the country read the results. Initially, there was disbelief. Some urban police departments were still committed Wilsonites. Kelling remembers the Los Angeles Police Chief standing up at one national law-enforcement conference and saying, "If those findings are true, every officer in Kansas City was asleep at the switch because I can assure you that's not how it is in Los Angeles."

But slowly resistance gave way to resignation. The study came out as violent crime was beginning its long, hard, two-decade surge across the United States, and it fed into the growing feeling among people in law enforcement that the task before them was overwhelming. They had thought they could prevent crime with police patrols, but now the Kansas City PD had tested that assumption empirically, and patrols turned out to be a charade. And if patrols didn't work, what did? Lee Brown, chief of the New York City Police Department, gave a famous interview in the middle of the crack epidemic in which he all but threw up his hands. "This country's social problems are well beyond the ability of the police to deal with on their own," Brown said. He had read George Kelling's Kansas City report. It was hopeless. No matter how many police officers a city had, Brown said, "You could never have enough to use traditional policing techniques to deter crime....If you don't have a police officer to cover every part of the city all the time, the chance of an officer on patrol coming across a crime in progress is very small."

In 1990, President George H. W. Bush came to Kansas City. He spent the morning in one of the city's poorest and most violent neighborhoods, then gave a speech to a group of local police officers. He tried to be upbeat. He failed. The homicide rate that year in Kansas City was three times the national average. It would go up again in 1991 and again in 1992, then once more in 1993. There wasn't much to say. Halfway through his remarks, Bush was reduced to simply listing the terrible things happening on the city's streets:

A four-year-old boy shot dead in a suspected crack house; an eleven-year-old kid gunned down outside another drug den, allegedly at the hands of a fourteen-year-old guard; in a downtown bar, a mother sells her baby for crack; and a firebombing leaves three generations dead, including a grandmother and three little kids—the headlines are horrifying, sickening, outrageous.

But in the early 1990s, twenty years after the first Kansas City experiment, Kansas City decided to try again. They hired another brilliant young criminologist named Lawrence Sherman. As they had with George Kelling, they gave him free rein. It was time for Kansas City Experiment Number Two. Why not? Nothing else was working.

2.

Lawrence Sherman thought the focus ought to be on guns. He believed the sheer number of guns in the city was what fueled its epidemic of violence. His plan was to try a number of ideas in sequence, rigorously evaluate their effectiveness—as Kelling had done—and pick a winner. He called a planning meeting with a group of the city's senior police officers. They chose as their testing ground Patrol District 144: a small, 0.64-square-mile neighborhood of modest single-family homes, bounded to the south by 39th Street and to the west by Highway 71. District 144 was as bad as Kansas City got in the early 1990s. The homicide rate there was *twenty* times the national average. The area averaged one violent felony a day and twenty-four drive-by shootings a year. A third of the lots were vacant. Just a few months before, an officer had been on patrol through 144 when he saw some kids playing basketball in the street. He stopped, got out, and asked them to move. One of the players threw the basketball at his head, then two others jumped him. It was that kind of place.

Sherman's first idea was for two-man teams to knock on every door in the neighborhood over a three-month period. The officers would introduce themselves, talk about gun violence, and give the residents a flyer with an 800 number on it: if they heard anything about guns, they were encouraged to call in an anonymous tip. The plan went off without a hitch. In many of the visits, the officers were trailed by a graduate student in criminology, James Shaw, whose job was to evaluate the program's effectiveness. Sometimes the officers stayed for as long as twenty minutes, chatting with people who had never had a police officer come to their door other than to make an arrest. In his subsequent write-up, Shaw was effusive:

> The police went to every residence in that community, some more than once, and talked to residents in a friendly, non-threatening manner. In response, people were very receptive and glad to see the police going door to door. People frequently responded with comments like "God bless you all, we shoulda' had a program like this before," or "Thank God! I didn't think you all would ever come."

In the end, 88 percent of the people visited said that they would use the hotline if they saw any guns. So how many calls came in—after 858 door-to-door visits over three months? Two. Both were about guns in another neighborhood.

The problem, everyone soon realized, was not that the residents of District 144 didn't want to help. They did. It was that they never left their houses. "It's starting to sound like Beirut around here," one homeowner told Shaw, and if you're so scared that you never leave your house, how on earth do you know who has guns or not? Shaw wrote:

> Not unlike residents in many other inner-city neighborhoods, these people have become like caged animals in their own homes; bars on the windows are the norm. One is not surprised even to see bars on second-story windows. More dismal however is the fact that in house after house the blinds are drawn and drapes closed up tightly, blocking out any trace of the outside world. These elderly people lock themselves up and shut themselves in. They hear the world outside, and it sometimes sounds like a battle zone. But they can't see anything.

The group's next idea was to train officers in the subtle art of spotting concealed weapons. The impetus came from a New York City police officer named Robert T. Gallagher, who in eighteen years on the force had disarmed an astonishing 1,200 people. Gallagher had elaborate theories, worked out over many years: street criminals overwhelmingly put their guns in their waist-bands (on the left side, in the case of a right-hander), causing a subtle but discernible hitch in their stride. The leg on the gun side takes a shorter step than the leg on the nongun side, and the corresponding arm follows a similarly constrained trajectory. When stepping off curbs or getting out of a car, Gallagher believed, gun carriers invariably glance toward their weapons or unconsciously adjust them.

Gallagher flew to Kansas City, with great fanfare, the month after the failed hotline experiment. He gave seminars. He made videos. The officers took notes. The television program *20/20* sent a camera crew to record the technique in action on the streets of Kansas City. Nobody spotted anything. *20/20* came back again. The same thing happened—nothing. Whatever magical skills Robert T. Gallagher possessed were not, apparently, transferable to the beat cops of Kansas City. Two of the team's best ideas for curbing gun violence had failed. They had one left.

3.

The winning entry in the Kansas City gun experiment was deceptively simple. It was based on a quirk in the American legal system.

The Fourth Amendment to the U.S. Constitution protects citizens from "unreasonable searches and seizures." That's why the police cannot search your home without a warrant. On the street, similarly, a police officer must have a good reason—"reasonable suspicion"—to frisk you.* But if you're in your car, that standard is not at all hard for a police officer to meet. Traffic codes in the U.S. (and in fact in most countries) give police officers literally hundreds of reasons to stop a motorist.

"There are moving violations: speeding, running a red light. There are equipment violations: a light that doesn't work, a tire not quite right," legal scholar David Harris writes.

> And then there are catch-all provisions: rules that allow police to stop drivers for conduct that complies with all the rules on the books, but that officers consider "imprudent" or "unreasonable" under the circumstances, or that describe the offense in language so broad as to make a violation virtually coextensive with the officer's unreviewable personal judgment.

There was even a Supreme Court case in which a police officer in North Carolina stopped what he thought was a suspicious driver, using the pretext that one of the car's

---

* To deal with that hurdle, for example, Gallagher developed all kinds of tricks. He and his partner would approach someone they thought was carrying a gun. They'd corner him, so he was feeling a little defensive. Then Gallagher would identify himself: *I'm a police officer.*

"When you stop a man with a gun, 99 out of 100 times he's going to do the same thing," Gallagher told a reporter years ago. "He's going to turn the side that the gun's on away from you—either several inches, just a quick turn of the hip, or halfway around. And the hand and arm are going to come naturally in the direction of the gun," in an instinctive protective motion. "At that point you don't have to wait to see if he goes under the shirt for the gun or if he's just going to keep it covered," he said. "At that point you have all the right in the world to do a frisk."

brake lights was out. As it turns out, it's perfectly permissible in North Carolina to drive with one brake light out, so long as the other one works. So what happened after the driver of the car sued, claiming he had been stopped illegally? The Supreme Court ruled in favor of the officer. It was enough that he *thought* driving with only one brake light seemed like an infraction. In other words, police officers in the United States not only have at their disposal a virtually limitless list of legal reasons to stop a motorist; they are also free to add any other reasons they might dream up, as long as they seem reasonable. And once they've stopped a motorist, police officers are allowed, under the law, to search the car, so long as they have reason to believe the motorist might be armed or dangerous.

Kansas City decided to take advantage of this latitude. Sherman's proposal was for the police department to detail four officers, in two squad cars. Their beat would be District 144. They were told not to stray outside the area's 0.64 square miles. They were freed from all other law-enforcement obligations. They didn't have to answer radio calls or rush to accident scenes. Their instructions were clear: watch out for what you think are suspicious-looking drivers. Use whatever pretext you can find in the traffic code to pull them over. If you're still suspicious, search the car and confiscate any weapon you find. The officers worked every night from 7 p.m. to 1 a.m., seven days a week, for 200 consecutive days. And what happened? Outside District 144, where police business was conducted as usual, crime remained as bad as ever. But inside 144? All of the new focused police work cut gun crimes—shootings, murders, woundings—in *half*.

Remember, the police had all but given up by that point. Hotline? Nobody calls it. Concealed-weapons detection? A crew from *20/20* comes down and twice goes home empty-handed. Lee Brown, up in New York City, was mourning the powerlessness of the police to do anything serious about violent crime. Everyone remembered the previous Kansas City experiment, which had plunged the law-enforcement community into twenty years of despair. But now the same city had come back, and this time they were declaring victory. "I don't know why it didn't occur to us to really focus on guns," the Kansas City police chief said after the results came in. He was as stunned as everyone else at what just two extra patrol cars had accomplished. "We usually focus on getting the bad guys after a crime. Maybe going after guns was too simplistic for us."

The first Kansas City experiment said that preventive patrol was useless, that having more police cars driving around made no difference. The second Kansas City experiment amended that position. Actually, extra patrol cars *did* make a difference—so long as officers took the initiative and stopped anyone they thought suspicious, got out of their cars as much as possible, and went out of their way to look for weapons. Patrol worked if the officers were *busy.* The statistics from the final report on the experiment were eye-opening. Over the seven months, each patrol car issued an average of 5.45 traffic citations per shift. They averaged 2.23 arrests per night. In just 200 days, the four officers had done more "policing" than most officers of that era did in their entire careers: 1,090 traffic citations, 948 vehicle stops, 616 arrests, 532 pedestrian checks, and 29 guns seized. That's one police intervention every forty minutes. On a given night in the tiny 0.64 square miles of 144, each squad car drove about twenty-seven miles. The officers weren't parked on a street corner, eating dough-nuts. They were in constant motion.

Police officers are no different from the rest of us. They want to feel that their efforts are important, that what they do matters, that their hard work will be rewarded. What happened in District 144 provided exactly what the profession of law enforcement had been searching for: validation.

"Officers who recovered a firearm received favorable notoriety from their peers, almost to the point that re-covery of a firearm came to be a measure of success," Shaw wrote in his account of the program. "Officers could frequently be heard making statements such as 'I've just got to get a gun tonight,' or 'I haven't gotten a gun yet; tonight will be the night!'"

In 1991 the *New York Times* ran a front-page story on the miracle in Kansas City. Larry Sherman says that over the next few days his phone rang off the hook: 300 police departments around the country bombarded him with requests for information on how he had done it. One by one, police departments around the country followed suit. To give one example, the North Carolina State Highway Patrol went from 400,000 to 800,000 traffic stops a year in the space of seven years.

The Drug Enforcement Agency used "Operation Pipe-line" to teach tens of thousands of local police officers across the United States how to use Kansas City–style traffic stops to catch drug couriers. Immigration officials started using police stops to catch undocumented immigrants.

Today, police officers in the United States make something like twenty million traffic stops a year. That's 55,000 *a day.* All over the United States, law enforcement has tried to replicate the miracle in District 144. The key word in that sentence is *tried.* Because in the transition from Kansas City to the rest of the country, something crucial in Lawrence Sherman's experiment was lost.

4.

The Lawrence Sherman who went to Kansas City is the same Larry Sherman who had worked with David Weisburd in Minneapolis a few years earlier, establishing the Law of Crime Concentration. They were friends. They taught together for a time at Rutgers, where their department chairman was none other than Ronald Clarke, who had done the pioneering work on suicide. Clarke, Weisburd, and Sherman—with their separate interests in English town gas, the crime map of Minneapolis, and guns in Kansas City—were all pursuing the same revolutionary idea of coupling.

And what was the principal implication of coupling? That law enforcement didn't need to be bigger; it needed to be more focused. If criminals operated overwhelmingly in a few concentrated hot spots, those crucial parts of the city should be more heavily policed than anywhere else, and the kinds of crime-fighting strategies used by police in those areas ought to be very different from those used in the vast stretches of the city with virtually no crime at all.

"If crime is concentrated on a few percent of the city streets," Weisburd asked, "why the hell are you wasting resources everywhere? If it's coupled to those places and doesn't move easily, even more so." The coupling theorists believed they had solved the problem that had so confounded the earlier days of preventive patrol. How do you effectively patrol a vast urban area with a few hundred police officers? Not by hiring more police officers, or by turning the entire city into a surveillance state. You do it by zeroing in on those few specific places where all the crime is.

But think back to those statistics from North Carolina. If you go from 400,000 traffic stops in one year to 800,000 seven years later, does that sound like focused and concentrated policing? Or does that sound like the North Carolina State Highway Patrol hired a lot more police officers and told everyone, everywhere, to pull over a lot more motorists? The lesson the law-enforcement community took from Kansas City was that preventive patrol worked if it was more aggressive. But the part they missed was that aggressive patrol was supposed to be confined to places where crime was concentrated. Kansas City had been a *coupling* experiment.

Weisburd and Sherman say they have trotted out their maps and numbers, trying to convince their peers of the Law of Crime Concentration, to little effect. Back in the 72nd precinct in Brooklyn where he began his work, after a long day roaming the neighborhood, Weisburd would turn to the police officers he had been walking with and say, "Isn't it strange how we're returning again and again to the same blocks?" They would look at him blankly.

"I was in a meeting with the deputy commissioner [of police] in Israel," Weisburd recalls.

Someone at the meeting said, "Well, David finds that crime doesn't just move around the corner. And that would suggest that you ought to become more focused." This guy turned around and he said, "My experience tells me that that's just not true. I don't believe that." That was the end of that.*

Is something wrong with Israel's deputy commissioner of police? Not at all. Because his reaction is no different from the behavior of the highway patrol in North Carolina, or the Golden Gate Bridge Authority, or the literary scholars who speak confidently of Sylvia Plath's doomed genius. There is something about the idea of coupling—of the notion that a stranger's behavior is tightly connected to place and context—that eludes us. It

---

* One of Weisburd's former students, Barak Ariel, went so far as to test resistance to the coupling idea in the Derry region of Northern Ireland. Law-enforcement officers in Derry are asked to identify specific troubled areas of their beats that they think are going to require additional police presence. Their predictions are called "waymarkers." Ariel wondered: how closely do the police officers' waymarkers match up with the hot spots where crime actually happens in Derry? I think you can guess. "The majority of streets included in 'Waymarkers' were neither 'hot' nor 'harmful,' resulting in a false positive rate of over 97 percent," Ariel concluded. This means that 97 percent of the blocks identified by police officers as being dangerous and violent were not dangerous and violent at all. The officers who drew these waymarkers were not sitting behind a desk, remote from the direct experience of the streets. This was their turf. These were crimes they investigated and criminals they arrested. Yet somehow they could not see a fundamental pattern in the location of the strangers they were arresting.

leads us to misunderstand some of our greatest poets, to be indifferent to the suicidal, and to send police officers on senseless errands.

So what happens when a police officer carries that fundamental misconception—and then you add to that the problems of default to truth and transparency?

You get Sandra Bland.

CHAPTER TWELVE

Sandra Bland

1.

At 4:27 on the afternoon of July 10, 2015, Sandra Bland was pulled over by a Texas State Trooper on FM 1098 in Waller County, Texas. She was driving a silver Hyundai Azera with Illinois license plates. She was twenty-eight years old and had just come from her hometown of Chicago to start a new job at Prairie View University. The name of the officer was Brian Encinia. He parked behind her, then approached Bland's Hyundai slowly along the curbside, leaning in to speak to her through the open passenger window.

Brian Encinia: Hello, ma'am. We're the Texas Highway Patrol, and the reason for your stop is because you failed to signal the lane change. Do you have your driver's license and registration with you? What's wrong? How long have you been in Texas?

Sandra Bland: Got here just yesterday.

Encinia: OK. Do you have a driver's license? [*Pause.*] OK, where you headed to now? Give me a few minutes.

Encinia takes her license with him to his patrol car. A few minutes pass. Then he returns, this time approaching Bland's car from the driver side.

Brian Encinia: OK, ma'am. [*Pause.*] You OK?

Bland: I'm waiting on you. This is your job. I'm waiting on you. When're you going to let me go?

Encinia: I don't know, you seem very, really irritated.

Bland: I am. I really am. I feel like it's crap what I'm getting a ticket for. I was getting out of your way. You were speeding up, tailing me, so I move over and you stop me. So yeah, I am a little irritated, but that doesn't stop you from giving me a ticket, so [*inaudible*] ticket.

In the many postmortems of the Bland case, this is generally identified as Encinia's first mistake. Her anger is steadily building. He could have tried to diffuse it. Later, during the investigation, it emerged that Encinia never intended to give her a ticket—only a warning. He could have told her that. He didn't. He could have explained, carefully, why she should have signaled. He could have smiled, joked with her. *Oh, ma'am. You don't think I'm going to give you a ticket for that, do you?* She has something to say and wants to be heard. He could have acknowledged that he was listening. Instead he waits a long, uncomfortable beat.

Encinia: Are you done?

That's the first missed opportunity. Then comes the second.

Bland: You asked me what was wrong, now I told you.
Encinia: OK.
Bland: So now I'm done, yeah.

She's done. Bland has said her piece. She's expressed her irritation. Then she takes out a cigarette and lights it. She's trying to calm her nerves. In the video we can't see any of this, because the camera is on the dashboard of Encinia's squad car; we see just the back of her car and Encinia, standing by her door. If you stopped the tape there and showed it to 100 people, 99 would guess that's where it ends.

But it doesn't.

Encinia: You mind putting out your cigarette, please? If you don't mind?

He's flat, calm, assertive. *Would you mind, said with an edge.*

Mistake Number Two: he should have paused, let Bland collect herself.

Bland: I'm in my car. Why do I have to put out my cigarette?

315

She's right, of course. A police officer has no authority to tell someone not to smoke. He should have said, "Yes. You're right. But do you mind waiting until after we've finished here? I'm not a fan of cigarette smoke." Or he could have dropped the issue entirely. It's only a cigarette. But he doesn't. Something about the tone of her voice gets Encinia's back up. His authority has been challenged. He snaps. Mistake Number Three.

> **Encinia:** Well, you can step on out now.
> **Bland:** I don't have to step out of my car.
> **Encinia:** Step out of the car.
> **Bland:** Why am I...
> **Encinia:** Step out of the car!
> **Bland:** No, you don't have the right. No, you don't have the right to do that.
> **Encinia:** Step out of the car.
> **Bland:** You do not have the right. You do not have the right to do this.
> **Encinia:** I do have the right, now step out or I will remove you.
> **Bland:** I refuse to talk to you other than to identify myself. [*crosstalk*] I am getting removed for a failure to signal?
> **Encinia:** Step out or I will remove you. I'm giving you a lawful order.

On the internet bulletin boards frequented by police officers after the case broke, Encinia's actions were supported by some. But just as many were dumbfounded by this final turn:

Dude, issue the f****n warning and move on. It's NOT WORTH IT....we're yankin females out of vehicles cause our ego got hurt cause she wouldn't tremble and put out the stupid cigarette????? Let's pose this question—suppose she had stepped out when he asked her to....THEN WHAT??? You were gonna scold her about the cigarette??? What was his plan?? What was going to be the purpose of pulling her out?

But Encinia has now given her a lawful order, and she has defied it.

Encinia: Get out of the car now or I'm going to remove you.
Bland: And I'm calling my lawyer.
Encinia: I'm going to yank you out of here. [*Reaches inside the car.*]
Bland: OK, you're going to yank me out of my car? OK, all right.

Encinia is now bent over, arms inside Bland's vehicle, tugging at her.

Bland: Let's do this.
Encinia: Yeah, we're going to. [*Grabs for Bland.*]

On the tape there's the sound of a slap, and then a cry from Bland, as if she's been hit.

Bland: Don't touch me!
Encinia: Get out of the car!

Bland: Don't touch me. Don't touch me! I'm not under arrest—you don't have the right to take me out of the car.

Encinia: You are under arrest!

Bland: I'm under arrest? For what? For what? For what?

Encinia [*To dispatch*]: 2547 county FM 1098 [*inaudible*] send me another unit. [*To Bland*]: Get out of the car! Get out of the car now!

Bland: Why am I being apprehended? You're trying to give me a ticket for failure...

Encinia: I said get out of the car!

Bland: Why am I being apprehended? You just opened my car door—

Encinia: I'm giving you a lawful order. I'm going to drag you out of here.

Bland: So you're threatening to drag me out of my own car?

Encinia: Get out of the car!

Bland: And then you're going to [*crosstalk*] me?

Encinia: I will light you up! Get out! Now! [*Draws stun gun and points it at Bland.*]

Bland: Wow. Wow. [*Bland exits car.*]

Encinia: Get out. Now. Get out of the car!

Bland: For a failure to signal? You're doing all of this for a failure to signal?

Encinia: Get over there.

Bland: Right. Yeah, let's take this to court, let's do this.

Encinia: Go ahead.

The encounter goes on for several more minutes. Bland becomes increasingly heated. He handcuffs her.

The second unit arrives. The yelling and struggling goes on—and on.

> **Encinia:** Stop now! Stop it! If you would stop resisting.
> **Female officer:** Stop resisting, ma'am.
> **Bland:** [*Cries.*] For a fucking traffic ticket, you are such a pussy. You are such a pussy.
> **Female officer:** No, you are. You should not be fighting.
> **Encinia:** Get on the ground!
> **Bland:** For a traffic signal!
> **Encinia:** You are yanking around, when you pull away from me, you're resisting arrest.
> **Bland:** Don't it make you feel real good, don't it? A female for a traffic ticket. Don't it make you feel good, Officer Encinia? You're a real man now. You just slammed me, knocked my head into the ground. I got epilepsy, you motherfucker.
> **Encinia:** Good. Good.
> **Bland:** Good? Good?

Bland was taken into custody on felony assault charges. Three days later she was found dead in her cell, hanging from a noose fashioned from a plastic bag. After a short investigation, Encinia was fired on the grounds that he had violated Chapter 5, Section 05.17.00, of the Texas State Trooper General Manual:

> An employee of the Department of Public Safety shall be courteous to the public and to other employees. An employee shall be tactful in the performance of duties, shall control behavior, and shall exercise the

319

utmost patience and discretion. An employee shall not engage in argumentative discussions even in the face of extreme provocation.

Brian Encinia was a tone-deaf bully. The lesson of what happened on the afternoon of July 10, 2015, is that when police talk to strangers, they need to be respectful and polite. Case closed. Right?

Wrong.

At this point, I think we can do better.

2.

A Kansas City traffic stop is a search for a needle in a haystack. A police officer uses a common infraction to search for something rare — guns and drugs. From the very beginning, as the ideas perfected in Kansas City began to spread around the world, it was clear that this kind of policing required a new mentality.

The person who searches your hand luggage at the airport, for example, is also engaged in a haystack search. And from time to time, the Transportation Security Administration (TSA) conducts audits at different airports. They slip a gun or a fake bomb into a piece of luggage. What do they find? That 95 percent of the time, the guns and bombs go undetected. This is not because airport screeners are lazy or incompetent. Rather, it is because the haystack search represents a direct challenge to the human tendency to default to truth. The airport screener sees something, and maybe it looks a little suspicious. But she looks up at the line of very ordinary-looking travelers waiting patiently, and she remembers that in two years on the job she's never seen a real gun. She knows, in fact, that in a typical year the TSA screens 1.7 billion carry-on bags, and out of that number finds only a few thousand handguns. That's a hit rate of .0001 percent—which means the odds are that if she kept doing her job for another 50 years she would never see a gun. So she sees the suspicious object inserted by the TSA's auditors, and she lets it go.

For Kansas City traffic stops to work, the police officer could not think that way. He had to suspect the worst of every car he approached. He had to *stop* defaulting to truth. He had to think like Harry Markopolos.

The bible for post–Kansas City policing is called *Tactics for Criminal Patrol*, by Charles Remsberg. It came out in 1995, and it laid out in precise detail what was required of the new, non-defaulting patrol officer. According to Remsberg, the officer had to take the initiative and "go beyond the ticket." That meant, first of all, picking up on what Remsberg called "curiosity ticklers"—anomalies that raise the possibility of potential wrongdoing. A motorist in a bad neighborhood stops at a red light and looks down intently at something on the seat next to him. What's *that* about? An officer spots a little piece of wrapping paper sticking out between two panels of an otherwise spotless car. Might that be the loose end of a hidden package? In the infamous North Carolina case, where the police officer pulled over a driver for a broken brake light—thinking, incorrectly, that this was against North Carolina law—the thing that raised his suspicions was that the driver was "stiff and nervous." The most savvy of criminals will be careful not to commit any obvious infractions. So traffic cops needed to be creative about what to look for: cracked windshields, lane changes without signaling, following too closely.

"One officer," Remsberg writes, "knowing that some of the most popular dope markets in his city are in dead-end streets and cul-de-sacs, just parks there and watches. Often drivers will get close before seeing his squad [car], then stop suddenly (improper stopping in a roadway) or hastily back up (improper backing in a roadway). 'There's two offenses,' he says, 'before I even pursue the car.'"

When he approached the stopped car, the new breed of officer had to be alert to the tiniest clues. Drug couriers often use air fresheners—particularly the kind shaped like little fir trees—to cover up the smell of drugs. (Tree air fresheners are known as the "felony forest.") If there are remains of fast food in the car, that suggests the driver is in a hurry and reluctant to leave his vehicle (and its valuable cargo) unattended. If the drugs or guns are hidden in secret compartments, there might be tools on the back seat. What's the mileage on the car? Unusually high for a car of that model year? New tires on an old car? A bunch of keys in the ignition, which would be normal—or just one, as if the car was prepared just for the driver? Is there too much luggage for what seems like a short journey? Or too little luggage for what the motorist says is a long journey? The officer in an investigatory stop is instructed to drag things out as long as possible. *Where you from? Where are you headed? Chicago? Got family there? Where?* He's looking for stumbles, nervousness, an implausible answer, and whether the driver's answer matches what he's seeing. The officer is trying to decide whether to take the next step and search the car.

Keep in mind that the overwhelming majority of people with food in their car, air fresheners, high mileage, new tires on an old car, and either too little or too much luggage are not running guns and drugs. But if the police officer is to find that criminal needle in a haystack, he has to fight the rational calculation that most of us make that the world is a pretty honest place.

So what is Brian Encinia? *He's the police officer who does not default to truth.* Here's a day from Brian Encinia's career, chosen at random: September 11, 2014.

> 3:52 p.m. The beginning of his shift. He stops a truck driver and tickets him for not having the appropriate reflective tape on his trailer.
>
> 4:20 p.m. He stops a woman for an improperly placed license plate.
>
> 4:39 p.m. He stops another woman for a license-plate infraction.
>
> 4:54 p.m. He notices a driver with an expired registration, stops him, and then also cites him for an expired license.
>
> 5:12 p.m. He stops a woman for a minor speeding infraction (that is, less than 10 percent over the speed limit).
>
> 5:58 p.m. He stops someone for a major speeding infraction.
>
> 6:14 p.m. He stops a man for an expired registration, then gives him three more tickets for a license

infraction and having an open container of alcohol in his vehicle.

8:29 p.m. He stops a man for "no/improper ID lamp" and "no/improper clearance lamp."

It goes on. Ten minutes later, he stops a woman for noncompliant headlamps, then two more minor speeding tickets over the next half hour. At 10 p.m. a stop for "safety chains," and then, at the end of his shift, a stop for noncompliant headlamps.

In that list, there is only one glaring infraction—the 5:58 stop for speeding more than 10 percent over the limit. Any police officer would respond to that. But many of the other things Encinia did that day fall under the category of modern, proactive policing. You pull over a truck driver for improper reflective tape, or someone else for "no/improper clearance lamp," when you are looking for something else—when you are consciously looking, as Remsberg put it, to "go beyond the ticket."

One of the key pieces of advice given to proactive patrol officers to protect them from accusations of bias or racial profiling is that they should be careful to stop everyone. If you're going to use trivial, trumped-up reasons for pulling someone over, make sure you act that way all the time. "If you're accused of profiling or pretextual stops, you can bring your daily logbook to court and document that pulling over motorists for 'stickler' reasons is part of your customary pattern," Remsberg writes, "not a glaring exception conveniently dusted off in the defendant's case."

That's exactly what Encinia did. He had day after day like September 11, 2014. He got people for improper mud flaps and for not wearing a seat belt and for straddling lanes and for obscure violations of vehicle-light regulations. He popped in and out of his car like a Whac-A-Mole. In just under a year on the job, he wrote 1,557 tickets. In the twenty-six minutes before he stopped Sandra Bland, he stopped three other people.

So: Encinia spots Sandra Bland on the afternoon of July 10. In his deposition given during the subsequent investigation by the Inspector General's office of the Texas Department of Public Safety, Encinia said he saw Bland run a stop sign as she pulled out of Prairie View University. That's his curiosity tickler. He can't pull her over at that point, because the stop sign is on university property. But when she turns onto State Loop 1098, he follows her. He notices she has Illinois license plates. That's the second curiosity tickler. What's someone from the other end of the country doing in East Texas?

"I was checking the condition of the vehicle, such as the make, the model, if it had a license plate, any other conditions," Encinia testified. He was looking for an excuse to pull her over. "Have you accelerated up on vehicles at that speed in the past, to check their condition?" Encinia is asked by his interrogator, Cleve Renfro. "I have, yes sir," Encinia replies. For him, it's standard practice.

When Bland sees Encinia in her rearview mirror coming up fast behind her, she moves out of the way to let him pass. But she doesn't use her turn signal. Bingo! Now Encinia has his justification: Title 7, subtitle C, Section 545.104, part (a) of the Texas Transportation Code, which holds that "An operator shall use the signal authorized by Section 545.106 to indicate an intention to turn, change

325

lanes, or start from a parked position." (In the event that Bland had used her turn signal at the very last moment, just before she changed lanes, Encinia even had a backup option: part (b) of Section 545.104 holds that "An operator intending to turn a vehicle right or left shall signal continuously for not less than the last 100 feet of movement of the vehicle before the turn." He could have stopped her for not signaling and he could have stopped her for not signaling enough.)*

Encinia gets out of his squad car and slowly approaches Bland's Hyundai from the passenger side, leaning in slightly to see if there's anything of interest in the car. He's doing the visual pat-down: Anything amiss? Fast-food wrappers on the floor? A felony forest hanging from the rearview mirror? Tools on the back seat? Single key on the key ring? Bland had just driven to Texas from Chicago; of course she had food wrappers on the floor. In the normal course of events, most of us looking in that window would cast our doubts aside. But Brian Encinia is the new breed of police officer. And we have decided that we would rather our leaders and guardians pursue their doubts than dismiss them. Encinia leans in the window, tells her why he pulled her over, and—immediately—his suspicions are raised.

---

* This is why Bland is so irritated, of course. "I feel like it's crap what I'm getting a ticket for. I was getting out of your way. You were speeding up, tailing me, so I move over and you stop me," she says. Meaning: a police car came speeding up behind her. She got out of its way, as a motorist is supposed to do, and now the same police officer who forced her to change lanes is giving her a ticket for improperly changing lanes. Encinia *caused* the infraction.

3.

Renfro: OK. After you asked Bland for her driver's license, you then asked her where she was headed and she replied, "It doesn't matter." You wrote in your report, "I knew at this point based on her demeanor that something was wrong."

In his deposition, Encinia is now being questioned by state investigator Cleve Renfro.

Renfro: Explain for the recording what you thought was wrong.
Encinia: ... It was an aggressive body language and demeanor. It appeared that she was not okay.

Brian Encinia believed in transparency—that people's demeanor is a reliable guide to their emotions and character. This is something we teach one another. More precisely, it is something we teach *police officers*. The world's most influential training program for law enforcement, for example, is called the Reid Technique. It is used in something like two-thirds of U.S. state police departments—not to mention the FBI and countless other law-enforcement agencies around the world—and the Reid system is based *directly* on the idea of transparency: it instructs police officers, when dealing with people they do not know, to use demeanor as a guide to judge innocence and guilt.

For example, here is what the Reid training manual says about eye contact:

In Western culture, mutual gaze (maintained eye contact) represents openness, candor, and trust. Deceptive suspects generally do not look directly at the investigator; they look down at the floor, over to the side, or up at the ceiling as if to beseech some divine guidance when answering questions....

Truthful suspects, on the other hand, are not defensive in their looks or actions and can easily maintain eye contact with the investigator.

The post–Kansas City textbook, *Tactics for Criminal Patrol*, instructs officers in police stops to conduct a "concealed interrogation," based on what they can gather from their initial observation of the suspect.

As you silently analyze their stories, their verbal mannerisms, and their body language for deception cues, you'll be trying to convince them that suspicion is far from your mind....The longer you can delay their tumbling to the fact that you are actually appraising them, their vehicle, and their reason for being in transit, the more likely they are to unwittingly provide you with incriminating evidence.

So that is exactly what Encinia does. He notices that she's stomping her feet, moving them back and forth. So he starts to stretch out their interaction. He asks her how long she has been in Texas. She says, "Got here just yesterday." His sense of unease mounts. She has Illinois plates. What is she doing in Texas?

Renfro: Did you have safety concerns at that point?

Encinia: I knew something was wrong but I didn't know what was wrong. I didn't know if a crime was being committed, had been committed, or whatnot.

He returns to his squad car to check her license and registration, and when he looks up and observes Bland through the rear window of her car, he says he sees her "making numerous furtive movements including disappearing from view for an amount of time." This is a crucial point, and it explains what is otherwise a puzzling fact from the video. Why does Encinia approach Bland's car from the passenger side the first time around, but from the driver side the second time? It's because he's getting worried. As he wrote in his report, "Officer safety training has taught me that it was much easier for a violator to attempt to shoot me on the passenger side of the vehicle."

Renfro: So explain for the recording why you would go from "This is a routine traffic stop with an aggravated person that in your opinion is not being cooperative or she's agitated," to your thought process that there's a possibility that you need to make a driver's-side approach due to the training on officers being shot.

Encinia: OK. Because when I was still inside the patrol car, I had seen numerous movements to the right, to the console, her right side of her body, that area as well as disappearing from sight.

His immediate thought was *Is she reaching for a weapon?* So now he approaches with caution.

Encinia: She has untinted glass on her windows so I can be able to see if anything could possibly be in her hands, if she had to turn over her shoulder or not. So that's why I chose that route...

To Encinia's mind, Bland's demeanor fits the profile of a potentially dangerous criminal. She's agitated, jumpy, irritable, confrontational, volatile. He thinks she's hiding something.

This is dangerously flawed thinking at the best of times. Human beings are not transparent. But when is this kind of thinking most dangerous? When the people we observe are mismatched: when they do not behave the way we expect them to behave. Amanda Knox was mismatched. At the crime scene, as she put on her protective booties, she swiveled her hips and said, "Ta-dah." Bernie Madoff was mismatched. He was a sociopath dressed up as a mensch.

What is Sandra Bland? She is also *mismatched*. She looks to Encinia's eye like a criminal. But she's not. She's just upset. In the aftermath of her death, it was revealed that she had had ten previous encounters with police over the course of her adult life, including five traffic stops, which had left her with almost $8,000 in outstanding fines. She had tried to commit suicide the year before, after the loss of a baby. She had numerous cut marks running up and down one of her arms. In one of her weekly "Sandy Speaks" video posts, just a few months before she left for Texas, Bland alluded to her troubles:

I apologize. I am sorry, my Kings and Queens. It has been two long weeks. I have been missing in action. But I gotta be honest with you guys. I am suffering from something that some of you all may be dealing with right now.... It's a little bit of depression as well as PTSD. I've been really stressed out these last couple of weeks...

So here we have a troubled person with a history of medical and psychiatric issues, trying to pull her life together. She's moved to a new town. She's starting a new job. And just as she arrives to begin this new chapter in her life, she's pulled over by a police officer—repeating a scenario that has left her deeply in debt. And for what? For failing to signal a lane change when a police car is driving up rapidly behind her. All of a sudden her fragile new beginning is cast into doubt. In the three days she spent in jail before taking her own life, Sandra Bland was distraught, weeping constantly, making phone call after phone call. She was in crisis.

But Encinia, with all of the false confidence that believing in transparency gives us, reads her emotionality and volatility as evidence of something sinister.

Renfro asks about the crucial moment—when Encinia requests that Bland put out her cigarette. Why didn't he just say, "Hey, your cigarette ashes are getting on me"?

Encinia: I wanted to make sure that she had it out without throwing it at me or just get it out of her hand.

Renfro then asks why, if that were the case, he didn't immediately tell her why she was under arrest.

Encinia: 'Cause I was trying to defend myself and get her controlled.

He's terrified of her. And being terrified of a perfectly innocent stranger holding a cigarette is the price you pay for not defaulting to truth. It's why Harry Markopolos holed up in his house, armed to the teeth, waiting for the SEC to come bursting in.

Renfro: I didn't ask you this earlier but I will now. When she tells you, "Let's do this," you respond, "We're going to." What did you mean by that?
Encinia: I could tell from her actions of leaning over and just she made her hand to me, even being a non-police officer if I see somebody balling fists, that's going to be confrontational or potential harm to either myself or to another party.
Renfro: Is there a reason why you just didn't take her down?
Encinia: Yes, sir.
Renfro: Why?
Encinia: She had already swung at me once. There was nothing stopping her from potentially swinging again, potentially disabling me.

Another of the investigators chimes in.

Louis Sanchez: Were you scared?
Encinia: My safety was in jeopardy at more than one time.

And then:

Sanchez: I don't want to put words in your mouth, so after this occurred, how long was your heart rate up, your adrenaline pumping? When did you calm down after this?

Encinia: Probably on my drive home, which was several hours later.

It was common, in the Bland postmortem, to paint Encinia as an officer without empathy. But that characterization misses the point. Someone without empathy is indifferent to another's feelings. Encinia is not indifferent to Bland's feelings. When he approaches her car, one of the first things he says to her is, "What's wrong?" When he returns to her car after checking her license, he asks again: "Are you okay?" He picks up on her emotional discomfort immediately. It's just that he completely misinterprets what her feelings mean. He becomes convinced that he is sliding into a frightening confrontation with a dangerous woman.

And what does *Tactics for Criminal Patrol* instruct the police officer to do under these conditions? "Too many cops today seem afraid to assert control, reluctant to tell anyone what to do. People are allowed to move as they want, to stand where they want, and then officers try to adapt to what the suspect does." Encinia isn't going to let that happen.

Encinia: Well, you can step on out now...Step out or I will remove you. I'm giving you a lawful order.

Brian Encinia's goal was to go beyond the ticket. He had highly tuned curiosity ticklers. He knew all about the visual pat-down and the concealed interrogation. And when the situation looked as if it might slip out of his control, he stepped in, firmly. If something went awry that day on the street with Sandra Bland, it wasn't because Brian Encinia didn't do what he was trained to do. It was the opposite. It was because he did exactly what he was trained to do.

4.

On August 9, 2014, one year before Sandra Bland died in her cell in Prairie View, Texas, an eighteen-year-old African American man named Michael Brown was shot to death by a white police officer in Ferguson, Missouri. Brown had been a suspect in a robbery at a nearby grocery store. When Darren Wilson—the police officer—confronted him, the two men struggled. Brown reached inside the driver's window of Wilson's patrol car and punched him. Wilson ended up shooting him six times. Seventeen days of riots followed. Prosecutors declined to press charges against Officer Wilson.

Ferguson was the case that began the strange interlude in American life when the conduct of police officers was suddenly front and center. And it should have served as a warning. The U.S. Department of Justice almost immediately sent a team of investigators to Ferguson—and their report, published six months later, is an extraordinary document. One of the leaders of the DOJ team was a lawyer named Chiraag Bains, and Bains says that what struck him, almost immediately, was that the anger in Ferguson wasn't just about Brown's death—or even largely about Brown. It was, instead, about a particular style of policing that had been practiced in the city for years. The Ferguson Police Department was the gold standard of Kansas City policing. It was a place where the entire philosophy of law enforcement was to stop as many people as possible for as many reasons as possible.

"It was very disturbing," Bains remembers.

One officer said, "It's all about the courts." Another said, "Yeah, every month they'll put up, our supervisors will put on the wall lists of officers and how many tickets they issued that month." We understood that productivity was the goal.

Ferguson had an entire police department full of Brian Encinias. Bains went on:

They knew that their job was to issue tickets and arrest people who hadn't paid their fines and fees and that's what they were going to be evaluated on.

Bains said one incident shocked him the most. It involved a young black man who had been playing basketball at a playground. Afterward, he was sitting in his car cooling off when a police car pulled up behind him. The officer approached the driver's window and demanded to see identification, accusing the driver of being a child molester.

I think [the police officer] said something to the effect like, "There are kids here and you're at the park, what are you, a pedophile?"...The officer then orders him out of the car and the guy says, "Well, I'm not doing anything. I mean, I have constitutional rights. I'm just sitting here just playing ball."

The officer then actually pulls his gun on the guy and threatening him and insisting that he get out of the car. The way the incident ends is that the officer writes him up for eight different tickets including not having a seatbelt on, he was sitting in his car at the park, not having a license, and also having a suspended license. He managed to issue both charges.

The man even got a ticket for "making a false declaration" because he gave his name as "Mike" when it was actually Michael.

He ends up carrying a lot of charges for quite a while. What happens to him is he gets charged with eight offenses in the Ferguson Municipal Code and tries to fight his case. He ends up, he was arrested on that occasion. He ends up losing his job where he was a contractor for the federal government. That arrest really derailed him.

Mike's arrest is a carbon copy of Sandra Bland's, isn't it? A police officer approaches a civilian on the flimsiest of pretexts, looking for a needle in a haystack—with the result that so many innocent people are caught up in the wave of suspicion that trust between police and community is obliterated. That's what was being protested in the streets of Ferguson: years and years of police officers mistaking a basketball player for a pedophile.[*]

Is this just about Ferguson, Missouri or Prairie View, Texas? Of course not. Think back to the dramatic increase in traffic stops by the North Carolina State Highway Patrol. In seven years they went from 400,000 to 800,000. Now, is that because in that time period the motorists of North Carolina suddenly started running more red lights, drinking more heavily, and breaking the speed limit more often? Of course not. It's because the state police changed tactics. They started doing far more haystack searches. They instructed their police officers to disregard their natural inclination to default to truth—and start imagining the worst: that young women coming from job interviews might be armed and dangerous, or young men cooling off after a pickup game might be pedophiles.

How many extra guns and drugs did the North Carolina Highway Patrol find with those 400,000 searches? Seventeen. Is it really worth alienating and stigmatizing 399,983 Mikes and Sandras in order to find 17 bad apples?

When Larry Sherman designed the Kansas City gun experiment, he was well aware of this problem. "You wouldn't tell doctors to go out and start cutting people up to see if they've got bad gallbladders," Sherman says. "You need to do lots of diagnosis first before you do

---

[*] There is significant evidence that African Americans are considerably more likely to be subjected to traffic stops than white Americans, meaning the particular indignity of the false positive is not equally distributed across all citizens. It is concentrated on those citizens who already suffer from other indignities.

any kind of dangerous procedure. And stop-and-search is a dangerous procedure. It can generate hostility to the police." To Sherman, medicine's Hippocratic oath—"First, do no harm"—applies equally to law enforcement. "I've just bought myself a marble bust of Hippocrates to try to emphasize every day when I look at it that we've got to minimize the harm of policing," he went on. "We have to appreciate that everything police do, in some ways, intrudes on somebody's liberty. And so it's not just about putting the police in the hot spots. It's also about having a sweet spot of just enough intrusion on liberty and not an inch—not an iota—more."

That's why the police officers involved in Sherman's Kansas City experiment underwent special training. "We knew that proactive policing was a legitimacy risk for the police, and I stressed that repeatedly," Sherman said.[*] Even more crucially, this is why the Kansas City gun experiment was confined to District 144. *That's where the crime was.* "We went through the effort of trying to reconstruct where the hot spots were," Sherman said. In the city's worst neighborhood, he then drilled down one step further, applying the same fine-grained analysis that he and Weisburd had used in Minneapolis to locate

---

[*] In later projects with Scotland Yard in London, when the police were trying to curb a wave of knife killings among teenagers, Sherman would insist that patrol officers leave their cards with everyone they talked to.

"They were sometimes doing five hundred stops a night," Sherman said, "and they were handing a receipt to everyone they stopped that said essentially, 'This is my name, this is my badge number. If you have any complaints or questions about anything I did, you can follow up with this receipt.'"

the specific street segments where crime was most concentrated. Patrol officers were then told to focus their energies on those places. Sherman would never have aggressively looked for guns in a neighborhood that wasn't a war zone.

In District 144, the "Mike and Sandra problem" didn't go away. But the point of confining the Kansas City gun experiment to the worst parts of the worst neighborhoods was to make the haystack just a little smaller, and to make the inevitable trade-off between fighting crime and harassing innocent people just a little more manageable. In an ordinary community, for the police to be as aggressive as Sherman wanted them to be would be asking for trouble. On the other hand, to people suffering in the 3 or 4 percent of streets where crime is endemic—where there might be as many as 100 or even 200 police calls in a year—coupling theory suggested that the calculus would be different.

"What happens in hot-spots policing? You tell the police, 'Go on the ten streets out of the one hundred in that neighborhood, or out of a thousand in that neighborhood, and spend your time there.' That's where things are happening," Weisburd says. "And if you do that, there's a good chance the neighborhood will say, 'Yeah, that intrusion is worthwhile because I don't want to get shot tomorrow.'"

The first question for Brian Encinia is: did he do the right thing? But the second question is just as important: was he in the right place?

5.

Prairie View, Texas, where Sandra Bland was pulled over, is sometimes described as being "outside" Houston, as if it were a suburb. It is not. Houston is fifty miles away. Prairie View is the countryside.

The town is small: no more than a few thousand people, short streets lined with modest ranch homes. The university sits at one end of the main street, FM 1098, which then borders the west edge of the campus. If you drive around the school on the ring road, there is a small Episcopal Church on the left, the college football stadium on the right, and after that lots of pasture land, populated with the occasional horse or cow. Waller County—where Prairie View is located—is predominantly Republican, white, middle- and working-class.

> **Renfro:** OK, talk to me about that area. Is it a high-crime area?
>
> **Encinia:** That portion of FM 1098 is a high-crime, high-drug area. It's—with my experience in that area, I have, in similar situations, with what I've seen, I've come across drugs, weapons, and noncompliant individuals.

Encinia then goes on to tell Renfro that he has made multiple arrests for "warrants, drugs, and numerous weapons, almost [all] within that vicinity."

Encinia's official record, however, shows nothing of the sort. Between October 1, 2014, and the Sandra Bland incident on July 10 of the following year, he stopped twenty-seven motorists on that mile-long stretch of highway. Six of those were speeding tickets. Those were compulsory stops: we can assume that any reasonably vigilant police officer, even in the pre–Kansas City era, would have done the same. But most of the rest are just Encinia on fishing expeditions. In March 2015 he cited a black male for "failure to drive in a single lane." Five times he pulled someone over for violating "FMVSS 571.108," the section of federal vehicle-safety regulations governing turn signals, license-plate lighting, and brake lights. The worst thing on the list are two cases of drunk driving, but let's keep in mind that this is a road that borders a college campus.

That's it. FM 1098 is not "a high-crime, high-drug area." You'd have to go three miles away to Laurie Lane—a half-mile stretch of trailer homes—to find anything in the vicinity that even remotely resembles a hot spot.

"Why are you stopping people in places where there's no crime?" Weisburd says. "That doesn't make sense to me."

Sherman is just as horrified. "At that hour of the day in that location, stopping [Sandra Bland] for changing lanes is not justifiable," he said. Even during the initial Kansas City gun experiment—in a neighborhood a hundred times worse than Prairie View—Sherman said that the special police officers made their stops solely at night. That's the only time of day when the crime rate was high enough to justify aggressive policing. Sandra Bland was pulled over in the middle of the afternoon.

Brian Encinia may have deliberately exaggerated the dangers of that stretch of road to justify his treatment of Sandra Bland. It seems just as likely, though, that it simply never occurred to him to *think* about crime as something so tightly tied to place. Literary theorists and bridge engineers and police chiefs struggle with coupling. Why would patrol officers be any different?

So it was that Brian Encinia ended up in a place he should never have been, stopping someone who should never have been stopped, drawing conclusions that should never have been drawn. The death of Sandra Bland is what happens when a society does not know how to talk to strangers.

6.

This has been a book about a conundrum. We have no choice but to talk to strangers, especially in our modern, borderless world. We aren't living in villages anymore. Police officers have to stop people they do not know. Intelligence officers have to deal with deception and uncertainty. Young people want to go to parties explicitly to meet strangers: that's part of the thrill of romantic discovery. Yet at this most necessary of tasks we are inept. We think we can transform the stranger, without cost or sacrifice, into the familiar and the known, and we can't. What should we do?

We could start by no longer penalizing one another for defaulting to truth. If you are a parent whose child was abused by a stranger—even if you were in the room—that does not make you a bad parent. And if you are a university president and you do not jump to the worst-case scenario when given a murky report about one of your employees, that doesn't make you a criminal. To assume the best about another is the trait that has created modern society. Those occasions when our trusting nature gets violated are tragic. But the alternative—to abandon trust as a defense against predation and deception—is worse.

We should also accept the limits of our ability to decipher strangers. In the interrogation of KSM, there were two sides. James Mitchell and his colleague Bruce Jessen were driven by the desire to make KSM talk. On the other side, Charles Morgan worried about the cost of forcing people to talk: what if in the act of coercing a prisoner to open up, you damaged his memories and made what he had to say less reliable? Morgan's more-modest expectations are a good model for the rest of us. There is no perfect mechanism for the CIA to uncover spies in its midst, or for investors to spot schemers and frauds, or for any of the rest of us to peer, clairvoyantly, inside the minds of those we do not know. What is required of us is restraint and humility. We can put up barriers on bridges to make it more difficult for that momentary impulse to become permanent. We can instruct young people that the kind of reckless drinking that takes place at a fraternity party makes the task of reading others all but impossible. There are clues to making sense of a stranger. But attending to them requires care and attention.

I said at the beginning of this book that I was not willing to put the death of Sandra Bland aside. I have now watched the videotape of her encounter with Brian Encinia more times than I can count—and each time I do, I become angrier and angrier over the way the case was "resolved." It was turned into something much smaller than it really was: a bad police officer and an aggrieved young black woman. That's not what it was. What went wrong that day on FM 1098 in Prairie View, Texas, was a collective failure. Someone wrote a training manual that foolishly encouraged Brian Encinia to suspect everyone, and he took it to heart. Somebody else higher up in the chain of command at the Texas Highway Patrol misread the evidence and thought it was a good idea to have him and his colleagues conduct Kansas City stops in a low-crime neighborhood. Everyone in his world acted on the presumption that the motorists driving up and down the streets of their corner of Texas could be identified and categorized on the basis of the tone of their voice, fidgety movements, and fast-food wrappers. And behind every one of those ideas are assumptions that too many of us share—and too few of us have ever bothered to reconsider.

> **Renfro:** OK. If Bland had been a white female, would the same thing have occurred?

It's the end of the deposition. Encinia and his interrogator are still fruitlessly trying to figure out what happened that day.

> **Encinia:** Color doesn't matter....We stop vehicles and people for law infractions, not based on any kind of race or gender at all. We stop for violations.

"We stop for violations," may be the most honest thing said in their entire episode. But instead of asking the obvious follow-up—*why* do we stop for all violations?—Renfro blunders on.

Renfro: What do you think that someone who's aggravated is going to do once you ask them, "Are you OK?" And she gives you that type of response, and then you come back with, "Are you done?" I mean, how's that building on rapport?

Renfro is firm but understanding, like a father chiding a small child for being rude to the dinner guests. The two of them have agreed to frame the tragic death of Sandra Bland as a personal encounter gone awry, and now they are at the stage where Renfro is critiquing Encinia's table manners.

Encinia: At no point was I ever trying to be discourteous or trying to downplay any of her response. I was just simply asking her if she was done, to make sure she had what she needed out, and that way I could move on with completing the traffic stop and/or identifying what possibly may or may not be in the area.
Renfro: Is it fair to say that she could have possibly taken that as being sarcastic?
Encinia: It is possible, yes, sir. Those were not my intentions.

Oh, so it was *her* mistake, was it? Apparently, Bland misinterpreted his intonation. If you are blind to the ideas that underlie our mistakes with strangers—and to the institutions and practices that we construct around those ideas—then all you are left with is the personal: the credulous Mountain Climber, the negligent Graham Spanier, the sinister Amanda Knox, the doomed Sylvia Plath. And now

Sandra Bland, who—at the end of the lengthy postmortem into that fateful traffic stop on FM 1098—somehow becomes the villain of the story.

> **Renfro:** Did you ever reflect back on your training at that point and think about that you may have stopped a subject that just didn't like police officers? Did that ever occur to you?
>
> **Encinia:** Yes sir.... That is a possibility, that she did not like police officers.

Because we do not know how to talk to strangers, what do we do when things go awry with strangers? We blame the stranger.

Acknowledgments

Talking to Strangers, like all books, was a team effort, and I am grateful that my teammates are among the best. The folks at Little, Brown were a delight to work with: my brilliant editor, Asya Muchnick, my champion Reagan Arthur, and all the others who supported this book from the beginning: Elizabeth Garriga, Pamela Marshall, Allan Fallow, and countless others at the best publishing house in America. Helen Conford at Penguin UK said the most British thing ever: "Lots of third rails! I love it!" Special thanks to Eloise Lynton, my tireless fact checker, Camille Baptista, who answered a million of my questions, and my agent, Tina Bennett, without whom I'd be writing longhand on parchment in an unheated garret somewhere. Countless friends took the time to read the manuscript and offer their advice: Adam Alter, Ann Banchoff, Tali Farhadian, Henry Finder, Mala Gaonkar, Emily Hunt, all the Lyntons, Brit Marling, Kate Moore, Wesley Neff, Kate Taylor, Lily and Jacob Weisberg, and Dave Wirtshafter.

I hope I haven't forgotten anyone.

Special thanks as always to my mother, who taught me to write clearly and simply. Sadly, my father died before I could finish. He would have read it carefully, mused about it, and then said something thoughtful or funny. Or possibly both. It is a lesser book without his contribution.

Notes

Talking to Strangers was written over a span of three years. In the course of my research, I conducted countless interviews and read many hundreds of books and articles. Unless otherwise attributed, quotations in the text are from my interviews.

What follows is not meant to be a definitive account of everything that influenced my thinking. It is simply a list of what I consider the most important of those sources. It is almost certainly the case that I have left some things out. Should you see anything that falls into that category or instances where I am plainly in error, please contact me at lbpublicity.generic@hbgusa.com and I will be happy to correct the record.

INTRODUCTION: "STEP OUT OF THE CAR!"

The Sandra Bland case was the subject of a 2018 HBO documentary, *Say Her Name: The Life and Death of Sandra Bland,* directed and produced by Kate Davis and David Heilbroner. *Say Her Name* was created with the full cooperation of Bland's family, and it does a very good job of describing her life and capturing her spirit. However, it feeds into the speculation—common in various corners of the internet—that there was something suspicious about Bland's death. I do not find those suspicions persuasive, and *Say Her Name* presents no real evidence to support them. The heartbreak of Sandra Bland is, as you have just read, more complicated—and, tragically, more systemic—than that.

"I am up today just praising God…": "Sandy Speaks on her birthday! February 7th, 2015," YouTube, February 7, 2015, accessed January 10, 2019, https://www.youtube.com/watch?v=KfrZM2Qjvtc.

has been viewed in one form or another several million times: See Texas Department of Public Safety video (963K views), *WSJ* video (42K views), second *WSJ* video (37k views), plus sites without video-view counts such as nytimes.com and nbc.com.

Transcript up to **"for a failure to signal?":** *"Sandra Bland Traffic Stop,"* Texas Department of Public Safety, YouTube, 2015, https://www.youtube.com/watch?v=CaW09Ymr2BA.

Michael Brown was shot to death: Rachel Clarke and Christopher Lett, "What happened when Michael Brown met Officer Darren Wilson," CNN, November 11, 2014, https://www.cnn.com/interactive/2014/08/us/ferguson-brown-timeline/.

In Baltimore, a young black man named Freddie Gray…Scott was killed on April 4, 2015: Peter Herman and John Woodrow Cox, "A Freddie Gray primer: Who was he, how did he die, why is there so much anger?" *Washington Post,* April 28, 2015, https://www.washingtonpost.com/news/local/wp/2015/04/28/a-freddie-gray-primer-who-was-he-how-did-he-why-is-there-so-much-anger. For

Philando Castile, see Mark Berman, "Minnesota officer charged with manslaughter for shooting Philando Castile during incident on Facebook," *Washington Post,* November 16, 2016, https://www.washingtonpost.com/news/post-nation/wp/2016/11/16/prosecutors-to-announce-update-on-investigation-into-shooting-of-philando-castile/?utm_term=.1e7914da2c3b. For Eric Garner, see Deborah Bloom and Jareen Imam, "New York man dies after chokehold by police," CNN, December 8, 2014, https://www.cnn.com/2014/07/20/justice/ny-chokehold-death/index.html. For Walter Scott, see Michael Miller, Lindsey Bever, and Sarah Kaplan, "How a cellphone video led to murder charges against a cop in North Charleston, S.C.," *Washington Post,* April 8, 2015, https://www.washingtonpost.com/news/morning-mix/wp/2015/04/08/how-a-cell-phone-video-led-to-murder-charges-against-a-cop-in-north-charleston-s-c/?utm_term=.476f73934c34.

"Good morning…and still be killed": "Sandy Speaks—April 8th 2015 (Black Lives Matter)," YouTube, April 8, 2015, https://www.youtube.com/watch?v=CIKeZgC8lQ4.

Confrontation between Cortés and Montezuma: William Prescott, *History of the Conquest of Mexico* (New York: Modern Library, 1980).

"When we saw so many cities": Bernal Diaz del Castillo, *The Discovery and Conquest of Mexico* (London: George Routledge & Sons, 1928), p. 270, https://archive.org/details/in.ernet.dli.2015.152204/page/n295.

Description of first meeting up to **"Yes, I am he":** Hugh Thomas, *Conquest: Cortés, Montezuma, and the Fall of Old Mexico* (New York: Simon & Schuster, 1995), p. 279.

"innumerable rooms inside…and admirable white fur robes": Thomas, *Conquest,* p. 280.

The idea that Montezuma considered Cortés a god (in footnote): Camilla Townsend, "Burying the White Gods: New Perspectives on the Conquest of Mexico," *American Historical Review* 108, no. 3 (2003): 659–87.

"The impossibility of adequately translating…Spanish surrender": Matthew Restall, *When Montezuma Met Cortés: The True Story of the Meeting That Changed History* (New York: Harper Collins, 2018), p. 345.

If you are interested in the **Cortés-Montezuma story,** I strongly recommend the last two of these sources. Restall's book is marvelous. And Townsend is that rarest of historians, able to write scholarly history in academic journals that reads like it was written for all of us.

CHAPTER ONE: FIDEL CASTRO'S REVENGE

"I am a case officer from Cuban Intelligence. I am an intelligence *comandante*": This account is taken from Brian Latell, *Castro's Secrets: Cuban Intelligence, the CIA, and the Assassination of John F. Kennedy* (New York: Palgrave Macmillan, 2013), p. 26.

one of the former Havana station chiefs: Herald Staff, "Spy work celebrated at museum in Havana," *Miami Herald*, July 16, 2001, http://www.latinamericanstudies.org/espionage/spy-museum.htm.

until he had listed dozens of names: Benjamin B. Fischer, "Doubles Troubles: The CIA and Double Agents during the Cold War," *International Journal of Intelligence and Counterintelligence* 21, no. 1 (2016): 48–74.

There were detailed explanations of which park bench: I. C. Smith, *Inside: A Top G-Man Exposes Spies, Lies, and Bureaucratic Bungling Inside the FBI* (Nashville: Nelson Current, 2004), pp. 95–96.

CIA officer stuffing cash: Herald Staff, "Spy work celebrated at museum in Miami," *Miami Herald*, July 16, 2001.

"we were in the enviable position…to the Americans.": Here Fischer quotes from Markus Wolf, with Anne McElvoy, *Man Without a Face: The Autobiography of Communism's Greatest Spymaster* (New York: Times Books/Random House, 1997), p. 285.

CHAPTER TWO: GETTING TO KNOW *DER FÜHRER*

The account of Chamberlain and Hitler is taken from a number of sources, but chiefly David Faber's excellent *Munich, 1938: Appeasement and World War II* (New York: Simon & Schuster, 2008), pp. 272–96; "so unconventional…breath away," p. 229; that 70 percent of the country thought Chamberlain's trip was a "good thing for peace" and the toast to Chamberlain's health, pp. 284–85; Chamberlain's speech at Heston Airport and the reaction to it, p. 296; "no signs of insanity…beyond a certain point," p. 302; "between a social gathering and a rough house," p. 300; "mixture of astonishment, repugnance, and compassion," p. 40. Faber is quoting from British diplomat Ivone Kirkpatrick's account of the event in his memoir, *The Inner Circle* (London: Macmillan & Company, 1959), p. 97; and "borderline into insanity," p. 257.

The people who were wrong about Hitler were the ones who had talked with him for hours. I suppose that makes a certain sense: you need to be exposed to a fraud before you can fall for a fraud. On the other hand, Hitler's dupes were all intelligent men, well experienced in world affairs, with plenty of suspicions going into their meeting. Why didn't whatever extra information they could gather on Hitler from a face-to-face meeting lead to an improvement in the accuracy of their opinion of him? See also Faber, *Munich, 1938*, pp. 285, 302, 351; Chamberlain's third and final visit to Germany, p. 414; "Herr Hitler was telling the truth," p. 302; "This morning…as mine," p. 4; "sleep quietly in your beds," pp. 6–7.

For King's admiration of Hitler (in footnote), see *W. L. Mackenzie King's Diary*, June 29, 1937, National Archives of Canada, MG 26 J Series 13, https://www.junobeach.org/canada-in-wwii/articles/aggression-and-impunity/w-l-mackenzie-kings-diary-june-29-1937/.

"In certain moods…marvelous drollery": Diana Mosley, *A Life of Contrasts: The Autobiography of Diana Mosley* (London: Gibson Square, 2002), p. 124.

"Halfway down the steps…the house painter he was": Neville Chamberlain to Ida

Chamberlain, September 19, 1938, in Robert Self, ed., *The Neville Chamberlain Diary Letters: Volume Four: The Downing Street Years, 1934–1940* (Aldershot, UK: Ashgate, 2005), p. 346; "In short...given his word," p. 348; "Hitler's appearance...friendly demonstrations" and "Hitler frequently...brought with me," Neville Chamberlain to Hilda Chamberlain, October 2, 1938, p. 350.

A good account of Halifax's visit to Berlin is here: Lois G. Schwoerer, "Lord Halifax's Visit to Germany: November 1937," *The Historian* 32, no. 3 (May 1970): 353–75.

Hitler even had a nickname for Henderson: Peter Neville, *Hitler and Appeasement: The British Attempt to Prevent the Second World War* (London and New York: Hambledon Continuum, 2006), p. 150.

Hitler, he believed, "hates war as much as anyone": Abraham Ascher, *Was Hitler a Riddle? Western Democracies and National Socialism* (Stanford: Stanford University Press, 2012), p. 73.

Göring "loved animals and children...teach squeamishness to the young" (in footnote): Sir Nevile Henderson, *Failure of a Mission: Berlin 1937–39* (New York: G. P. Putnam and Sons, 1940), p. 82.

Anthony Eden...saw the truth of him: See D. R. Thorpe, *The Life and Times of Anthony Eden, First Earl of Avon, 1897–1997* (New York: Random House, 2003).

For Sendhil Mullainathan's study, see Jon Kleinberg et al., "Human Decisions and Machine Predictions," NBER Working Paper 23180, February 2017; this is an early version of Kleinberg et al., "Human Decisions and Machine Predictions," *The Quarterly Journal of Economics* 133, no. 1 (February 2018): 237–93.

Pronin had them fill in the blank spaces: Emily Pronin et al., "You Don't Know Me, But I Know You: The Illusion of Asymmetric Insight," *Journal of Personality and Social Psychology* 81, no. 4 (2001): 639–56, APA PsychNET.

I quoted part of Pronin's conclusion. But the whole paragraph is worth considering:

> The conviction that we know others better than they know us—and that we may have insights about them they lack (but not vice versa)—leads us to talk when we would do well to listen and to be less patient than we ought to be when others express the conviction that they are the ones who are being misunderstood or judged unfairly. The same convictions can make us reluctant to take advice from others who cannot know our private thoughts, feelings, interpretations of events, or motives, but all too willing to give advice to others based on our views of their past behavior, without adequate attention to their thoughts, feelings, interpretations, and motives. Indeed, the biases documented here may create a barrier to the type of exchanges of information, and especially to the type of careful and respectful listening, that can go a long way to attenuating the feelings of frustration and resentment that accompany interpersonal and intergroup conflict.

Those are wise words.

Chapter Three: The Queen of Cuba

"Homeland or death, you bastards": Transcript taken from the documentary *Shoot Down,* directed by Cristina Khuly (Palisades Pictures, 2007). That Juan Roque was the Cubans' source inside Hermanos al Rescate is also from the documentary.

The U.S. government was aware of **growing Cuban anger about the Hermanos al Rescate missions** for some time before the shoot-down occurred and had alerted the organization, mainly by communicating directly with its leader, Jose Basulto. Through the summer and fall of 1995, the State Department and the Federal Aviation Administration (FAA) made public statements and cautioned the organization that no flight plan to Cuba was acceptable. At one point the FAA tried to revoke Basulto's pilot license. Government warnings slowed in the fall of 1996, however, because officials felt that further alerts were "more likely to provoke Basulto than to quiet him down." By this period, the Clinton administration and Hermanos al Rescate were at odds because of Clinton's 1995 "wet feet, dry feet policy," which forced Cuban rafters to repatriate.

The State Department knew about the shoot-down threat after meeting with Rear Admiral Eugene Carroll on the 23rd, but the government did not contact Hermanos al Rescate. Instead, the State Department warned the FAA the night before the attack that "it would not be unlikely that [Hermanos al Rescate would] attempt an unauthorized flight into Cuban airspace tomorrow." In response, the FAA arranged for radar centers to pay special attention to flights over the Florida Straits. However, when radar monitors spotted the MiGs on the 24th, still no warning was issued to the pilots. Despite the fact that F-15 fighter jets were ready for action, the go-ahead to protect the planes never came. The U.S. government later blamed communication issues for its failure to protect the Hermanos al Rescate pilots. Basulto, who survived the incident, suggested the attack was the result of a conspiracy between Cuban leaders and the U.S. government. This account is taken from Marifeli Pérez-Stable, *The United States and Cuba: Intimate Enemies* (New York: Routledge, 2011), p. 52.

This was an embarrassing revelation: Scott Carmichael, *True Believer: Inside the Investigation and Capture of Ana Montes, Cuba's Master Spy* (Annapolis: Naval Institute Press, 2007), p. 5.

"CNN Interview with Admiral Eugene Carroll—U.S. Navy Rear Admiral (Ret.)," CNN, February 25, 1996, Transcript #47-22, http://www.hermanos.org/CNN%20Interview%20with%20Admiral%20Eugene%20Carroll.htm.

Montes's nickname was the "Queen of Cuba"; DIA found codes in her purse and radio in her closet; and postmortem quote "Her handlers...work for Havana" are all from Jim Popkin, "'Queen of Cuba' Ana Montes did much harm as a spy. Chances are you haven't heard of her," *Washington Post,* April 8, 2013.

For a complete list of **Tim Levine's deception experiments,** see "Deception and Deception Detection," https://timothy-levine.squarespace.com/deception, accessed March 7, 2019.

For **video of "Philip"** and other interview subjects, see T. R. Levine, *NSF funded cheating tape interviews* (East Lansing, Mich.: Michigan State University, 2007–2011).

Levine had people watch **twenty-two liars and twenty-two truth-tellers.** The viewers correctly identified the liars 56 percent of the time. See Experiment 27 in Chapter 13 of Timothy R. Levine, *Duped: Truth-Default Theory and the Social Science of Lying and Deception* (Tuscaloosa, AL: University of Alabama Press, 2019). The average for similar versions of the same experiment by other psychologists is 54 percent. C. F. Bond, Jr. and B. M. DePaulo, "Accuracy of deception judgments," *Review of Personality and Social Psychology* 10 (2006): 214–34.

Tim Levine's answer is called the "Truth-Default Theory": Timothy Levine, "Truth-Default Theory (TDT): A Theory of Human Deception and Deception Detection," *Journal of Language and Social Psychology* 33, no. 4 (2014): 378–92.

Stanley Milgram's obedience experiment: Stanley Milgram, "Behavioral Study of Obedience," *Journal of Abnormal and Social Psychology* 64, no. 4 (1963): 371–78.

The account of **the second lesson from Milgram's experiment** was largely drawn from Gina Perry's definitive *Behind the Shock Machine: The Untold Story of the Notorious Milgram Psychology Experiments* (New York: The New Press, 2013); "mild and submissive," pp. 55–56; "…I might have killed that man in the chair," p. 80; "'Maybe it really was true,'" pp. 127–29.

the full statistics from the Milgram experiment: Stanley Milgram, *Obedience to Authority: An Experimental View* (New York: Harper Torchbooks, 1969), p. 172.

CHAPTER FOUR: THE HOLY FOOL

The source of the following quotes is U.S. Securities and Exchange Commission, Office of Investigations, "Investigation of Failure of the SEC to Uncover Bernard Madoff's Ponzi Scheme—Public Version," August 31, 2009, www.sec.gov/news/studies/2009/oig-509.pdf: "told us in confidence" and "Throw in that his brother-in-law," p. 146; "None of it seems to add up," p. 149; "I came to the conclusion…any evidence we could find," p. 153; "I never…truly fraudulent," p. 158; "Sollazzo did not find…'ridiculous,'" p. 211; "It would have been so easy…that was the case," p. 427; "This is not rocket science…$10 billion of options," p. 155.

"I gift-wrapped…their priorities": "Opening Statement of Harry Markopolos," Public Resource Org, YouTube, video provided courtesy of C-SPAN, February 4, 2009, https://www.youtube.com/watch?v=AF-gzN3ppbE&feature=youtu.be, accessed March 8, 2019.

Markopolos biographical info: Harry Markopolos, *No One Would Listen: A True Financial Thriller* (Hoboken, N.J.: John Wiley & Sons, 2010), p. 11; account of trying to approach Spitzer with brown envelope, pp. 109–111.

"a great deal for us…doing business" and **"Being deceived…a trade-off"** are both from Chapter 11 of Timothy R. Levine, *Duped: Truth-Default Theory and the Social Science of Lying and Deception* (University of Alabama Press, 2019).

" 'Most of the officers…qualified staff' " and " 'The division…shrank dramatically' ":
The account and quotes in the footnote about Angleton's search for a mole in
the CIA are from Tom Mangold, *Cold Warrior: James Jesus Angleton—The CIA's
Master Spy Hunter* (New York: Simon & Schuster, 1991), pp. 263–264.

CHAPTER FIVE: CASE STUDY: THE BOY IN THE SHOWER

The source of the following material is *Commonwealth of Pennsylvania vs. Graham
Basil Spanier* vol. 1 (March 21, 2017): McQueary transcript through "P: Stomach
to back? McQueary: Yes," pp. 105–8; McQueary's father's testimony, pp. 141–42;
McQueary transcript through "just kind of went sad," pp. 115–16; prosecution's
closing statement, pp. 86–87; Dranov questioning by defense counsel, pp. 155,
163–65; Wendell Courtney testimony, pp. 174–75, 189; Tim Curley and John
Raykovitz quotes (in footnote), pp. 381, 203; Gary Schultz testimony, p. 442.

Sandusky interview with Costas: "Sandusky addresses sex abuse allegations in
2011 interview," NBC News, June 21, 2012, https://www.nbcnews.com/video/
sandusky-addresses-sex-abuse-allegations-in-2011-interview-44570179907,
accessed March 12, 2019.

"Dad would get every single kid…could not keep track of them all":
Malcolm Gladwell, "In Plain View," *The New Yorker*, September 24, 2012,
https://www.newyorker.com/magazine/2012/09/24/in-plain-view.

"They took in so many…part of his persona": Joe Posnanski, *Paterno* (New York:
Simon & Schuster, 2012), p. 251.

"Wherever I went…part of me": Jerry Sandusky, *Touched: The Jerry Sandusky
Story* (Champaign, Ill.: Sports Publishing Inc., 2000), pp. 33, 210.

"If Sandusky…canonize him": Jack McCallum, "Last Call: Jerry Sandusky,
the Dean of Linebacker U, is leaving Penn State after 32 years to
devote himself to a different kind of coaching," *Sports Illustrated*, December
20, 1999, https://www.si.com/vault/1999/12/20/271564/last-call-jerry-sandusky-
the-dean-of-linebacker-u-is-leaving-penn-state-after-32-years-to-devote-
himself-to-a-different-kind-of-coaching.

"In more than one motel hallway…done without public notice": Bill Lyon,
"Penn State defensive coordinator Jerry Sandusky is the Pied Piper of his time,"
Philadelphia Inquirer, December 27, 1999.

This was not unusual for Sandusky (in footnote): *Commonwealth v. Gerald A.
Sandusky*, June 11, 2012, p. 53; Brett Swisher Houtz testimony, June 11, 2012,
p. 70; Dorothy Sandusky testimony, June 19, 2012, p. 257.

The mother told her son's psychologist…"luckiest boy in the world": According
to one of the numerous postmortems on the case, "The boy said that he did
not want to get Sandusky in 'trouble' and that Sandusky must not have meant
anything by his actions. The boy did not want anyone to talk to Sandusky

because he might not invite him to any more games." Freeh Sporkin & Sullivan, LLP, *Report of the Special Investigative Counsel Regarding the Actions of the Pennsylvania State University Related to the Child Sexual Abuse Committed by Gerald A. Sandusky*, July 12, 2012, https://assets.documentcloud.org/documents/396512/report-final-071212.pdf, p. 42; "wasn't anything sexual about it" and "Honest to God, nothing happened," pp. 43–46.

Aaron Fisher biographical info and **felt uneasy about some of Sandusky's behavior:** Aaron Fisher, Michael Gillum, and Dawn Daniels, *Silent No More: Victim 1's Fight for Justice Against Jerry Sandusky* (New York: Ballantine Books, 2012).

Fisher met with his therapist repeatedly: Mark Pendergrast, *The Most Hated Man in America: Jerry Sandusky and the Rush to Judgment* (Mechanicsburg, Penn.: Sunbury Press, 2017), pp. 90, 52, 55; Fisher changes story, p. 59; "Myers said…get some money," quoted from Pennsylvania State Police interview with Allan Myers, September 2011, p. 147; footnote regarding the prosecution's report on Allan Myers is from Anthony Sassano, Supplemental Report on Allan Myers, April 11, 2012, Penn State Police, quoted on p. 168 of Pendergrast's book. The full passage in *The Most Hated Man in America* reads as follows:

> "Corricelli indicated that Attorney Shubin advised him that Myers had related to him incidents of oral, anal, and digital penetration by Sandusky," Sassano wrote in his report. "Shubin showed Corricelli a three page document purported to be Myers's recollection of his sexual contact with Sandusky. Corricelli examined the document and indicated to me that he suspected the document was written by Anthony Shubin. I advised that I did not want a copy of a document that was suspected to be written by Attorney Shubin." Sassano concluded: "At this time, I don't anticipate further investigation concerning Allan Myers."

For more on the controversy over repressed traumatic memories (in footnote), see, for example, C. J. Brainerd and V. F. Reyna, *The Science of False Memory* (Oxford: Oxford University Press, 2005); E. F. Loftus and K. Ketcham, *The Myth of Repressed Memory: False Memories and Allegations of Sexual Abuse* (New York: St Martin's Press, 1994); R. J. McNally, *Remembering Trauma* (Cambridge, Mass.: Harvard University Press, 2003); R. Ofshe and E. Watters, *Making Monsters: False Memories, Psychotherapy, and Sexual Hysteria* (New York: Scribner, 1994); D. L. Schacter, *The Seven Sins of Memory: How the Mind Forgets and Remembers* (Boston: Houghton Mifflin, 2001).

"I am contacting you…Jerry Sandusky and a child": Geoffrey Moulton, Jr., *Report to the Attorney General of the Investigation of Gerald A. Sandusky*, May 30, 2014, Appendix J, http://filesource.abacast.com/commonwealthofpa/mp4_podcast/2014_06_23_REPORT_to_AG_ON_THE_SANDUSKY_INVESTIGATION.pdf.

Let's be clear. The Sandusky case is *weird*. Ever since Sandusky's arrest and conviction, a small group of people have insisted that he is innocent. The most outspoken is the radio talk-show host John Ziegler, a conservative-leaning journalist. Ziegler is involved with three others in the website www.framingpaterno.com, which is devoted to poking holes in the prosecution's case against Sandusky.

As I mention in my discussion of the Sandusky case, Ziegler is the one who persuasively argues that there was at least a five-week lag between McQueary's spotting Sandusky in the shower and his telling anyone in the Penn State leadership about it. See John Ziegler, "New Proof that December 29, 2000, Not February 9, 2001, was the Real Date of the McQueary Episode," *The Framing of Joe Paterno* (blog), February 9, 2018, http://www.framingpaterno.com/new-proof-december-29-2000-not-february-9th-2001-was-real-date-mcqueary-episode. Ziegler thinks this is evidence that McQueary didn't see what he thought he saw. I think it suggests—in the context of default to truth—that McQueary had *doubts* about what he saw. Needless to say, there is a big difference between those two interpretations.

Ziegler has uncovered a number of other facts, which for reasons of space and focus I did not include in the chapter. (The Sandusky case is a very very deep and winding rabbit hole.) According to Ziegler's reporting, at least some of Sandusky's victims are not credible. They appear to have been attracted by the large cash settlements that Penn State was offering and the relatively lax criteria the university used for deciding who would get paid.

In the course of reporting this chapter, I corresponded on several occasions with Ziegler and chatted with him on the phone. He generously shared a number of documents with me—including the memo written by private investigator Curtis Everhart. I'm not convinced of Ziegler's ultimate conclusion—that Sandusky is innocent. But I do agree with him that the case is much more ambiguous and unusual than the conventional press accounts suggest. If you would like to go down the Sandusky rabbit hole, you may want to start with Ziegler.

A second (and perhaps more mainstream) Sandusky skeptic is author Mark Pendergrast, who published *The Most Hated Man in America: Jerry Sandusky and the Rush to Judgment* in 2017. Pendergrast argues that the Sandusky case was a classic example of a "moral panic" and the frailty of human memory. I drew heavily from Pendergrast's book in my account of the Aaron Fisher and Allan Myers cases. One of the noteworthy things about Pendergrast's book, I must say, is the back cover, which has blurbs from two of the most influential and respected experts on memory in the world: Richard Leo of the University of San Francisco, and Elizabeth Loftus of the University of California at Irvine.

Here is what Loftus had to say: "*The Most Hated Man in America* tells a truly remarkable story. In all the media coverage the Sandusky case has received, it's amazing that no one else has noticed or written about so many of these things, including all the 'memories' that were retrieved through therapy and litigation. One would think that the sheer insanity of so much of this will have to eventually come out."

What do I think? I have no idea. I will let others tackle the morass of conflicting evidence and speculation and ambiguity that is the Sandusky case. My interest is simply this: if the case is such a mess, how on earth can you put Spanier, Curley, and Schultz behind bars?

the "graduate assistant…reported what he had seen": Sandusky Grand Jury Presentment, November 5, 2011, https://cbsboston.files.wordpress.com/2011/11/sandusky-grand-jury-presentment.pdf, pp. 6–7.

McQueary's email to Jonelle Eshbach was obtained by Ray Blehar, a blogger in the Penn State area. Ray Blehar, "Correcting the Record: Part 1: McQueary's 2001 Eyewitness Report," *Second Mile – Sandusky Scandal (SMSS): Searching for the Truth through a Fog of Deception* (Blog), October 9, 2017, https://notpsu.blogspot.com/2017/10/correcting-record-part-1-mcquearys-2001.html#more.

Rachael Denhollander's statement: "Rachael Denhollander delivers powerful final victim speech to Larry Nassar," YouTube, January 24, 2018, https://www.youtube.com/watch?v=7CjVOLToRJk&t=616s.

"And unfortunately, I was right…deepest, darkest hole and hide": "Survivor reported sexual assault in 1997, MSU did nothing," YouTube, January 19, 2018, https://www.youtube.com/watch?v=OYJIx_3hbRA.

"This just goes to show…patients lie to get doctors in trouble": Melissa Korn, "Larry Nassar's Boss at Michigan State Said in 2016 That He Didn't Believe Sex Abuse Claims," *Wall Street Journal,* March 19, 2018, https://www.wsj.com/articles/deans-comments-shed-light-on-culture-at-michigan-state-during-nassars-tenure-1521453600.

Quotes from *Believed* podcast: Kate Wells and Lindsey Smith, "The Parents," *Believed,* NPR/Michigan Radio, Podcast audio, November 26, 2018, https://www.npr.org/templates/transcript/transcript.php?storyId=669669746.

"He does that to me all the time!": Kerry Howley, "Everyone Believed Larry Nassar," *New York Magazine/The Cut,* November 19, 2018, https://www.thecut.com/2018/11/how-did-larry-nassar-deceive-so-many-for-so-long.html.

"I had to make an extremely hard choice…your dark, broken soul": "Lifelong friend, longtime defender speaks against Larry Nassar," YouTube, January 19, 2018, https://www.youtube.com/watch?v=H8Aa2MQORd4.

"I asked the specific question…as far away from him as possible": Allan Myers interview with Curtis Everhart (Criminal Defense Investigator), November 9, 2011.

The only time Myers ever appeared…he didn't recall thirty-four times: *Commonwealth v. Gerald A. Sandusky* (Appeal), November 4, 2016, p. 10.

"Are you sure…like that before" and "Every one of you…would back them up": Jeffrey Toobin, "Former Penn State President Graham Spanier Speaks," *The New Yorker,* August 21, 2012, https://www.newyorker.com/news/news-desk/former-penn-state-president-graham-spanier-speaks.

CHAPTER SIX: THE *FRIENDS* FALLACY

Dialogue is from *Friends,* "The One with the Girl Who Hits Joey" (episode 15, season 5), directed by Kevin Bright, NBC, 1998.

It was developed by legendary psychologist (in footnote): Paul Ekman and Wallace V. Friesen, *Facial Action Coding System, parts 1 and 2* (San Francisco: Human Interaction Laboratory, Dept. of Psychiatry, University of California, 1978).

In my second book, *Blink* (Little, Brown and Company, 2005), I devoted a large chunk of Chapter Six, "Seven Seconds in the Bronx: The Delicate Art of Mind Reading," to a discussion of the work of Paul Ekman, one of the most important psychologists of the last century. He is the coinventor of FACS, which I asked Jennifer Fugate to use to analyze that episode of *Friends*. FACS has become the gold standard for understanding and cataloging how human emotion is displayed on the face. Ekman's principal scientific contribution was to demonstrate the idea of "leakage"— that the emotions we feel are often, involuntarily, displayed on our faces in some distinctive configuration of facial muscles. And if you are trained in the "language" of the face and have the opportunity to break down videotape of someone's expressions millisecond by millisecond, you can identify those configurations.

Here is what I wrote on p. 210 of *Blink*: "Whenever we experience a basic emotion, that emotion is automatically expressed by the muscles of the face. That response may linger on the face for just a fraction of a second or be detectable only if electrical sensors are attached to the face. But it's always there."

Ekman was making two bold claims. First, that emotion is necessarily expressed on the face—that if you feel it, you'll show it. And second, that these kinds of emotional expressions are universal—that everyone, everywhere, uses their face to display their feelings in the same way.

These propositions had always left some psychologists uneasy. But since *Blink* was written, there has been growing reaction in the psychology community against Ekman's position.

For example, why did Ekman believe that emotions were universal? In the 1960s, he and two colleagues traveled to Papua New Guinea, armed with a stack of thirty photographs. The pictures were headshots of Westerners making facial expressions corresponding to the basic emotions: anger, sadness, contempt, disgust, surprise, happiness, and fear.

The New Guinea tribe that Ekman's group visited was called the Fore. As recently as a dozen years earlier, they had still been effectively living in the Stone Age, completely cut off from the rest of the world. Ekman's idea was that if the Fore could identify anger or surprise in the photographed faces as readily as someone in New York City or London can, emotions must be universal. Sure enough, they could.

"Our findings support Darwin's suggestion that facial expressions of emotion are similar among humans, regardless of culture, because of their evolutionary origin," Ekman and his colleagues wrote in a paper published in *Science,* one of the most prestigious academic journals. (See P. Ekman et al., "Pan-Cultural Elements in Facial Display of Emotions," *Science* 164 [1969]: 86–88.)

This idea—that there is a universal set of human emotional reactions—is the principle that lies behind an entire category of tools that we use to understand strangers. It's why we have lie detectors. It's why lovestruck couples stare deeply into each other's eyes. It's why Neville Chamberlain made his daring visit to see Hitler in Germany. And it's why Solomon looked hard at the defendant in the child-abuse case.

But there's the problem. Ekman was leaning awfully hard on what he saw with the Fore. Yet the emotion-recognition exercise he did with them wasn't nearly as conclusive as he said it was.

Ekman went to New Guinea with another psychologist, Wallace Friesen, and an anthropologist, Richard Sorenson. Neither Ekman nor Friesen spoke the language of the Fore. Sorenson knew only enough to understand or say the simplest things. (See James Russell, "Is There Universal Recognition of

Emotion from Facial Expression? A Review of the Cross Cultural Studies," *Psychological Bulletin* 115, no. 1 [1994]: 124.) So there they are, showing headshots to tribesmen of white people making faces—and they are utterly reliant on their translator. They can't just have each tribesman free-associate about what he thinks is happening in each photo. How would they make sense of that? They have to keep things simple. So Ekman and his group use what's called "forced choice." They show each Fore person the pictures, one by one, and for every image they asked the viewer to choose the right answer from a short list of emotions. Is what you are looking at anger, sadness, contempt, disgust, surprise, happiness, or fear? (The Fore didn't really have a word to describe *disgust* or *surprise,* so the three researchers improvised: *disgust* was *something that stinks; surprise* was *something new.*)

Now, is forced choice a good method? For example, suppose I want to find out whether you know which city is the capital of Canada. (A surprising number of Americans, in my experience, have no idea.) I could ask you straight out: What is the capital of Canada? That's a *free* choice question. In order to answer it correctly, you really have to know the capital of Canada. Now here's the forced-choice version of that question.

> The capital of Canada is:
> Washington, DC
> Kuala Lumpur
> Ottawa
> Nairobi
> Toronto

You can guess, can't you? It's not Washington, DC. Even someone with no knowledge whatsoever of geography probably knows that's the capital of the United States. It's probably not Kuala Lumpur or Nairobi, since those names don't *sound* Canadian. So it's down to Toronto or Ottawa. Even if you have no idea what the capital of Canada is, you have a 50 percent chance of getting the answer right. So is that what was happening with Ekman's survey of the Fore?

Sergio Jarillo and Carlos Crivelli—the two researchers I write about in Chapter Six of this book—began their research by attempting to replicate Ekman's findings. Their idea was: let's correct the flaws in his exercise and see if it still holds up. Their first step was to pick a isolated tribe—the Trobriand Islanders—whose language and culture at least one of them (Jarillo) knew well. That was their first advantage over Ekman: they knew an awful lot more about whom they were talking to than Ekman's group had. They also decided not to use "forced choice." They would use the far more rigorous methodology of free choice. They laid out a set of headshots (with people looking happy, sad, angry, scared, and disgusted) and asked, "Which of these is the sad face?" Then they asked the next person, "Which of these is the angry face?" And so on. Finally, they tallied all the responses.

And what did they find? That when you redo Ekman's foundational experiment—only this time, carefully and rigorously—the case for universalism disappears. Over the past few years the floodgates have opened, which is where much of the research I described in this chapter comes from.

A few additional points:

Ekman's original *Science* paper is, upon reflection, a little strange. He argued that what he found in the Fore was evidence of universalism. But if you examine his data, it doesn't look like he's describing universalism.

The Fore were really good at correctly identifying happy faces, but only about half of them correctly identified the "fear" face as being an expression of fear. Forty-five percent of them thought the surprised face was a fearful face. Fifty-six percent of them read sadness as anger. This is universalism?

Crivelli made a very insightful remark when we were talking about the people (like Ekman) who so favored the universalism idea. Many of them belonged to the generation that grew up in the aftermath of the Second World War. They were born into a world obsessed with human difference—in which black people were thought to be genetically inferior and Jews were held to be damaged and malignant—and they were powerfully drawn to a theory that maintained we are all the same.

It is important to note, however, that the work of anti-universalists is *not* a refutation of Ekman's contributions. Everyone in the field of human emotion is in some crucial sense standing on his shoulders. People like Jarillo and Crivelli are simply arguing that you can't understand emotion without taking culture into account.

To quote psychologist Lisa Feldman Barrett—one of the leaders in challenging the Ekman view—"emotions are…made and not triggered." (See her book *How Emotions Are Made* [New York: Houghton Mifflin Harcourt, 2017], p. xiii.) Each of us, over the course of our lives, builds our own set of operating instructions for our face, based on the culture and environment we inhabit. The face is a symbol of how different human beings are, not how similar we are, which is a big problem if your society has created a rule for understanding strangers based on reading faces.

For a good summary of this new line of research, see L. F. Barrett et al., "Emotional expressions reconsidered: Challenges to inferring emotion in human facial movements," *Psychological Science in the Public Interest* (in press), as well as Barrett's *Emotions* (cited above).

Photos of Pan-Am smile and Duchenne smile: Jason Vandeventer and Eric Patterson, "Differentiating Duchenne from non-Duchenne smiles using active appearance models," *2012 IEEE Fifth International Conference on Biometrics: Theory, Applications and Systems (BTAS)* (2012): 319–24.

Facial Action Coding System units for Ross looking through door: Paul Ekman and Erika L Rosenberg, eds., *What the Face Reveals: Basic and Applied Studies of Spontaneous Expression Using the Facial Action Coding System (FACS)*, Second Edition (Oxford University Press: New York, 2005), p.14.

a kind of billboard for the heart: Charles Darwin, *The Expression of the Emotions in Man and Animals* (London: J. Murray, 1872). Ekman has written extensively on Darwin's contributions to the understanding of emotional expression. See Paul Ekman, ed., *Darwin and Facial Expression* (Los Altos, Calif.: Malor Books, 2006).

The plaintiff was Ginnah Muhammad (in footnote): *Ginnah Muhammad v. Enterprise Rent-A-Car*, 3–4 (31st District, 2006).

For an introduction to the Jarillo-Crivelli study on Trobriand islanders, see Carlos Crivelli et al., "Reading Emotions from Faces in Two Indigenous Societies," *Journal of Experimental Psychology: General* 145, no. 7 (July 2016): 830–43, doi:10.1037/xge0000172. Also from this source is the chart comparing success rate of Trobrianders with that of Madrid students.

dozens of videotapes of judo fighters: Carlos Crivelli et al., "Are smiles a sign of happiness? Spontaneous expressions of judo winners," *Evolution and Human Behavior* 2014, doi:10.1016/j.evolhumbehav.2014.08.009.

he watched videotapes of people masturbating: Carlos Crivelli et al., "Facial Behavior While Experiencing Sexual Excitement," *Journal of Nonverbal Behavior* 35 (2011): 63–71.

Anger photo: Job van der Schalk et al., "Moving Faces, Looking Places: Validation of the Amsterdam Dynamic Facial Expression Set (ADFES)," *Emotion* 11, no. 4 (2011): 912. Researchgate.

Namibia study: Maria Gendron et al., "Perceptions of Emotion from Facial Expressions Are Not Culturally Universal: Evidence from a Remote Culture," *Emotion* 14, no 2 (2014): 251–62.

"This is not to say...freighted with significance": Mary Beard, *Laughter in Ancient Rome: On Joking, Tickling, and Cracking Up* (Oakland: University of California Press, 2015), p. 73.

Two German psychologists...ran sixty people through it: Achim Schützwohl and Rainer Reisenzein, "Facial expressions in response to a highly surprising event exceeding the field of vision: A test of Darwin's theory of surprise," *Evolution and Human Behavior* 33, no. 6 (Nov. 2012): 657–64.

"The participants...emotion-face associations": Schützwohl is drawing from a previous study: R. Reisenzein and M. Studtmann, "On the expression and experience of surprise: No evidence for facial feedback, but evidence for a reverse self-inference effect," *Emotion*, no. 7 (2007): 612–27.

Walker put a gun to his ex-girlfriend's head: Associated Press, " 'Real Smart Kid' Jailed, This Time for Killing Friend," *Spokane (Wash.) Spokesman-Review*, May 26, 1995, http://www.spokesman.com/stories/1995/may/26/real-smart-kid-jailed-this-time-for-killing-friend/.

"Whatever these unobserved variables...create noise, not signal": Kleinberg et al., "Human Decisions," op. cit.

CHAPTER SEVEN: A (SHORT) EXPLANATION OF THE AMANDA KNOX CASE

"A murder always...want in a story?": *Amanda Knox*, directed by Rod Blackhurst and Brian McGinn (Netflix, 2016). Also from that documentary are the following: Knox's list of lovers (in footnote); "She started hitting...suspect Amanda" (in footnote); "Every piece of proof...no doubt of this"; and "There is no trace...not objective evidence."

"The amplified DNA...borderline for interpretation": Peter Gill, "Analysis and Implications of the Miscarriages of Justice of Amanda Knox and Raffaele Sollecito," *Forensic Science International: Genetics* 23 (July 2016): 9–18. *Elsevier*, doi:10.1016/j.fsigen.2016.02.015.

Judges correctly identify liars: Levine, *Duped,* chapter 13.

Levine found this pattern: This refers to experiment 27 in Levine's *Duped,* chapter 13. See also Timothy Levine, Kim Serota, Hillary Shulman, David Clare, Hee Sun Park, Allison Shaw, Jae Chul Shim, and Jung Hyon Lee, "Sender Demeanor: Individual Differences in Sender Believability Have a Powerful Impact on Deception Detection Judgments," *Human Communication Research* 37 (2011): 377–403. Also from this source is the performance of trained interrogators on matched and mismatched senders.

In a survey of attitudes toward deception: The Global Deception Research Team, "A World of Lies," *Journal of Cross-Cultural Psychology* 37, no. 1 (January 2006): 60–74.

"It wasn't so much...care about this": Markopolos, *No One Would Listen,* p. 82.

"And though it's risky...Tsarnaev smirked" (in footnote): Seth Stevenson, "Tsarnaev's Smirk," *Slate,* April 21, 2015, https://slate.com/news-and-politics/2015/04/tsarnaev-trial-sentencing-phase-prosecutor-makes-case-that-dzhokhar-tsarnaev-shows-no-remorse.html.

"In the Boston Marathon Bombing...remained stony-faced": Barrett, *How Emotions Are Made,* p. 231.

"I'd do things...fall-over hilarious": Amanda Knox, *Waiting to Be Heard: A Memoir* (New York: Harper, 2013), pp. 11–12; "'You seem really flexible'...full of contempt," p. 109; "But what drew laughs...accepting of differences" (in footnote), p. 26; "Ta-dah" moment, p. 91.

Just listen to a handful of quotations: John Follain, *Death in Perugia: The Definitive Account of the Meredith Kercher Case from Her Murder to the Acquittal of Raffaele Sollecito and Amanda Knox* (London: Hodder and Stoughton, 2011), pp. 90–91, 93, 94.

Diane Sawyer interview: "Amanda Knox Speaks: A Diane Sawyer Exclusive," ABC News, 2013, https://abcnews.go.com/2020/video/amanda-knox-speaks-diane-sawyer-exclusive-19079012.

"What's compelling to me...distance ourselves from" (in footnote): Tom Dibblee, "On Being Off: The Case of Amanda Knox," *Los Angeles Review of Books,* August 12, 2013, https://lareviewofbooks.org/article/on-being-off-the-case-of-amanda-knox.

"We were able...other kinds of investigation": Ian Leslie, "Amanda Knox: What's in a face?" *The Guardian,* October 7, 2011, https://www.theguardian.com/world/2011/oct/08/amanda-knox-facial-expressions.

"Her eyes...could have been involved": Nathaniel Rich, "The Neverending Nightmare of Amanda Knox," *Rolling Stone,* June 27, 2011, https://www.rollingstone.com/culture/culture-news/the-neverending-nightmare-ofamanda-knox-244620/?print=true.

CHAPTER EIGHT: CASE STUDY: THE FRATERNITY PARTY

The Jonsson testimony and description of the incident are from *People v. Turner,* vol. 6 (March 18, 2016), pp. 274–319. Emily Doe testimony about waking in hospital, vol.

6, p. 445; Brock Turner testimony about amount he drank, vol. 9 (March 23, 2016), pp. 836, 838; police estimate of Turner BAC, vol. 7 (March 21, 2016), p. 554; Julia's testimony about amount she drank, vol. 5 (March 17, 2016), pp. 208–9, 213; Doe and Turner BAC (in footnote), vol. 7, pp. 553–54; Doe testimony about amount she drank, vol. 6, pp. 429, 433–34, 439; Turner testimony about sexual escalation, vol. 9, pp. 846–47, 850–51, 851–53; prosecution's closing arguments, vol. 11, March 28, 2016, pp. 1072–73; Turner testimony about grinding, vol. 9, pp. 831–32; Doe testimony about blackout, vol. 6, pp. 439–40; Turner testimony about blackout, vol. 11, pp. 1099–1100; Turner testimony about Doe voice mail, vol. 9, p. 897.

An estimated one in five…victim of sexual assault: This figure has been supported by dozens of studies since 1987, including the 2015 *Washington Post*/Kaiser Family Foundation poll. A 2015 study by the Association of American Universities (AAU) found that 23 percent of undergraduate women are sexually assaulted while in college. A 2016 study released by the Department of Justice puts the number even higher, at 25.1 percent, or 1 in 4. See David Cantor et al., "Report on the AAU campus climate survey on sexual assault and sexual misconduct," Westat, 2015, https://www.aau.edu/sites/default/files/%40%20Files/Climate%20Survey/AAU_CampusClimate_Survey_12_14_15.pdf; Christopher Krebs et al., "Campus Climate Survey Validation Study Final Technical Reports," U.S. Department of Justice, 2016, http://www.bjs.gov/content/pub/pdf/ccsvsftr.pdf.

Poll about establishing consent and defining sexual assault: Bianca DiJulio et al., "Survey of Current and Recent College Students on Sexual Assault," *Washington Post*/Kaiser Family Foundation, June 12, 2015, pp. 15–17, http://files.kff.org/attachment/Survey%20Of%20Current%20And%20Recent%20College%20Students%20On%20Sexual%20Assault%20-%20Topline.

"How can we expect students…as to what they are?": Lori E. Shaw, "Title IX, Sexual Assault, and the Issue of Effective Consent: Blurred Lines—When Should 'Yes' Mean 'No'?," *Indiana Law Journal* 91, no. 4, Article 7 (2016): 1412. "It is not enough…'too much to drink,'" p. 1416. Shaw quotes from *People v. Giardino* 98, Cal. Rptr. 2d 315, 324 (Cal. Ct. App. 2000) and Valerie M. Ryan, "Intoxicating Encounters: Allocating Responsibility in the Law of Rape," 40 CAL. W.L. REV. 407, 416 (2004).

The story of Dwight Heath in Bolivia was first told by me in "Drinking Games," *The New Yorker*, February 15, 2010, https://www.newyorker.com/magazine/2010/02/15/drinking-games.

Heath wrote…a now-famous article: Dwight B. Heath, "Drinking patterns of the Bolivian Camba," *Quarterly Journal of Studies on Alcohol* 19 (1958): 491–508.

"Although I probably…embrace each other": Ralph Beals, *Ethnology of the Western Mixe* (New York: Cooper Square Publishers Inc., 1973), p. 29.

The myopia theory was first suggested: Claude Steele and Robert A. Josephs, "Alcohol Myopia: Its Prized and Dangerous Effects," *American Psychologist* 45, no. 8 (1990): 921–33.

A group of Canadian psychologists…his sober counterpart (in footnote): Tara K. MacDonald et al., "Alcohol Myopia and Condom Use: Can Alcohol Intoxication

Be Associated With More Prudent Behavior?," *Journal of Personality and Social Psychology* 78, no. 4 (2000): 605–19.

"I was hoping...she was enjoying it": Helen Weathers, "I'm No Rapist...Just a Fool," *Daily Mail,* March 30, 2007, www.dailymail.co.uk/femail/article-445750/Im-rapist--just-fool.html.

"He insisted...she removed them altogether": *R v Bree* [2007] EWCA Crim 804 [16]–[17]; "She had no idea...for how long," [8]; "Both were adults...legislative structures," [25]–[35]; further quotes from ruling (in footnote), [32], [35], [36].

Memory test with three dead mice: Donald Goodwin, "Alcohol Amnesia," *Addiction* (1995): 90, 315–17. (No ethics board would approve this experiment today.) The story about the salesman who experienced a five-day blackout is also drawn from this source.

Police sobriety checkpoints (in footnote): Joann Wells et al., "Drinking Drivers Missed at Sobriety Checkpoints," *Journal of Studies on Alcohol* (1997): 58, 513–17.

one of the first comprehensive surveys of college drinking: Robert Straus and Selden Bacon, *Drinking in College* (New Haven: Yale University Press, 1953), p. 103.

Aaron White recently surveyed more than 700 Duke students: Aaron M. White et al., "Prevalence and Correlates of Alcohol-Induced Blackouts Among College Students: Results of an E-Mail Survey," *Journal of American College Health* 51, no. 3 (2002): 117–31, doi:10.1080/07448480209596339.

In a remarkable essay (in footnote): Ashton Katherine Carrick, "Drinking to Blackout," *New York Times,* September 19, 2016, www.nytimes.com/2016/09/19/opinion/drinking-to-blackout.html.

the consumption gap between men and women...has narrowed: William Corbin et al., "Ethnic differences and the closing of the sex gap in alcohol use among college-bound students," *Psychology of Addictive Behaviors* 22, no. 2 (2008): 240–48, http://dx.doi.org/10.1037/0893-164X.22.2.240.

Nor is it just a matter of weight (in footnote): "Body Measurements," National Center for Health Statistics, Centers for Disease Control and Prevention, U.S. Department of Health & Human Services, May 3, 2017, https://www.cdc.gov/nchs/fastats/body-measurements.htm.

There are also meaningful differences (in footnote): Numbers found using online blood-alcohol calculator at http://www.alcoholhelpcenter.net/program/bac_standalone.aspx.

"Let's be totally clear...prevent more victims": Emily Yoffe, "College Women: Stop Getting Drunk," *Slate,* October 16, 2013, slate.com/human-interest/2013/10/sexual-assault-and-drinking-teach-women-the-connection.html.

Adults feel quite differently (in footnote): Statistic is from *Washington Post*/Kaiser Family Foundation poll.

"Persons learn about drunkenness...deserve what they get": Craig MacAndrew and Robert B. Edgerton, *Drunken Comportment: A Social Explanation* (Chicago: Aldine Publishing Company, 1969), pp.172–73.

"My independence, natural joy...not how to drink less": Emily Doe's

Victim Impact Statement, pp. 7–9, https://www.sccgov.org/sites/da/newsroom/ newsreleases/Documents/B-Turner%20VIS.pdf.

CHAPTER NINE: KSM: WHAT HAPPENS WHEN THE STRANGER IS A TERRORIST?

"Call me Mukhtar...the 9/11 attacks": James Mitchell, *Enhanced Interrogation: Inside the Minds and Motives of the Islamic Terrorists Trying to Destroy America* (New York: Crown Forum, 2016), p. 7.

portions of a videotaped deposition: Sheri Fink and James Risen, "Psychologists Open a Window on Brutal CIA Interrogations," *New York Times,* June 21, 2017, https://www.nytimes.com/interactive/2017/06/20/us/cia-torture.html.

From Wikipedia: "Water intoxication, also known as water poisoning, hyperhydration, overhydration, or water toxemia[,] is a potentially fatal disturbance in brain functions that results when the normal balance of electrolytes in the body is pushed outside safe limits by excessive water intake."

"The realistic stress of...actual combat": Charles A. Morgan et al., "Hormone Profiles in Humans Experiencing Military Survival Training," *Biological Psychiatry* 47, no. 10 (2000): 891–901, doi:10.1016/s0006-3223(99)00307-8.

Rey-Osterrieth figures drawn before and after interrogation: Charles A. Morgan III et al., "Stress-Induced Deficits in Working Memory and Visuo-Constructive Abilities in Special Operations Soldiers," *Biological Psychiatry* 60, no. 7 (2006): 722–29, doi:10.1016/ j.biopsych.2006.04.021. The Rey-Osterrieth figure was first developed by Andre Rey and published in his article "L'examen psychologique dans les cas d'encephalopathie traumatique (Les problemes)," *Archives de Psychologie* 28 (1941): 215-85.

In another, larger study (in footnote): Charles Morgan et al., "Accuracy of eyewitness memory for persons encountered during exposure to highly intense stress," *International Journal of Law and Psychiatry* 27 (2004): 264–65.

KSM made his first public confession: *Verbatim Transcript of Combatant Status Review Tribunal Hearing for ISN 10024,* March 10, 2007, http://i.a.cnn.net/cnn/ 2007/images/03/14/transcript_ISN10024.pdf.

"might induce some form...wishes to have access to": Shane O'Mara, *Why Torture Doesn't Work: The Neuroscience of Interrogation* (Cambridge, Mass.: Harvard University Press, 2015), p. 167.

KSM was "making things up": Robert Baer, "Why KSM's Confession Rings False," *Time,* March 15, 2007, http://content.time.com/time/world/article/0,8599,1599861,00.html.

"He has nothing...problem since he was captured": Adam Zagorin, "Can KSM's Confession Be Believed?" *Time,* March 15, 2007, http://content.time.com/time/ nation/article/0,8599,1599423,00.html.

Chapter Ten: Sylvia Plath

"I am writing from London...he lived there!": Sylvia Plath to Aurelia Plath, November 7, 1962, in Peter K. Steinberg and Karen V. Kukil, eds., *The Letters of Sylvia Plath Volume II: 1956–1963* (New York: Harper Collins, 2018), p. 897.

"She seemed different...never seen her so strained": Alfred Alvarez, *The Savage God: A Study of Suicide* (New York: Random House, 1971), pp. 30–31; "She talked about...how to ski," pp. 18–19; "the poet as a sacrificial victim...the sake of her art," p. 40.

Plath poems: "The woman is perfected...it is over" from "Edge," in *The Collected Poems of Sylvia Plath*, edited by Ted Hughes (New York: Harper Perennial Modern Classics, 2008), p. 272; "And like the cat...Number Three," from "Lady Lazarus," pp. 244–45; and "If you only knew...my veins with invisibles..." from "A Birthday Present," p. 207.

poets have far and away the highest suicide rates: Mark Runco, "Suicide and Creativity," *Death Studies* 22 (1998): 637–54.

"A poet has to adapt himself" (in footnote): Stephen Spender, *The Making of a Poem* (New York: Norton Library, 1961), p. 45.

"She could never again...ultimately her undoing" (in footnote): Ernest Shulman, "Vulnerability Factors in Sylvia Plath's Suicide," *Death Studies* 22, no. 7 (1988): 598–613. ("When she killed herself...a broken home" [in footnote] is from this source too.)

"Had she supposed...laid her cheek on it": Jillian Becker, *Giving Up: The Last Days of Sylvia Plath* (New York: St. Martin's Press, 2003), pp. 80, 291.

"The victims...the top of the cozy": Douglas J. A. Kerr, "Carbon Monoxide Poisoning: Its Increasing Medico-Legal Importance," *British Medical Journal* 1, no. 3452 (March 5, 1927): 416.

United Kingdom suicide rate in 1962: Ronald V. Clarke and Pat Mayhew, "The British Gas Suicide Story and Its Criminological Implications," *Crime and Justice* 10 (1988): p. 88, doi:10.1086/449144; graph "Relation between gas suicides in England and Wales and CO content of domestic gas, 1960–77," p. 89; graph "Crude suicide rates (per 1 million population) for England and Wales and the United States, 1900–84," p. 84; "[Town] gas had unique advantages...in front of trains or buses," p. 99; graph of "Suicides in England and Wales by domestic gas and other methods for females twenty-five to forty-four years old," p. 91.

"the greatest peacetime operation in this nation's history": Malcolm E. Falkus, *Always under Pressure: A History of North Thames Gas Since 1949* (London: Macmillan, 1988), p. 107.

Town gas to natural gas conversion, 1965–1977: Trevor Williams, *A History of the British Gas Industry* (Oxford: Oxford University Press, 1981), p. 190.

our inability to understand suicide costs lives (in footnote): See, for example, Kim Soffen, "To Reduce Suicides, Look at Gun Violence," *Washington Post,* July 13, 2016, https://www.washingtonpost.com/graphics/business/wonkblog/suicide-rates/.

the inexplicable saga of the Golden Gate Bridge: John Bateson, *The Final Leap: Suicide on the Golden Gate Bridge* (Berkeley: University of California Press, 2012), p. 8; history of suicide barrier (or lack of it) on bridge, pp. 33, 189, 196.

wound up filming twenty-two suicides (in footnote): Director Eric Steel's documentary is starkly titled *The Bridge* (More4, 2006).

Seiden followed up on 515 people: Richard H. Seiden, "Where are they now? A follow-up study of suicide attempters from the Golden Gate Bridge," *Suicide and Life-Threatening Behavior* 8, no. 4 (1978): 203–16.

"If a physical barrier...replaced by another": These five quotes are from a set of public comments on the Transportation District's proposal to erect a suicide net: http://goldengatebridge.org/projects/documents/sds_letters-emails-individuals.pdf.

In one national survey...would simply take their life some other way: Matthew Miller et al., "Belief in the Inevitability of Suicide: Results from a National Survey," *Suicide and Life-Threatening Behavior* 36, no. 1 (2006).

Weisburd spent a year walking: David Weisburd et al., "Challenges to Supervision in Community Policing: Observations on a Pilot Project," *American Journal of Police* 7 (1988): 29–50.

Sherman had been thinking along these lines as well: Larry Sherman et al., *Evidence-Based Crime Prevention* (London: Routledge, 2002). (Both Sherman and Weisburd are enormously prolific. I've included a small sample of their work here; if it interests you, there's much more to read!)

"We chose Minneapolis": L. W. Sherman et al., "Hot spots of predatory crime: Routine activities and the criminology of place," *Criminology* (1989): 27–56.

Half the crime in the city [of Boston]: Glenn Pierce et al., "The character of police work: strategic and tactical implications," *Center for Applied Social Research Northeastern University,* November 1988. Although the study authors weren't aware that their data supported the Law of Crime Concentration, Weisburd put the pieces together when he looked at their conclusions.

Weisburd map of Seattle crime patterns:

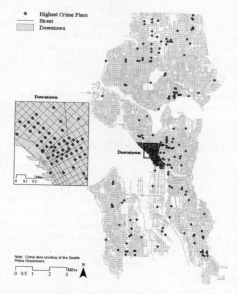

See Figure 2 in David Weisburd et al., "Understanding and Controlling Hot Spots of Crime: The Importance of Formal and Informal Social Controls," *Prevention Science* 15, no. 1 (2014): 31–43, doi:10.1007/s11121-012-0351-9. The map shows crime over the period from 1989 to 2004. For more on Weisburd's research on crime and place, see David Weisburd et al., *The Criminology of Place: Street Segments and Our Understanding of the Crime Problem* (Oxford: Oxford University Press, 2012), and David Weisburd et al., *Place Matters: Criminology for the Twenty-First Century* (New York: Cambridge University Press, 2016).

Not long after I met Weisburd in 2018, he arranged for me to spend a day with a colleague of his, Claire White. The two of them have been running a multimillion-dollar "hot spot" research project in Baltimore since 2012 — studying 450 street segments all over the city. "It's becoming well established that crime is highly concentrated," White explained. "[Weisburd] has shown us that across numerous cities with different types of data. The big question is why? What is it about these places that have such a high concentration of crime?"

White and Weisburd hired forty student interviewers. They send them out every day to document the condition of those 450 segments, gathering as much information as they can on their residents. "We ask about what we call collective efficacy, willingness to intervene," White said. "If there's kids climbing on a parked car, how willing are your neighbors to say something? If the local fire station was going to be shut down, how willing are your neighbors to do something about it? Kind of this willingness to be involved as well as trusting. Do you trust your neighbors? Do you share the same values as your neighbors?...We have questions about the police: Do you think the police treat you fairly? Do you think the officers treat people with respect?"

For comparison purposes, some of those street segments are "cold" spots, defined as blocks with fewer than four police calls a year. A hot spot is anything with more than eighteen police calls a year. Keep in mind that Baltimore is an eighteenth-century city—the blocks are really short. So that's a minimum of eighteen police calls along a street segment that you could walk in less than a minute. White said that some of the streets in the study had over *six hundred* calls for service in one year. That's what Weisburd means by the Law of Crime Concentration. Most streets have none. A small number of streets are home to virtually all the crime in the area.

White and I began our tour in West Baltimore, not far from the city's downtown.

"It's notorious for being one of the pretty high crime areas. It's where Freddie Gray was arrested and where the riots took place," she said, referring to the 2015 case of a young African American who died in police custody, under suspicious circumstances, leading to angry protests. "If you've seen *The Wire*, they always talk about West Baltimore." The area was typical of an older northeastern city: narrow streets, red-brick townhouses. Some blocks had been gentrified, others not. "There's definitely many areas where you'll be walking and you feel you're in a nice neighborhood, right? You feel comfortable," White said, as she drove through the heart of the neighborhood. "Then you turn the corner and you're in a street that's all boarded up. It's a ghost town. You wonder if anyone even lives on the street."

She took me to the first of the street segments being studied and parked there. She wanted me to guess whether it was a hot spot or a cold spot. On the corner was an exquisite nineteenth-century church, and behind it a small park. The block had elegant European proportions. The sun was shining. I said I thought it must be a cold spot. She shook her head. "This is a violent street."

She drove on.

Sometimes a street's identity was obvious: a bedraggled block with a bar at one end and Slick Rick's Bail Bonds at the other was exactly as it looked—a double hot spot, bad for both crime and drugs. "There's ones where it's very clear, right?" White asked me. "You get out of the car and the people on the street start shouting out their codes for a police officer coming." She started laughing. "I love going out with the field researchers when they're like, 'That's the code for *us* being on the street.'" Once, in broad daylight, White's field workers found themselves in the middle of a gun battle; there was little ambiguity about that segment.

But some bedraggled streets were perfectly fine. Once, in the midst of a particularly dismal stretch, we came across a little oasis: two consecutive street segments of manicured lawns and freshly painted houses. One large abandoned building had a sign posted in its window, a reference to John 14: 2, 3: "In my father's house there are many rooms." Was a glimpse of irony evidence of function or dysfunction?

I asked White to explain what tipped a street segment one way or the other. Sometimes she could. Usually she couldn't. "That's exactly it," she said. "The environment doesn't always speak to what's going on. In our pilot study, one of the streets we selected was a violent hot spot. The police officer and clinician were like, 'No way is this a violent hot spot.' All the homes are well kept. It's this beautiful street. I went and checked to make sure. I thought maybe there was something wrong with our data. I have this officer saying no way is this a violent hot spot, and it is. You can't always tell."

The lesson of an afternoon driving around Baltimore with Claire White was that it is really easy to make mistakes about strangers. Baltimore is a city where the homicide rate is many times the national average. The simplest thing in the world is to look at the abandoned buildings and the poverty and the drug dealers calling out their codes, then write off those areas and everyone in them. But the point of the Law of Crime Concentration is that most of the streets in "those areas" are perfectly fine. The hot spot is a *spot,* not a region. "We focus on all the bad people," White said of Baltimore's reputation, "but in reality there's mostly good people." Our ignorance of the unfamiliar is what fuels our fear.

"Cal seemed pleased…I turned back": Sylvia Plath, *The Bell Jar* (London: Faber and Faber, 1966), pp. 175, 179, 181.

as high as the suicide rate for women…has ever been: See Figure 3 in Kyla Thomas and David Gunnell, "Suicide in England and Wales 1861–2007: A time-trends analysis," *International Journal of Epidemiology* 39, issue 6 (2010): 1464–75, https://doi.org/10.1093/ije/dyq094.

Weisburd's Jersey City map: See Figure 2 in David Weisburd et al., "Does Crime Just Move Around the Corner? A Controlled Study of Spatial Displacement and Diffusion of Crime Control Benefits." *Criminology* 44, no. 3 (08, 2006): 549–92. doi: http://dx.doi.org.i.ezproxy.nypl.org/10.1111/j.1745-9125.2006.00057.x.

"I would park illegally…like moths to an electric light bulb": Anne Sexton, "The Barfly Ought to Sing," *TriQuarterly* no. 7 (1996): 174–75, quoted in Diane Wood Middlebrook, *Anne Sexton: A Biography* (New York: Houghton Mifflin, 1991), p. 107. Also from the Middlebrook biography: "to be prepared to kill herself," p. 165; "She stripped…asleep in familiar arms" and "surprised by her suicide," p. 397; "For Ernest Hemingway…that fear," "woman's way out," "I'm so fascinated…dying perfect," and "a Sleeping Beauty," all from p. 216.

Chart of **suicide methods by fatality rate:** "Lethality of Suicide Methods," Harvard T. H. Chan School of Public Health, January 6, 2017, https://www.hsph.harvard.edu/means-matter/means-matter/case-fatality, accessed March 17, 2019.

"Sleepmonger, deathmonger…I'm on a diet from death": Anne Sexton, "The Addict," in *The Complete Poems* (New York: Open Road Media, 2016), p. 165.

Look at how suicides from carbon-monoxide poisonings declined in the years after 1975. It's just like the chart of British suicides at the end of the town-gas era. See Figure 4 in Neil B. Hampson and James R. Holm, "Suicidal carbon monoxide poisoning has decreased with controls on automobile emissions," Undersea and Hyperbaric Medical Society, Inc. 42 (2): 159-64, March 2015.

CHAPTER ELEVEN: CASE STUDY: THE KANSAS CITY EXPERIMENTS

"Many of us...knew much about": George Kelling et al., "The Kansas City Preventive Patrol Experiment: A Summary Report" (Washington, DC: Police Foundation, 1974), p. v, https://www.policefoundation.org/wp-content/uploads/2015/07/Kelling-et-al.-1974-THE-KANSAS-CITY-PREVENTIVE-PATROL-EXPERIMENT.pdf.

"This country's social problems...progress is very small": Alan M. Webber, "Crime and Management: An Interview with New York City Police Commissioner Lee P. Brown," *Harvard Business Review* 63, issue 3 (May–June 1991): 100, https://hbr.org/1991/05/crime-and-management-an-interview-with-new-york-city-police-commissioner-lee-p-brown.

"A four-year-old boy...sickening, outrageous": George Bush, "Remarks to the Law Enforcement Community in Kansas City, Missouri," January 23, 1990, in *George Bush: Public Papers of the Presidents of the United States*, January 1–June 30, 1990, p. 74.

The description of Kansas City's Patrol District 144 is from Lawrence Sherman et al., "The Kansas City Gun Experiment," National Institute of Justice, January 1995, https://www.ncjrs.gov/pdffiles/kang.pdf; new strategy halves gun crimes in District 144, Exhibit 4, p. 6; statistics for 200 days of Gun Experiment, p. 6.

"The police went...'would ever come'": James Shaw, "Community Policing Against Crime: Violence and Firearms" (PhD dissertation, University of Maryland College Park, 1994), p. 118; "Not unlike residents...can't see anything," pp. 122–23; statistics for seven months of Kansas City Gun Experiment, p. 136; "Officers who recovered...'will be the night!'" pp. 155–56.

"When you stop...to do a frisk" (in footnote): Erik Eckholm, "Who's Got a Gun? Clues Are in the Body Language," *New York Times,* May 26, 1992, https://www.nytimes.com/1992/05/26/nyregion/who-s-got-a-gun-clues-are-in-the-body-language.html.

"There are moving violations...personal judgment": David A. Harris, "Driving While Black and All Other Traffic Offenses: The Supreme Court and Pretextual Traffic Stops," *Journal of Criminal Law and Criminology* 87, issue 2 (1997): 558, https://scholarlycommons.law.northwestern.edu/cgi/viewcontent.cgi?article=6913&context=jclc.

The Supreme Court ruled in favor of the officer: *Heien v. North Carolina,* 135 S. Ct. 534 (2014), https://www.leagle.com/decision/insco20141215960.

"I don't know why...too simplistic for us": Fox Butterfield, "A Way to Get the Gunmen: Get the Guns," *New York Times,* November 20, 1994, https://www.nytimes.com/1994/11/20/us/a-way-to-get-the-gunmen-get-the-guns.html.

In 1991 the *New York Times:* Don Terry, "Kansas City Police Go After Own 'Bad

Boys,'" September 10, 1991, https://www.nytimes.com/1991/09/10/us/kansas-city-police-go-after-own-bad-boys.html.

For the rise in North Carolina traffic stops in the early 2000s, see Deborah L. Weisel, "Racial and Ethnic Disparity in Traffic Stops in North Carolina, 2000–2001: Examining the Evidence," North Carolina Association of Chiefs of Police, 2014, http://ncracialjustice.org/wp-content/uploads/2015/08/Dr.-Weisel-Report.compressed.pdf.

One of Weisburd's former students (in footnote): E. Macbeth and B. Ariel, "Place-based Statistical Versus Clinical Predictions of Crime Hot Spots and Harm Locations in Northern Ireland," *Justice Quarterly* (August 2017): 22, http://dx.doi.org/10.1080/07418825.2017.1360379.

CHAPTER TWELVE: SANDRA BLAND

"Dude, issue the…pulling her out?": Nick Wing and Matt Ferner, "Here's What Cops and Their Supporters Are Saying about the Sandra Bland Arrest Video," *HuffPost*, July 22, 2015. https://www.huffingtonpost.com/entry/cops-sandra-bland-video_us_55afd6d3e4b07af29d57291d.

"An employee of the Department…extreme provocation": Texas Department of Public Safety General Manual, Chapter 5, Section 05.17.00, https://www.documentcloud.org/documents/3146604-DPSGeneralManual.html.

TSA haystack searches: DHS Press Office, "DHS Releases 2014 Travel and Trade Statistics," January 23, 2015, https://www.dhs.gov/news/2015/01/23/dhs-releases-2014-travel-and-trade-statistics, accessed March 2019.

"go beyond the ticket" and other Remsberg quotes: Charles Remsberg, *Tactics for Criminal Patrol: Vehicle Stops, Drug Discovery, and Officer Survival* (Northbrook, Ill.: Calibre Press, 1995), pp. 27, 50, 68. Also from this source: "If you're accused…the defendant's case," p. 70; "concealed interrogation" and "As you silently analyze…incriminating evidence," p. 166; and "Too many cops…what the suspect does," pp. 83–84.

the driver was "stiff and nervous": *Heien v. North Carolina*, 135 S. Ct. 534 (2014), https://www.leagle.com/decision/insco20141215960.

When he approached the stopped car: Gary Webb, "DWB: Driving While Black," *Esquire* 131, issue 4 (April 1999): 118–27. Webb's article was really the first to document the growing use of Kansas City techniques. It is superb—and chilling. At one point he sits down with a Florida officer named Vogel who was a particularly aggressive proponent of proactive searches. Vogel was proud of his sixth sense in spotting potential criminals. Webb writes: Other indicators, [Vogel] said, are adornments like "earrings, nose rings, eyelid rings. Those are things that are common denominators with people who are involved with crimes. Tattoos would go along with that," particularly tattoos of "marijuana leaves." Bumper stickers also give him a feel for the soul of the driver. "Deadhead stickers are things that almost—the people in those kinds of vehicles are almost always associated with drugs."

Give me a break.

a day from Brian Encinia's career: *Los Angeles Times* Staff, "Citations by Trooper Brian Encinia," *Los Angeles Times,* August 9, 2015, http://spreadsheets.latimes.com/citations-trooper-brian-encinia/.

"I was checking...yes sir" (and all Encinia/Renfro Q&A quotes from Brian Encinia): Interview with Cleve Renfro (Texas Department of Public Safety Lieutenant), October 8, 2015. Audio obtained by KXAN-TV of Austin, https://www.kxan.com/news/investigations/trooper-fired-for-sandra-bland-arrest-my-safety-was-in-jeopardy/1052813612, accessed April 2019.

"An operator shall use the signal...": Texas Transportation Code, Title 7: Vehicles and Traffic, Subtitle C: Rules of the Road, Chapter 545: Operation and Movement of Vehicles, Sections 104, 105, p. 16, https://statutes.capitol.texas.gov/?link=TN.

"In Western culture...the investigator": John E. Reid et al., *Essentials of the Reid Technique: Criminal Investigation and Confessions* (Sudbury, Mass.: Jones and Bartlett Publishers, 2005), p. 98.

The Reid Manual is full of assertions about lie detection that are, to put it plainly, nonsense. The Reid "system" teaches interrogators, for example, to be alert to nonverbal cues, which have the effect of "amplifying" what a suspect says. By nonverbal cues, they mean posture and hand gestures and the like. As the manual states, on page 93, "hence the commonplace expressions, 'actions speak louder than words' and 'look me straight in the eye if you're telling the truth.'"

If you stacked all the scientific papers refuting this claim on top of each other, they would reach the moon. Here is one of my favorite critiques, from Richard R. Johnson, a criminologist at the University of Toledo. (Johnson's research can be found here: "Race and Police Reliance on Suspicious Non-Verbal Cues," *Policing: An International Journal of Police Strategies and Management* 30, no. 2 [June 2007]: 277–90.)

Johnson went back and looked at old episodes of the half-hour television documentary *Cops.* You may remember this show: it began in 1989 and still airs today, making it one of the longest-running programs on American television. A camera crew rides along with a police officer and films—*cinema verité*–style, without narration—whatever happens on that particular shift. (It's strangely riveting, although it's easy to forget that what you see on a typical *Cops* show is heavily edited; police officers simply aren't that busy.) Johnson watched 480 old episodes of *Cops.* He was looking for interactions between a police officer and a citizen in which the citizen was on camera, from the waist up, for at least sixty seconds. He found 452 segments like that. Then he divided the segments into "innocent" and "suspect," based on the information provided in the show. Was this the mother, child in arms, whose home had just been burglarized? Or was this the teenager who ran the instant he saw the police, and was found with the woman's jewelry in his backpack? Then he subdivided his collection of clips one more time by race—white, black, and Hispanic.

It should be pointed out that there is a small mountain of research on so-called demeanor cues. But Johnson's study is special because it was not done in a college psychology lab. It's real life.

Let's start with what many police officers believe to be the most important demeanor cue—eye contact. The Reid Technique's training manual—the most widely used guide for law enforcement—is clear on this: People who are lying look away. Truthful suspects maintain eye contact.

So what does Johnson find when he examines this idea in the light of real-world interactions on *Cops*? Are the innocent more likely to look an officer in the eye than the guilty?

Johnson calculated the total number of seconds of eye contact per minute of footage.

Black people who are perfectly innocent are actually *less* likely to look police in the eye than black people who are suspected of a crime. Now let's look at white people:

The first thing to note here is that Caucasians on *Cops*, as a group, look police officers in the eye far more than black people do. In fact, whites suspected of a crime spend the most time, of all four groups, looking the police officer in the eye. If you use gaze aversion as a cue to interpret someone's credibility, you're going to be a lot more suspicious of black people than white people. Far worse, you're going to be most suspicious of all of *perfectly innocent* African Americans.

OK. Let's look at facial expressions. The Reid Technique teaches police officers that facial expressions can provide meaningful clues to a suspect's inner state. Have I been found out? Am I about to be found out? As the manual states:

"The mere fact of variation of expressions may be suggestive of untruthfulness, where the lack of such a variation may be suggestive of truthfulness" (Reid et al., *Essentials of the Reid Technique*, p. 99).

This is a version of the common idea that when someone is guilty or being evasive, they smile a lot. Surveys of police officers show that people in law enforcement are very attuned to "frequent smiling" as a sign that something is awry. To use the language of poker, it's considered a "tell." Here is Johnson's *Cops* analysis of smiling. This time I've included Johnson's data on Hispanics as well.

Once again, the rule of thumb relied upon by many police officers has it exactly backward. The people who smile the most are innocent African Americans. The people who smile the least are Hispanic suspects. The only reasonable conclusion from that chart is that black people, when they are on *Cops*, smile a lot, white people smile a little bit less, and Hispanic people don't smile much at all.

Let's do one more: halting speech. If someone is trying to explain themselves, and they keep nervously stopping and starting, we take that as a sign of evasion or deception. Right? So what does the *Cops* data say?

The African American suspects speak fluidly. The innocent Hispanics are hemming and hawing nervously. If you do what the Reid manual says, you'll lock up innocent Hispanics and be fooled by guilty African Americans.

Does this mean we simply need a better, more specific set of interpretation rules for police officers? *Watch out for the smooth-talking black guy. White people who don't smile are up to no good.* No! That doesn't work either, because of the enormous variability Johnson uncovered.

Take a look, for example, at the range of responses that make up those averages. Eye contact for innocent African Americans ranged from 7 seconds to 49.41 seconds. There are innocent black people who almost never make eye contact, and innocent black people who make lots of eye contact. The range for smiling for innocent black people is 0 to 13.34. There are innocent black people who smile a *lot*—13.34 times per minute. But there are also innocent black people who never smile. The "speech disturbances" range for innocent Caucasians is .64 to 9.68. There are white people who hem and haw like nervous teenagers, and white people who speak like Winston Churchill. The only real lesson is that people are all over the map when it comes to when and how much they smile, or look you in the eye, or how fluidly they talk. And to try to find any kind of pattern in that behavior is impossible.

Wait! I forgot one of the Reid Technique's big clues: watch the hands!

> During a response, a subject's hands can do one of three things. They can remain uninvolved and unmoving, which can be a sign that the subject lacks confidence in his verbal response or is simply not talking about something perceived as very significant. The hands can move away from the body and gesture, which is called illustrating. Finally, the hands can come in contact with some part of the body, which is referred to as adaptor behavior. (Reid et al., p. 96).

What follows is an explanation of how hand movements do and don't contribute to our understanding of truthfulness. The Reid Technique assumes there is a pattern to hand movement. Really? Here are Johnson's hand-movement data. This time I've included the range of responses—the shortest recorded response in the second column and the longest in the third column. Take a look:

Hand gestures per minute

	Average time (in seconds)	Shortest time (in seconds)	Longest time (in seconds)
African American/innocent	28.39	00.00	58.46
African American/suspect	23.98	00.00	56.00
Caucasian/innocent	07.89	00.00	58.00
Caucasian/suspect	17.43	31.00	56.00
Hispanic/innocent	22.14	23.00	57.00
Hispanic/suspect	31.41	13.43	53.33
Entire sample	23.68	00.00	58.46

If you can make sense of those numbers, you're smarter than I am.

By the way, the weirdest of all Reid obsessions is this: "Changes in [foot] bouncing behavior—whether it be a sudden start or stop—that occur in conjunction with a verbal response can be a significant indication of deception.... The feet are also involved in significant posture changes called 'shifts in the chair.' With this behavior, the subject plants his feet and literally pushes his body up, slightly off the chair to assume a new posture. Gross shifts in the chair of this nature are good indications of deception when they immediately precede or occur in conjunction with a subject's verbal response" (Reid et al., *Essentials of the Reid Technique,* p. 98).

What? I happen to be someone who is constantly, nervously jiggling his foot. I do it when I'm excited, or when I'm on a roll, or when I'm a little jumpy after too much coffee. What on earth does this have to do with whether or not I'm telling the truth?

One more shot at the Reid Technique. Let me just quote from Brian Gallini's devastating law-review article, "Police 'Science' in the Interrogation Room: Seventy Years of Pseudo-Psychological Interrogation Methods to Obtain Inadmissible Confessions," *Hastings Law Journal* 61 (2010): 529. The passage is a description of a study done by Saul Kassin and Christina Fong: "'I'm Innocent!': Effects of Training on Judgments of Truth and Deception in the Interrogation Room," *Law and Human Behavior* 23, no. 5 (October 1999): 499–516.

> More substantively, Professors Kassin and Fong videotaped one group of participants interrogated pursuant to the Reid method to determine whether they committed a mock crime. A second group of participants, some of whom were trained in the Reid method, watched the videos and opined on (1) the guilt or innocence of each subject, and (2) their confidence in their assessment of guilt or innocence. The results were as predictable as they were disturbing: First, judgment accuracy rates were comparable to chance. Second, "training in the use of verbal and nonverbal cues did not improve judgment accuracy." In an effort to explain why training did nothing to improve judgment accuracy, the authors stated pointedly, "There is no solid empirical basis for the proposition that these same cues reliably discriminate between criminals and innocent persons accused of crimes they did not commit."

Finally, the authors reported, participants were overconfident in their assessment of guilt or innocence. In the authors' words:

> [W]e found among both trained and naive participants that judgment accuracy and confidence were not significantly correlated, regardless of whether the measure of confidence was taken before, after, or during the task. Further demonstrating the meta-cognitive problems in this domain is that confidence ratings were positively correlated with the number of reasons (including Reid-based reasons) articulated as a basis for judgments, another dependent measure not predictive of accuracy. *Training had a particularly adverse effect in this regard. Specifically, those who were trained compared to those in the naive condition were less accurate in their judgments of truth and deception. Yet they were more self-confident and more articulate about the reasons for their often erroneous judgments.*

"I apologize...these last couple of weeks...": "Sandy Speaks— March 1, 2015," YouTube, posted July 24, 2015, https://www.youtube.com/ watch?v=WJw3_cvrcwE, accessed March 22, 2019.

DOJ report on Ferguson, Missouri: United States Department of Justice Civil Rights Division, "Investigation of the Ferguson Police Department," March 4, 2015, https://www.justice.gov/sites/default/files/opa/press-releases/attachments/2015/03/04/ferguson_police_department_report.pdf.

African Americans are considerably more likely to be subjected to traffic stops (in footnote): Charles R. Epp, Steven Maynard-Moody, and Donald Haider-Markel, *How Police Stops Define Race and Citizenship* (Chicago: University of Chicago Press, 2004).

North Carolina State Highway Patrol statistics: "Open Data Policing: North Carolina," accessed March 2019, https://opendatapolicing.com/nc/, accessed March 2019.

FM 1098 is not "a high-crime, high-drug area": This crime map reflects Waller County data from 2013 to 2017 collected by Baltimore-based crime data aggregator SpotCrime, which sources data from local police departments.

More on the dilemmas caused by haystack searches: Middle-aged women, in most countries, are encouraged to get regular mammograms. But breast cancer is really rare. Just under 0.5 percent of women who get a mammogram actually have the disease. Looking for breast cancer is therefore a haystack search.

Epidemiologist Joann Elmore recently calculated just what this means. Imagine, she said, that a group of radiologists gave a mammogram to 100,000 women. Statistically, there should be 480 cancers in that 100,000. How many will the radiologists find? 398. Believe me, for a task as difficult as reading a mammogram, that's pretty good.

But in the course of making those correct diagnoses, the radiologists will also run up 8,957 false positives. That's how haystack searches work: if you want to find that rare gun in someone's luggage, you're going to end up flagging lots of hair dryers.

Now suppose you want to do a better job of spotting cancers. Maybe getting 398 out of 480 cases isn't good enough. Elmore did a second calculation, this time using a group of radiologists with an extra level of elite training. These physicians were very alert, and very suspicious—the medical equivalent of Brian Encinia. They correctly identified 422 of the 480 cases—much better! But how many false positives did that extra suspicion yield? 10,947. An extra two thousand perfectly healthy women were flagged for a disease they didn't have, and potentially exposed to treatment they didn't need. The highly trained radiologists were better at finding tumors not because they were more accurate. They were better because they were more suspicious. They saw cancer everywhere.

If you are a woman, which group of radiologists would you rather have read your mammogram? Are you more concerned about the tiny chance that you'll have a cancer that will be missed, or the much larger probability that you'll be diagnosed with a cancer you don't have? There's no right or wrong answer to that question. Different people have different attitudes toward their own health, and toward risk. What's crucial, though, is the lesson those numbers teach us about haystack searches. Looking for something rare comes with a price.

Index

Note: Page numbers in *italics* refer to illustrations.

The author is grateful for permission to use the following copyrighted material:

Photos: Duchenne and non-Duchenne smiles. Reprinted by permission of Paul Ekman, Ph.D./ Paul Ekman Group, LLC.

Photo: "Anger" from Job van der Schalk et al., "Moving Faces, Looking Places: Validation of the Amsterdam Dynamic Facial Expression Set (ADFES)," Emotion 11, no. 4 (2011): 912. Reproduced by permission of author.

Images: "Rey-Osterrieth Complex Figure," "Sample ROCF immediate recall drawings from the Pre/Post-stress groups," "Sample ROCF immediate recall drawings from the Stress Group," from Charles A. Morgan et al., "Stress-Induced Deficits in Working Memory and Visuo-Constructive Abilities in Special Operations Soldiers," Biological Psychiatry 60, no. 7 (2006): 722–29. Reproduced by permission of Dr. Charles A. Morgan III and Elsevier.

Excerpts from "Edge" [6l.], "Lady Lazarus" [2], "A Birthday Present" [6] from The Collected Poems of Sylvia Plath, edited by Ted Hughes. Copyright © 1960, 1965, 1971, 1981 by the Estate of Sylvia Plath. Editorial material copyright © 1981 by Ted Hughes. Reprinted by permission of Harper Collins.

Excerpt from "The Addict," by Anne Sexton from Live or Die (Boston: Houghton Mifflin, 1966). Reprinted by permission of SLL/Sterling Lord Literistic, Inc. Copyright by Anne Sexton.

Graphs: "Relation between gas suicides in England and Wales and CO content of domestic gas, 1960–77"; "Crude suicide rates (per 1 million population) for England and Wales and the United States, 1900–84"; "Suicides in England and Wales by domestic gas and other methods for females twenty-five to forty-four years old" from Ronald V. Clarke and Pat Mayhew, "The British Gas Suicide Story and Its Criminological Implications," Crime and Justice 10 (1988): 79–116. Reproduced by permission of Ronald V. Clarke, Pat Mayhew, and the University of Chicago Press.

Map: Weisburd Jersey city map from David Weisburd, et al., "Does Crime Just Move Around The Corner? A Controlled Study of Spatial Displacement and Diffusion of Crime Control Benefits," Criminology 44, no. 3 (2006): 549–91. Reproduced by permission of David Weisburd and the American Society of Criminology.

Also by Malcolm Gladwell

Blink

> *Blink* is about all those moments when we 'know' something without knowing why. Here Malcolm Gladwell explores the phenomenon of 'blink', showing how a snap judgement can be far more effective than a cautious decision. By trusting your instincts, he reveals, you'll never think about thinking in the same way again.

> 'A global phenomenon … there is, it seems, no subject over which he cannot scatter some magic dust' *Observer*

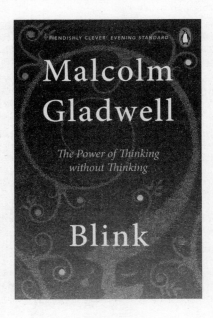